P9-DWF-093

THE
SPOTTED
SPHINX

By the same author

BORN FREE
LIVING FREE
FOREVER FREE
THE PEOPLES OF KENYA
THE STORY OF ELSA
ELSA AND HER CUBS

JOY ADAMSON

THE SPOTTED SPHINX

A Helen and Kurt Wolff Book
Harcourt, Brace & World, Inc.
NEW YORK

TO ALL *who work to preserve the lives of*
wild animals whose survival is endangered
by the activities of man

COPYRIGHT © 1969 BY JOY ADAMSON

ALL RIGHTS RESERVED. NO PART OF THIS PUBLICATION MAY BE REPRODUCED
OR TRANSMITTED IN ANY FORM OR BY ANY MEANS, ELECTRONIC OR MECHANICAL,
INCLUDING PHOTOCOPY, RECORDING, OR ANY INFORMATION STORAGE AND
RETRIEVAL SYSTEM, WITHOUT PERMISSION IN WRITING FROM THE PUBLISHER.

FIRST AMERICAN EDITION

LIBRARY OF CONGRESS CATALOG CARD NUMBER: 77-85008

PRINTED IN THE UNITED STATES OF AMERICA

THE AUTHOR WOULD LIKE TO EXPRESS HER GRATITUDE TO MISS
SALLY CARRIGHAR AND TO HOUGHTON MIFFLIN COMPANY, BOSTON,
AND HAMISH HAMILTON LTD, LONDON FOR PERMISSION
TO QUOTE FROM HER *Wild Heritage.*

CONTENTS

WITHDRAWN

694411

THE
SPOTTED
SPHINX

CHAPTER

1

I Take Charge of Pippa

IN SEPTEMBER, 1964, I was asked by a friend to adopt an eight-months-old female cheetah cub owned by a family who were moving to England and wanted their pet to remain in Kenya. At this time I was camping on location with Columbia Pictures at the foot of Mount Kenya, where the company was making the film version of *Born Free*. Since my position at the film unit excluded any handling of the lions, I was free to have a pet and accepted the offer with joy.

Although cheetahs are the easiest of all wild cats to tame, little is known about their habits when in the wild. They are unique in that they combine characteristics of the dog with those of the cat, and although they are classed as cats, they do not really fit into any category with other animals. They are the fastest mammals in the world over a short distance and have been timed to run at sixty miles an hour and more. (The limit of a racehorse is forty miles an hour.) The cheetah is built for speed, with light bones, a small head, a minute chin and long, slender legs. Like a dog, it cannot retract its claws: it sits in doglike fashion and hunts like a canine; however, its pugmarks are characteristic of a cat, as well as its use of the dewclaw and its possibly acquired ability to climb trees. Its sandy-colored coat is sleek like that of a short-haired dog, while its black spots are fluffy like a cat's fur.

Cheetahs are solitary animals inhabiting open plains and are seldom seen in company except when mating or with young. The cubs, usually numbering up to four, are born after a gestation period of

3

ninety to ninety-three days, with a long, fluffy mane and grayish coat which covers the upper half of the body from head to tail and is in strong contrast to the dark-colored, short-haired, spotted coat which covers the lower part of the body. For the first two or three months of their life the cubs look almost like silver-backed jackals with a fancy spotted undercarriage. Then their coat becomes sand-colored, spotted all over, and the ruff remains only along the top of their neck and shoulders.

The name "cheetah" originated in India and means "the spotted one." Its history is intriguing, for we find cheetahs used as emblems on the reliefs and friezes of the ancient Egyptians, where they exemplify courage. There are only two records of a cheetah becoming a royal pet; they belonged to Genghis Khan and Charlemagne. Until recently Indian princes used to hunt with cheetahs trained to run down game, but since 1930 there has been no record of a cheetah living wild in India; the species now survives only in Africa. During a recent census it was found that the cheetah still stands its ground in certain parts of East Africa but will survive only if protected.

The cheetah female cub offered to me had been found abandoned in Wajir, a desert region of the Northern Frontier District of Kenya. The Major of a regiment stationed in the area took the tiny orphan and reared her with his children at his home near Nairobi. Soon the cub began to accompany the family on their shopping visits to the city and became a popular guest in the dining rooms of several Nairobi restaurants.

Major and Mrs. Dunkey asked me to meet them on the seventeenth of October, 1964, at the New Stanley Hotel. When I saw a couple drinking tea in the company of a cheetah cub who squatted pertly on a chair opposite them, with its golden eyes intently watching everything that went on, I needed no introduction.

I fell in love with the cat at first sight, but kept to an old rule of mine when meeting children and animals and waited for the cub to take the initiative. Giving her time to make up her mind about me, I chatted with the Dunkeys, trying to learn all I could about her habits. I was told that Kitten, as they called her, loved children and played hide-and-seek with them among the rosebushes in the garden but that she was inclined to chase strangers and dogs. I also learned that Kitten slept on Mrs. Dunkey's bed and when she had her morning tea the cat drank milk out of a dish. Unfortunately, she

By permission of East African Newspapers, Nairobi

Pippa as I first met her

had the habit of wetting the bed, so I was promised a plastic sheet as protection. I was told that Kitten adored a rabbit doll made of plush which might be useful in diverting her attention should she do something she was not supposed to do. Finally, I was advised that if she went on strike and wouldn't budge, I was to lift her by her tail and scruff, a proceeding to which she had become quite used. She ate three pounds of raw meat a day and drank a lot of milk to which four drops of Abidec (vitamins) were to be added; as an occasional treat I was to give her a mousebird.

While we talked, Kitten scrutinized me, her eyes half closed under her heavy brows, then she came over to me, purred loudly, and licked my face. While I stroked her soft fur I felt her body vibrating like an engine; breathing in and out, she gave the famous cheetah purr; finally she nibbled at my ear. That, I was assured, was a sign of great affection. We now all felt relieved, knowing that I was accepted and that we soon would be good friends.

The Dunkeys told me that they had been offered up to four hundred pounds for their pet by people who wanted to take her to England or America. Though they were not rich, they declined these offers, preferring to find a home for Kitten in Kenya where she could live in as much freedom as possible. Knowing of my love for animals and of our relationship with Elsa, they hoped I would adopt Kitten and give her a happy life. I was deeply touched by their trust and the precious gift of their much-loved pet and promised that I would do all within my power to fulfill their hopes.

It was at this moment that the plan of rehabilitating Kitten to the wild life she had been born to came into my mind, but as I did not know if this would be possible I did not mention it to the Dunkeys. In fact, I said that I would be obliged, while living with the film unit, to confine her because of all the lions in the camp and would only be able to free her when taking her out for exercise to the neighboring plains. This was agreed on.

A few days later the Dunkeys brought Kitten to the film location at Naro Moru, a hundred and twenty miles north of Nairobi. This was where the film of *Born Free* was being shot and where I was staying at the time. I had prepared a large wire enclosure adjoining my two tents. I had built it around a tree among whose branches we had erected a wooden platform to satisfy a cheetah's climbing instinct. We also, as substitute for rocks, placed a few wooden benches in the compound. To make Kitten comfortable during the night I had a big wooden crate built, with a sliding door made of wire on the side facing the inside of my tent. Another door opened onto the compound; this way, she could keep in touch with me should she feel lonely.

I thought that the change of foster parents would be the right moment for altering her bed-sleeping habit, and so I padded the sleeping crate with her familiar blankets, cushion, and the toys the Dunkeys had brought, and I placed my bed along the wired side of the crate, thus being within the cub's reach during night.

I also asked the Dunkeys if I might change her name from Kitten to Pippa, which was phonetically similar and easier to pronounce when calling her over long distances, and this too was agreed on.

I realize, in retrospect, that most of the names I had given my previous pets started with a P: Pippin, Pati, Pampo, etc. If they got lost an explosive consonant carried more easily across a distance.

Poor Pippa, how much she would now have to learn.

When all had been arranged I suggested we should have lunch. Having seen Pippa quite at ease in the Stanley Hotel lounge, among a crowd of people, I took it as a matter of course that she should join us and I expected to introduce her to the film unit who knew of her arrival. But when we reached the farmhouse at the far end of the film location, we saw people leaving the dining hall and walking across the lawn to their rooms, and as soon as Pippa hopped out of the car there was a rush. By the slamming and banging of doors I realized that the cheetah's arrival was causing some alarm among the personnel of the unit and I felt rather embarrassed by this welcome, but Pippa walked into the dining room unconcerned by all the dash for safety, sat in a ladylike fashion at our table, and behaved with perfect manners throughout our meal. Indeed, she appeared to be so intrigued by her new environment that she did not want to go away, and Major Dunkey had finally to demonstrate the "tail and scruff" lifting operation and carry her into the car. Later, the Dunkeys returned to Nairobi. I admired their self-control and the way in which they parted with their friend Kitten, knowing what it must have meant for both of them.

Now Pippa was my responsibility.

Back at the Simba Camp she aroused great interest among the lions who were playing parts in the film; of these there were a considerable number, since it was impossible to know in advance which could be trained to re-create the various incidents of Elsa's life. Her nearest neighbors, two old lionesses, paced up and down inside their enclosure to get the best view of the strange, spotted creature. The various compounds were separated not only by great distances and had trees between them, but some also had screens to prevent the animals from seeing each other; it was hoped that this would reassure them. But I wondered how these precautions could prevent the lions from hearing and scenting each other, particularly as after dark their roars often shook the stillness of the night. Although I found this chorus, which built up to awe-inspiring crescendos and ebbed away to synchronized whuffings, fascinating, poor Pippa was terrified. Tense with fear, she stared in the direction of the sounds. Although I sat close to her, talking calmly and stroking her, it took the best part of the night before she relaxed and settled down.

Lions and cheetahs do not get on well when living wild, so Pippa's reaction was understandable.

It was therefore a great relief to be leaving, on the following day, with part of the film unit for the coast to film the scenes in which Elsa is supposed to play with her human foster parents in the ocean. Not being sure if the film lions would enter the sea, it was decided to take two lionesses, Girl and Mara, to the coast in the hope that one might oblige. The camp for the filming of these scenes had already been prepared, and while the majority of the unit flew to the coast the animals traveled to Malindi in a convoy of five cars by road.

Pippa was used to cars and quickly settled on the front seat between my servant, Muguru, and myself. She took a great interest in everything she could see along the way; certainly she was happy, for she often rubbed her silky head affectionately against mine or licked my face. We broke the long journey—540 miles—at Mtito Ndei, which is halfway, and spent the night at the hotel. It was easy to get permission for Pippa to walk around the grounds, join us for dinner, to the delight of the other guests, and share my room. The poor lions were less fortunate and had to be confined inside the cars. We parked them outside our bungalows so that we could give the animals moral support and throughout the night often visited them but they never stopped restlessly pacing around. At dawn we continued our safari. Hoping to shorten the journey and reduce their discomfort to the minimum, we took a short cut through the National Park at Voi but unfortunately lost our way among the many tracks and arrived very much later than we expected at our destination. Then, at last, the exhausted lions were able to relax in their compounds which were at the film camp, built along the Blue Lagoon. I drove on another five miles to the open sea, where a bungalow had been rented for Pippa and myself.

The film camp was fenced in by wire which extended far into the sea at either side. This was done less to confine the animals than to keep the local people away, for they, who had never before seen a lion, swarmed around the place. Pippa aroused an equal interest, not only among people but also among dogs. The news of her arrival must have spread like bush fire, and, worse than any bitch in heat, she was soon besieged by every dog in the vicinity. Luckily for her, the owner of the place agreed to attach a wire enclosure to the bungalow to give her some space to walk about in without being molested by the dogs.

While this was being erected, I took her to the beach together with Muguru, but unfortunately I had to keep her on a sixty-foot-long nylon line. I was curious as to how she would respond to the sea as I had never heard of a cheetah swimming, and in fact Pippa did not seem to like sea bathing, for after a few attempts to wet her paws when trying to follow me into the ocean she decided to wait on the beach with Muguru until I returned from my swim. Meanwhile her curiosity was aroused by all the busy crabs around her; she was very surprised to see them disappear into holes just at the moment she was about to pounce on them. Perplexed, she looked at me, then suddenly decided to have a full-speed run along the beach. That was all right for her but not much fun for me, for I had to keep up with her by hanging on to the nylon line.

Luckily, our race was stopped by a large coral rock which, at low tide, stood isolated on the beach. Pippa investigated it, first sniffing around its base, then climbing swiftly to its top regardless of the sharp surface of the coral. She looked superb as she stood silhouetted against the sky, gazing at the ocean. Indeed, she seemed as much impressed by the vastness of the scene as I was. Then suddenly she squatted, delivered her droppings and quickly jumped off the rock while I tried to disentangle the nylon line before it was cut to threads by the sharp-edged coral.

While I was still engaged in doing this, Pippa, rolling in the sand

Pippa at the seaside

She loved the sand and the rocks

and clasping a rotten coconut, started a new game. Covered with wet sand, she looked so comical that I laughed aloud. This seemed to hurt her feelings; unexpectedly she pushed her legs with such force against me that I somersaulted backwards and when I got up was so bedraggled that I felt properly put in my place. I had barely time to scramble to my feet when she raced off and I had to run after her at what seemed to me not sixty, but a hundred, miles an hour. It would have been great fun but for the ghastly nylon line. This had been given to me by the Dunkeys, who had used it on a previous holiday when they had taken Pippa to the coast. They had advised me not to let her loose because she might chase people walking on the beach and because of the thick belt of vegetation which grew along the shore in which she might get lost. The precaution was justified so far as the local fishermen were concerned; however often I assured them that Pippa was a harmless pet, at her sight they bolted, thus inviting her to chase them.

Next day we visited the film camp. To everyone's delight, Girl and Mara had taken to the sea as if they had been born to it, and the difficulty was not how to induce them to enter the water but to get them out of it. In spite of all the fun, poor Girl was so distressed at being separated from her brother, Boy (another star of the animal cast), that it was decided to arrange for him to join her. While he was on his way, Mara and Girl rested in their compounds.

This gave all of us an opportunity to take a swim. For some time Pippa watched us splashing in the water, then suddenly she joined us, her mouth tightly closed. Soon she got out of her depth, but paddling frantically she swam after me. I felt very proud that she should have done so just to keep close to me, and I thought that by swimming in the ocean she had probably set a precedent in cheetah habits.

Next morning, while walking with Pippa and Muguru along the beach, I left her for a short time in charge of the boy. On my return, he showed me her empty harness dangling from the nylon line: she had slipped out of it in her attempt to follow me. We were about a mile from home and I was alarmed as it was impossible to trace her spoor in the dense vegetation. We called and searched as best we could for a long time and later were joined by our host. In the end we all got too thirsty to continue, so I suggested going home for a drink and carrying on the search afterward. As soon as we approached the bungalow I had a strange feeling that I was being watched and, bending low, saw Pippa hiding under a bush. She seemed as happy as I was that we were together again and, after a lot of face licking, she followed us home. I was astonished that after such a short time in a new environment she had been able to find her way back, and felt humbled at having so underestimated her innate homing instinct.

She soon developed another habit which puzzled me. We usually took our morning walks along the beach at early dawn when the air was cool and hardly any people were on the beach. The afternoon walks were less private and more strenuous because of the heat. But at whatever time of the day we passed the big coral rock, Pippa made a rush for it and deposited her droppings on its top. Later I observed that she always preferred to do her droppings on elevations, either on anthills or tree stumps. Possibly this was due to either an instinctive preference for a safe strategic position while handicapped in movement or to mark her territory. But how she could make the release of her movements coincide with whatever time we happened to pass the chosen spot, I could not understand.

Within the next few days Pippa grew less nervous about the water and, especially at low tide, enjoyed exploring the exposed beaches around the larger coral rocks, of which there were several close to the coast. Unfortunately, I had always to control her by the nylon line as she was only too keen to climb these islands from which I would have had no means of bringing her back should she decide to stay there when the tide came in. Meanwhile, she had a lot of fun poking at little fish in shallow pans, chasing after the provoking crabs or just splashing about in the water. Obviously, I was never able to photograph her swimming as she did this only to follow me and I could not take a photograph in these circumstances.

One night the sea got very rough, and the roaring of the crashing waves ebbed away only at dawn when the tide receded. On our morning walk we found large piles of seaweed, up to six feet high, deposited along the line of the tide, separated by narrow gaps. Pippa seemed to think that they had been put there for her entertainment and leapt from one pile to the next across the gaps with such speed that she seemed almost to fly. Having still to control her by the nylon line, Muguru and I took breathless turns at keeping up with her, and dreaded these heaps as much as Pippa favored them. As she interrupted our exercises only when other distractions diverted her interest, I now welcomed all holidaymakers in sight as they usually stopped to admire Pippa or take photographs. Although she was camera-shy, she tolerated this but then took her revenge by catching her admirers off guard, advancing on them from the back and then, with a quick movement of her front leg, swiping at their knees.

The filming of the lions in the sea went off splendidly and everybody was very pleased with the results. Toward the end of our stay I too wanted to take photographs of these marvelous scenes. Trying to keep out of the way of the filming unit, I awaited my opportunity near a coral rock while the camera crew floated on a raft close to the actors. According to the script, Mara was supposed to swim, with Bill and Ginny Travers (acting George and myself), and then all were to walk together to the beach. But Mara was far more interested in the rolling waves, which, as they reached the shore, broke high into spraying foam, then dissolved into little ripples, soaked up by the sand. She dived powerfully through the breakers, letting them roll over her, and bobbed up and down in the glistening foam waiting for the next wave to swamp her again. The Traverses had a tough time keeping up with her until they could direct her toward the cameras and wade with her into the picture. At this moment Mara saw me: she knew me well, but as I was wearing an unfamiliar bathing suit she seemed not to recognize me and, judging by her flattened ears, as she waded over determinedly, I knew that I was in for a rough game. Hoping to break the impact of her final rush and avoid landing on the sharp coral I pretended to feel at ease and walked slowly behind the rock, only just in time to rescue my camera from her reach before she bounced on me and knocked me into the shallow water. Then, having identified me, she sat on me and licked me gently while I stroked her. Finally she got up and waded back to the raft.

It was only then that I discovered she had accidentally slightly scratched my arm, which started to bleed as soon as I lifted it out of the water. Making use of the salt water as a disinfectant, I washed it repeatedly, then waded to the beach to take some photographs of the filming from the car of the White Hunter who had transported Mara to the scene. After this I swam out to the raft to congratulate everyone on the marvelous shots they must have got that morning.

On returning to the beach I was surprised to see our nursing Sister arriving with the first-aid box. Apparently she had been summoned by the White Hunter. I was very fond of Sister and appreciated her concern about my scratches but explained that I did not need all the injections which she was preparing to give me and suggested that all I needed was sulfanilamide. This had always proved very effective in dealing with the various injuries I had received during the years in which I had lived among wild animals, and these injuries had been much worse than today's superficial wound. Sister, however, insisted that I must be in great pain and therefore needed morphia and that I must also be treated for delayed shock since, considering my lacerated arm, my behavior was abnormal; next I was to be injected with penicillin to prevent blood poisoning and have inoculations against tetanus. In fact, I had to have the lot, for who was I to know what should be done in such an emergency?

Although I sympathized with Sister, who seemed to sense that this might be her only opportunity to use the lavish assortment of medical supplies with which she had been equipped for such a potentially dangerous film as ours was, with twenty lions starring as co-partners, I did not see why I should be the victim.

But all my protests were silenced, and after being duly injected with all those powerful drugs I was taken to the Malindi hospital to be stitched up as well. During the twenty-mile drive I felt very sick and only just managed to stagger into the hospital. I was so full of drugs that the doctor decided to give me one more injection to counteract the previous ones. By this time I was beyond caring and only vaguely conscious of having my arm attended to.

Eventually I was allowed to go home and to bed. Dizzy from all the treatment, I dozed off. But not for long, for soon visitors arrived to ask how I felt. Though this must have been obvious, they chatted on until another party came, followed by yet another. All I longed for was to be left alone. It took me two days to recover from the drugs, during which Pippa spent most of her time close to me. Since we had only known each other for two weeks, I was very touched at this proof of her affection.

All my life I had wanted to have a cheetah as a friend—then Elsa arrived. After her death I determined never again to become attached to any animal. But as cheetahs have such a different temperament and character from lions, I felt I could become attached to

Pippa without feeling disloyal to Elsa. If the lion is gregarious, demonstrative in its actions, ritual in its habits, fearful of no natural enemy, and placidly self-possessed, the cheetah is elusive, high-strung, always on the alert, and with an instinct for concealing itself. Listening now to Pippa purring, I was as content as she seemed to be.

The film unit went back to Naro Moru, but I stayed on for a little longer to do some TV scenes for a program intended to show the attractions of Kenya. Among the sites chosen were the ruins of Godi, an ancient Arab town which had recently been excavated. Its atmosphere was ghostly, but Pippa brought gaiety to it as she skipped among the broken, ornate gates and palace walls, her golden, spotted fur in beautiful contrast to the gray stones. She also helped me when doing scenes of the shore, for she gave an unusual touch to beach-combing.

When we were ready to return I found myself left to drive alone with Pippa from Mombasa to Naro Moru, a distance of 420 miles. After some hours she became very restless and, besides jumping about in the car, insisted on sitting on the steering wheel and on my bandaged arm. Finally I had no choice but to put her into the wired traveling crate I had taken along for such an emergency. Pippa resented this very much. Never before had she been confined in a crate, and she protested furiously, uttering a great variety of sounds which simulated bird calls. Among them I identified the call of the yellow-neck, a partridge (francolin). It was about two hours before she became exhausted and settled down.

At this time I knew very little about the habits of cheetahs and took her vocal performance as a normal reaction to distress. But later, when I asked cheetah and bird experts about it, I learned that I had been privileged to listen to a unique demonstration of a wild mammal imitating bird calls. Although on two later occasions I heard Pippa mock yellow-necks, she never again gave voice to such a variety of sounds; but neither has she since been in such distress.

Cheetahs live largely on birds and small mammals, and it may be that in the wild they imitate a bird in order to deceive and attract it. Yet whenever I have watched Pippa stalking birds, she has never uttered a sound. Perhaps this is because she has only been playing with the birds, not actually hunting them for food. The metallic chirp of the cheetah is well known; it is used to communicate or when alarmed. When Pippa defends her meat she growls and breathes heavily, but when she is content her purring shakes her body.

She had a cozy sleeping box, but even if it was raining she liked best to sleep outside in her compound. This was encouraging as it proved that she preferred natural conditions to living as a pet. Further to break her domestic habits, I stopped taking her to the main farmhouse where the unit lived; in any case, neither she nor the film people enjoyed each other's company. Pippa also never came to be at ease with the lions which lived close to the Simba Camp, but as there was nothing I could do about this, I spent as much time as I could with her on the plains where she was truly happy.

As soon as I let her out of the car she raced off into space, enjoying her freedom. She also loved the colored balloons I brought along for her. Carried by the wind, they bobbed wildly across the grass until she touched them with her claws and then, with a pop, they burst. Perplexed, she would sniff at the shriveled remains until I inflated a new balloon, then off she went on another chase. Other sources of fun were the ant-bear and wart-hog holes with freshly piled earth around to prove they were occupied. By the way in which Pippa almost disappeared into them I could judge how attractive their scent must be to her. She certainly did not share my worry about what would happen should one of the occupants come out to investigate. But the best fun of all was provided by the antelopes who grazed around in numerous herds. The little Thomson's gazelles especially intrigued Pippa. But after a few days they realized that we represented no danger to them and, exasperatingly disinterested, paid no attention to Pippa's stalking. However cleverly she crept through the grass, wriggling close to the ground and taking the best advantage of wind and cover, they ignored her and went on busily whisking their little tails until she was almost on top of them. Then, hopping off on stiff legs, they would turn around and wait until she had caught up again, only to repeat their provocation. I watched fascinated and was glad to see that Pippa's previous life as a pet had not impaired her natural instincts so I could hope that, with more opportunities and practice, she might someday hunt her prey like a wild cheetah.

CHAPTER

2

Early Training

TOWARD THE END of November George and I visited our home at Isiolo and took Pippa with us. During the sixty-mile drive we dropped sixty-five hundred feet to an altitude of three thousand feet in the semi-desert scrub country of the Northern Frontier. Pippa had no sooner arrived than she seemed to be quite at home and rolled delightedly in the reddish sand. Next she climbed the few acacia trees which grew close to the house and then investigated the nearby river. Fearing she might get lost, I called her back and put on her nylon line. But as she pleaded insistently to be released, after a short time I let her off, deciding to rely on her instinct to enable her to find her way home in her new environment. Later we took her for a stroll along the river, which seemed sheer paradise for her. Dashing into the undergrowth beneath the palm and fig trees, she found some yellow-necks; unfortunately for her, they flew across the river. Though it was only a narrow stream, we had seen crocodiles in its deeper pools and therefore did not encourage Pippa to cross it. Her attention was diverted by some guinea fowls and, rushing among them, she stirred the birds to flight. George shot one which, still flapping its wings, fell almost on top of Pippa. To our surprise she took no interest in it but made a face of disgust and walked away. A little later she spotted a few gerenuks. These graceful gazelles live only in hot, arid country; they are common around Wajir, where Pippa had been born. Perhaps her instinct told her that they were her natural prey, for she pursued the slender bucks determinedly and disappeared for such a long time that I feared she might have got lost in the dense acacia bush and lava boulders. When she returned, panting but happy, we were satisfied that we could trust her instinct, and thereafter I only confined her in my room after it had become dark. We had to do this because we often heard lions during the night and could not risk leaving her unprotected at her age.

George and I loved the Northern Frontier and our home at its southern border. Seeing how happy Pippa was here, too, we hoped that one day we might be able to rehabilitate her in this neighborhood, which seemed ideal since there were no livestock in the area and the ecological conditions were perfect for her. Our home was eight miles distant from the house we had occupied when Elsa lived with us. After George retired from the Game Department we had handed it over to his successor and, since then, had rented our present home. It belonged to the National Parks and stood out in the blue, the only human dwelling visible in all this vast country. Here we were a thousand feet higher than at Isiolo. Our house stood at the foot of an escarpment leading up toward Mount Kenya, whose glacier peaks we could see when looking south; to the north we overlooked the immense plain and the mountains of the Northern Frontier District, which stretched out to the horizon, and in the foreground we could see the hills which had been Elsa's playground. We had the amenities of civilization, such as a telephone, plenty of water from the river, a generator which provided electricity, a good library and a piano, but at the same time we enjoyed the happiness of living close to nature. From our veranda we could watch the wild animals during the hours of daylight or wake up during the night to the snorting of antelope or the sound of elephant browsing in our garden.

Unfortunately, owing to the remoteness, our ideal home had recently become unsafe because the Shifta were operating in the vicinity. Shifta was the term currently used to describe Somali bandits. In the past it simply meant any raiding party of any tribe which had entered Kenya illegally from the north and indulged in poaching, stealing livestock, or killing people. These raiders had always been one of the problems of this part of the N. F. D. I remember that whenever we were traveling in the northern boundary area and stopped for a break, four Game Scouts automatically took up positions at the four points of the compass, facing the horizon, to be on the lookout for any danger, and there they remained until we moved on. This was common practice for all safaris near the border, though luckily it was usually only a routine precaution. Since Kenya has become independent, the term "Shifta" has acquired a political significance and now describes any Somali or Boran tribesman who claims the N. F. D. as his country and is not willing to come under the rule of the Kenya Government. As the Somalis had no legal right to their claim, they hoped to establish it by guerrilla warfare. This racial conflict between the Nilo-Hamitic nomads of the semi-desert regions north of the equator and the rural, agricultural Bantu people south of it is not new but has developed in intensity since Kenya has become independent. Though the Kenyatta Government had taken action to control the Shifta, we were advised to remove our valuables from Isiolo to Naro Moru, where the film company had kindly offered to store our boxes. This was the purpose of our present visit, so, after having completed our packing, we returned.

A few days later the rains started and flooded the area. The land around Mount Kenya is rich, black cotton soil which turns into a sticky clay after the first downpour. The roads soon became almost impassable, and it was no fun slithering through the muck while driving Pippa to the plains. The lion trainers had no choice but to churn along with their charges when exercising them. I searched for a new playground where Pippa would be able to run free and which we could reach on foot. About a mile from my tent I discovered a plain on which the owner had cleared an airstrip. He seldom grazed his cattle there and agreed that I could let Pippa play on it provided she did not chase his stock when they were around.

My only remaining difficulty was how to coax her past the two lionesses whose compound we passed on our way. Pippa panicked when, on our first walk, the lionesses growled at her and sprang against the wire. Bolting with unbelievable strength, she almost tore my arm out as I hung on to her leash and struggled after her through the border fence into the thick bush of the adjoining farm. After calming her down we made a long detour before we returned to my tent, which, like Pippa's and the lionesses' compound, was close to the boundary fence. For the next few days we used this longer route, then Pippa grew less frightened and was willing to venture nearer the lionesses so long as I walked between her and them. But still there were times when she would stop as if paralyzed and stare at the lionesses until, without warning, she jerked my arm and we were off.

I was interested to see how conservative Pippa was, always using the same reeds to brush herself against, the same rocks for a lengthy rubbing, the same favorite bushes for a rest—to me they looked just like any other bush. Was this habit of hers the sign of an instinct to establish a territory?

Once we reached the plain I let her loose, and off she shot. It was wonderful to watch her effortless movements as she darted with lightning speed into the open. She soon made friends with two crowned plovers and a secretary bird who teased her mercilessly. The stately, long-legged secretary delighted in standing motionless while she stalked him until she made her final rush, then he took off swiftly, lunged at her from the air, and caused her to jump fruitlessly at him. Day after day they played together, then one day there was no secretary bird. Knowing the tree where he nested, I looked for him but never saw him again.

Pippa also had some fun with a family of wart hogs which included five tiny piglets. She always waited for them to move out from cover, then, as soon as the parents, followed by the little ones, in single file, tails erect, trotted into the open, she dashed at them and scattered the military formation of their procession. On one occasion she came very close to a youngster but left the battlefield hurriedly when the boar charged her with his formidable tusks.

One afternoon a small airplane landed close to us. Instantly Pippa rushed up to investigate this strange bird. When the pilot saw her circling the machine he entered into the game and turned the plane parallel with her. This delighted Pippa and she went on circling with the pilot until I had to put her on the leash. She seemed to have no fear of anything unknown and even boldly charged the freight train which puffed its noisy way along the nearby railway line; this gave me cause to worry.

She was already an excellent tree climber, and after inspecting all the trees in sight to find a suitably rough bark, she climbed swiftly into the top branches. I often marveled to see her turning around so sure-footedly on the slender boughs. Only once did she come to any harm, straining her ankle when jumping from a considerable height. I decided to confine her for a few days in her enclosure. But she hated this and, scrambling up the wire whenever I approached, did further harm to her injured leg. Realizing that rest was out of the question, I took her on the leash for short walks to give her exercise, which, apart from food and sleep, was obviously her greatest need.

From infancy Pippa had been used to walking on the leash, but since she had come to Naro Moru she had had so much freedom that she now disliked being controlled even for short distances. For one thing, this forced her to walk so close to me that any possibility of teasing me was prevented. On the plains she often ran out of my view, but when I called her she always responded and came trotting back until she saw me waiting for her, then she would stop and sniff, with a show of indifference. I was obliged to walk on, pretending to be equally indifferent. I knew, however, that she would follow me until I turned around to see what she was up to, when she would instantly freeze, look away, and wait until I moved on. This game was typical of Pippa's character and of her instinct to conceal her intentions. She was most affectionate and responded to affection, like all other creatures, but she disliked showing her feelings except by purring or nibbling my hand or ears. Sometimes she clasped me with her front legs in an embrace, but when I made a fuss over her she would walk away or look through me as if I did not exist.

She loved any game. For instance, she would carry a piece of rag around and shake it at me until I tried to catch it, and after I had chased her around the compound she would rush onto her tree platform, where she would crouch and hold the rag between her paws, plainly expecting me to grab at it. If I did she would jump quickly to the ground and, dancing around me, try to recover the rag, which I hid behind my back, until she won the game. Then there was an old tire dangling on a rope from a beam. It took her some time before she trusted this evasive toy, but in time she found she could control it by holding on to it with her front legs, after which she would walk around in circles on her hind legs with it or even somersault through it. I placed some solid rubber balls of varying sizes inside the tire for her to poke out and then chase, but on the whole she preferred games in which I took part, such as a tug-of-war over a stick.

To increase her opportunities for exercising I had a tripod ladder made, but she refused to climb it. Obviously she was afraid of the gaps between the bars although she showed no fear when stepping from one branch to another branch. During most of the hot hours of the day she slept on her platform, from which she could watch the many things which went on at the Simba Camp.

Feeding time was in the evening after we had returned from our walk. Knowing that cheetahs need a diet which includes birds to keep them fit, I added to her three or four pounds of meat and her milk some mousebirds, which lived in great flocks near the tent; she did not like them nor did she touch the chickens I offered her. She went on hunger strike until I gave in and again fed her only lean meat, substituting a dose of Abidec for the gristle and quills which she would have eaten in her wild state.

Pippa's sanitary habits were strange. She never slept inside her comfortable box but wetted the blankets inside it every night, and when I removed them she went on using the box as a lavatory. Her droppings she placed on the wooden benches or even sometimes on her tree platform.* This fouling of her lay-ups was odd, for otherwise she was as clean as any cat could be. She loved being brushed by me, and this became a ritual. Whenever she was in an obstreperous mood, I had only to stroke her with the brush and she relaxed and purred.

By now the weather had deteriorated and heavy rains made filming very difficult. So we looked forward to the Christmas break, when we would be able to relax.

George and I had intended spending the holidays with Pippa at Elsa's camp, but the road proved impassable so we drove instead to Isiolo. While I prepared a Christmas tree, I thought of how last year I had been traveling on an extended lecture tour around the world and had found myself in Fiji at this time.

How different was this Christmas Day. We decided to go across the hills where we had so often walked with Elsa. I had never returned there since she had left Isiolo. It was a beautiful, sunny morning. Pippa, eager not to be left behind, jumped quickly into the Land-Rover and, sitting between George and me on the front seat, excited the sleepy inhabitants of Isiolo, who crowded around the car to get a better look at her as we passed by. We left the Land-Rover at our old home, three miles from the township, and walked into the hills which surround the house like a horseshoe. Since the rains the coun-

* This might be interpreted as marking her territory.

An old tire was a favorite toy

try had turned a luscious green, flowers covered the ground, and almost every bush was in bloom. Myriads of insects hummed around the blossoms and brilliantly colored birds flew among the aloes to get the nectar from their waxen flowers, like crimson candelabra on the rocks.

I had little time to reflect on the past for Pippa was in high spirits. She dashed to and fro among the eroded watercourses and granite boulders and kept me busy anticipating her ambushes or her swipings. It was not long before she discovered that elephant balls were much more fun to play with than rubber balls; rolling the droppings around and around, somersaulting frantically from one to the other, she tossed the heavenly-smelling toys around until they fell apart. Then there were ground squirrels to be chased even though they were far too quick for her and always scampered into a hole before she could catch up with them. There were also many trees to climb as well as many anthills to investigate; in short, she had a very busy morning. Playing hide-and-seek with Pippa and seeing her so happy, I felt as though Elsa's spirit were joining our fun.

Climbing up a pass between two hills, we found the fresh footprint of a shoe. Having heard that a gang of Shifta was hiding some distance away, we suspected that this had been made by one of them; the local people usually wore rubber sandals of a different shape. After looking without success for more traces of the men, we climbed a hill which had been one of Elsa's favorite lookouts. Standing there, we overlooked the valley below, which was an emerald green color with dark patches where acacias clustered together, and reddish-brown threads where watercourses cut through the ground. To the north were more mountains, some with ragged shapes, some flat like giant boxes, while still others looked like pyramids. The distant plains were so level that they looked like a sea with anchored mountains floating on their surface. Toward the west the horizon was bounded by the Lorogi Plateau, which is part of the Great Rift. Southward, Mount Kenya towered into the sky, while the eastern view was limited by the volcanic Jombeni range on the other side of which lie the plains which became Elsa's final home.

While Pippa strained her eyes to see what was going on in the bush below, through our field glasses we observed several groups of elephants and giraffes resting under trees during the midday heat. Feeling hot too, we settled for lunch in a shady cleft among the rocks.

Pippa also found a cool spot from which she watched two bateleur eagles soaring into the sky. Then she relaxed and, resting her head on her front paws, purred contentedly. All we saw was vast and very beautiful: except for the twitter of birds and Pippa's purring, no sound broke the stillness. Looking at her and at George, I thought of Elsa and felt very happy. Here, truly, was my home.

On our return along the crest of the hills, Pippa stirred up some francolins. George shot one and, after wringing its neck, held it out of Pippa's reach; jumping, she tore it away and to our surprise ate it to the last bone. She obviously liked the francolin as much as she detested guinea fowl. Later in the afternoon George shot a guinea fowl. Pippa became very excited and sniffed around the thicket where it had fallen, paying no attention to the bird but investigating the area. We found this had been the lair of three lions. They must have left recently, for the grass was still warm where they had rested. Probably George's shot had alarmed them. It was interesting to see that Pippa, here, where she was free and in control of the situation, was not afraid of exploring their hide-out, whereas the lions at Naro Moru had filled her with such terror.

Next day we took Pippa into the newly established Isiolo Game Reserve. It was a splendid morning and the plains glistened. On this sandy ground the water was quickly absorbed except for a few puddles, and the climate was so warm that the rainy season never brought with it the gloom it does at higher altitudes. Driving along the plain and then along the swamp and doum-palm-sheltered rivulets, Pippa craned her neck and jumped around excitedly to see the herds of Grévy's zebras (the handsomest of the kind), oryxes, impalas, and antelopes—animals that were new to her—and saliva dribbled from her mouth. By the time it became hot and she had calmed down we looked for a tree by the Uaso Nyiro. The shade beneath an isolated, large acacia growing at a bend in the river, with a fine view in both directions, seemed an ideal picnic place. Through the foliage peeped a troop of vervet monkeys who became very agitated when Pippa left the car. The vervets have always been my favorites among all the monkeys of Kenya. I never tired of watching them moving gracefully among the trees and looking, their black faces contrasting with their light-colored fur, as though they were wearing masks.

Pippa hardly glanced at them and at once settled down to sleep beneath the tree. The vervets, however, were evidently very surprised at finding a cheetah in the company of human beings and, timid as these little creatures usually are, curiosity prevailed. Boldly they came nearer and nearer and made such a din that finally Pippa moved away in disgust and settled under a shady bush hidden from their view. Not daring to leave the safety of the tree, they now concentrated their attention on us. There were a great many of them, and we were constantly hit by their droppings. I bore with them until one landed inside my hat. That was too much for me; so I told the vervets in not too gentle a voice just what I thought of them, whereupon I was interrupted by George, who asked me not to make the monkeys nervous! In the circumstances I left George to his noisy friends and went to join Pippa.

Neither of us had any rest, for soon a herd of elephants arrived. Scenting us, they turned away with piercing screams and crossed the river downstream. It was a magnificent sight to see them wading through the shallow water in single file, the little ones chaperoned by their mothers and all holding their trunks high up until they reached the opposite bank. Here they felt sufficiently safe to spray water over their bodies, splash about, wrestle with each other, and toboggan down the bank until they had had enough fun and disappeared into the bush. During this performance, Pippa sat tense with excitement; she had never seen an elephant before, and I wondered if she associated these giants with the droppings she loved to play with. It was such a happy day that I felt like joining Pippa in her purring.

Next morning we had to return to Naro Moru. In the direction of Mount Kenya the country was still wrapped in heavy rain clouds. Pippa seemed not at all keen on returning to the world of cold and mud and the bustle of human activities; indeed, we had quite a job enticing her into the car.

When we arrived at Naro Moru I received news which made it necessary for me to fly to London, so I arranged with a young animal trainer employed by the film company who had previously shown interest in Pippa for him to look after her during my absence. He was to sleep in my tent so as to be close to her at night and take her for some walks, which he and George agreed to share between them.

I returned after three weeks and was just in time to watch George bringing Pippa back in his car from exercise. She gave me a terrific welcome, bouncing around me and nibbling at my hands and ears. George told me that while I was away she had once disappeared for two days. Although a large party spent most of the night searching for her, she was found only next morning and then near the main road where lots of traffic was passing. As she was so fond of traveling by car, she might well have run up to one, and I decided that in future we would never take her in that direction.

During our next afternoon's walk Pippa pulled me along at such a speed that I could hardly follow. As soon as we arrived at the plain our usual games began and her behavior was just as friendly as before I left for London. As the sun was setting some animals emerged from the bush, and Pippa promptly stalked them. When it got really late I called to her to come, but she ignored me, and however cunningly I tried to get close enough to slip the leash onto her harness, she immediately jumped away and went off for another chase. This went on until it was almost dark and I was desperate. Luckily, the farmer who owned the land passed by on his way to the Simba Camp, so I sent a message to George asking him to pick us up in his Land-Rover. While I was waiting I succeeded in securing Pippa to the leash, but then she stubbornly sat put and I was quite unable to move her. When George arrived he waved a piece of fresh meat at her, but she ignored it, showed no intention of jumping into the car, and followed our movements with hard, cold eyes. Whenever we tried to approach her she struck at us with her sharp claws, ripped our skin, and sent us bowling. Finally George threw a blanket over her and lifted her into the car.

I was shocked. What had come over Pippa? I had never before seen her so obstinate or so fierce, with such a murderous expression in her eyes. George then told me that while I was away they had often had difficulty in bringing Pippa back from the plains, but he had not been alarmed because she did not know him or the trainer as well as she knew me. When, next day, Pippa behaved in the same way, I realized that something had gone very wrong and that her trust in people had been injured. How could I restore it? The best way seemed to me to make use of our bluffing game. Next day, I took Muguru along with me to the plain, and we had great games until it was time to return. Then Pippa, sensing that I meant to put her on the leash again, avoided me most cunningly until I finally outwitted her and—hiding behind a bush—grabbed her quickly when she came to look for me. Realizing that she had lost the game, she now sat put in doglike fashion, digging her front toes firmly into the ground whenever I pulled the leash. I handed it over to Muguru and walked away. I had gone quite a distance before I heard her racing along with the panting boy trying to keep up with her. To give him time to regain his wind I walked ahead again, and thus we repeated the procedure until we reached home.

This method worked well for a few days, after which Pippa was no longer to be fooled. As soon as I handed the leash to Muguru she struck out with her legs at the poor fellow and sent him flying, then she just sat and would not budge. I tried without success to entice her into the car, but she kicked at us whenever we came close to her. The only way left was for me to try to handle her on my own again, since obviously she was at her worst when other persons were involved.

During the next weeks I was often exasperated as I stood at dusk in the icy wind, or in the drizzling rain, waiting for her to move, talking softly to her and petting her until she responded and slowly trotted home. Here she would find a big chunk of meat waiting for her, which she sometimes allowed me to hold while she chewed away at it. After her meal we sat together on a heap of fresh straw until she dozed off.

It is often said that cheetahs can never be house-trained, perhaps because they have no lairs; if they had, they might keep them clean as lions do. Although Pippa was clean as to her body and had no smell, she continued not to care where she left her droppings and still often fouled her platform or the wooden benches. Because, even during heavy rains, she never used her sleeping box but preferred to lie on straw, I had a wooden hut made in which the straw could be kept dry and where she could have shelter during the icy nights. But the only use she made of the hut was as a vantage point from the roof of which she could observe the neighborhood.

Every day Pippa became more restless. She would climb up the twelve-foot-high wire of her compound, and one day I found her actually hanging on its top. Although I sympathized with her wish to be free, I had quickly to get an overhang attached to prevent her climbing out.

During this time a group from the American TV program "Today" visited us to make a film of our animals. At dawn I took them out with Pippa to the plain to catch the sun rising behind

Mount Kenya, against which splendid spectacle they wished to film her. The grass till glistened with the heavy dew as we stood shivering in the cold morning air and Pippa raced around, using up her unspent energy. I was asked to join in her game. Though I realized what a contrast there would be between my movements and her effortless grace, I skipped about and rolled in the wet grass hoping the scene would help to illustrate the amazing elegance and sheer beauty of a cheetah's movements set against the vastness of the plains with Mount Kenya now silhouetted in the rising sun. For me, this was a symbol of freedom, of the freedom I wanted to give to all animals but especially to the ones which had been used in our film. During the last ten months we had accumulated twenty-one lions and we expected another litter of cubs within a few days. What would become of all these animals when filming was completed? For us and for Virginia and Bill Travers the only solution was to rehabilitate all the lions to a natural life in the way in which we had succeeded in rehabilitating Elsa and her cubs.

We expected that the film company would be only too glad to let the lions live the lives they had been acting in *Born Free* and were shocked when we learned that all the lions owned by the company were to go to zoos, while those few which were privately owned would be returned, with the exception of Boy and Girl. These had been the mascots of the 2nd Battalion of the Scots Guards; now through the kindness of Sgt. Ron Ryves and R. S. M. Campbell Graham they were given to George to rehabilitate to their natural wild heritage.

While we were desperately trying to save as many of our friends as we could from a future in captivity, the international press took up the story, and headlines concerning the *"Rumpus about the Born Free Lions"* circled the world. During the ensuing correspondence it became obvious that many letter-writers confused the meaning of release with that of rehabilitation: some believed that we were cruel to want to expose the lions to the hazards of wild life, which they were unlikely to survive after their pampered past with human foster parents. We were also accused of endangering people's lives by wanting to set free lions which had lost all fear of men. These criticisms are justified in the cases of animals simply released in Game Reserves regardless of whether they can fend for themselves or not. But we wanted to *rehabilitate* the lions. This is a long process

which involves very close contact with the animals until one is satisfied that they are able to hunt and kill efficiently, have established their territorial rights in competition with the local lions,
and have acquired immunity against local diseases. In the early
stages we knew we would have to help with food, protect them
against wild lions, and treat them against possible infections. Wild
lions do not usually leave their pride and hunt on their own before
the age of two years. We therefore planned to stay with our lions
until their hunting instincts were well developed.

Ever since we had successfully rehabilitated Elsa and her cubs,
I had been looking forward to having similar opportunities in the
course of which I hoped to discover new methods of conservation. At
the moment, while the wild beasts are decreasing at an alarming
rate, the zoo-born cubs are often destroyed for lack of a market. This
is partly due to the fact that in captivity a lioness will breed every
three and a half months just out of boredom, while in the wild she
is fully occupied rearing her young and will not mate for two years,
that being the time when they become independent of her help.
With more experience in rehabilitating lions the present vicious circle might be broken by restocking the African bush with zoo-born
animals before they lose their virility and while they are still at a
manageable age. Cheetahs are in an even greater need of help,
since they not only decrease alarmingly under natural conditions but,
with the exception of those in the Whipsnade and Krefeld zoos and
a private zoo in Rome (Dr. Spinelli's), they do not breed in captivity. So far as I knew no one had yet attempted to rehabilitate a
cheetah pet. This was a challenge, and besides there was the fascinating problem of whether a cheetah that had been reared by
human beings would revert to normal breeding habits.

After a heartbreaking, losing fight to ensure a free life at least
for Ugas, a magnificent lion, and Henrietta and Mara, splendid
lionesses who had taken the part of Elsa in many scenes, we had to
reconcile ourselves to the fact that of all the animals used in
the film, only Girl and Boy would leave the film location for
a wild life.* Our next step was to find a place suitable for their rehabilitation. After approaching some of the National Parks with neg-

* Later, Ugas joined them.

ative results, we met with enthusiastic co-operation from the Warden of the Meru Game Reserve.

By now only a few shots remained to be done. One of these
was a courting scene between Ugas and Henrietta. While the camera
crew were arranging the setting, George and a trainer took the animals to a plain and exercised them until they had used up most of
their energy and seemed sufficiently relaxed for the filming to take
place. Then confining each one in its Land-Rover cage, we drove to
the place where the camera crew were waiting, secured inside their
vehicles.

According to the script, Ugas was to rest under a bush where Henrietta was to join him for a love scene. He was a formidable lion and
no playmate for anybody who did not know him well. George, who
was Ugas's "pal," got a good share of his vigorous affection as soon
as he was let out of the car. Standing on his hind legs and resting
his four hundred pounds of weight on George's shoulders, he licked
his face almost raw with his rasping tongue. While enduring this
demonstration, George gradually coaxed Ugas to the bush, where
finally he lay down.

All this was watched by Henrietta; still inside her Land-Rover, she
had become increasingly restless, and as soon as she was free she
went for Ugas and showed very clearly that she was not prepared to
share his love with George. She chased the poor fellow from his comfortable position, dashed at him repeatedly, at one moment making a
lightning strike at him, the next crouching low, growling with bared
teeth while preparing for another vigorous attack. Ugas tolerated
Henrietta's provocation like a gentleman, but certainly she was behaving more like an outraged Xanthippe than an amorous partner.
What was she up to? Why was she biting and clawing at him? George
assured me that she was making love; to me it looked as though she
were very angry, and I became concerned about poor Ugas. I
thought that if this was lion-style wooing, it was a rough way of showing one's affection, and Ugas seemed to agree with me. Stopping
Henrietta in mid-air during her next assault, he bowled her over
with a stroke of his powerful paw. She was not in the least upset
but, landing on her back, caressed him gently and seemed as happy
and content as any loving female might be who had been put in
her place by her lord and master. Ugas had hardly moved during

31

Henrietta's love play, and only his perplexed expression showed his surprise and bewilderment. In the end, looking down at her with an embarrassed and bemused expression, he might have been saying: "You foolish darling, why this pretense when I know all the time how much you love me?"

This scene was not only amusing but it also gave me an insight into Henrietta's character. She was devoted to George, whom she accepted as perhaps the favorite among her pride, allowing him all sorts of familiarities which normally she would permit only from other lions. But this morning he had unwittingly become her rival. The fact that she ignored him and concentrated on Ugas seemed to indicate her differentiating between her kin and her human friend, who in a sexual contest was of no interest.

When the film unit broke up, George and I were, together with the animals, among the last to remain on location. We hoped up to the very end to save some more lions from the zoos, but we had to watch the prides being split up with a total disregard to the extent to which the lions were devoted to and dependent on each other. When I stressed how unhappy these animals were going to be when they were separated I was asked what I knew about a lion's feelings. I mentioned that Elsa's sons, Jespah and Gopa, lost their manes after her death and that this was a reaction similar to that of cats who molt when under a great strain. I pointed out that Elsa's sisters, having been brought up by us in freedom for five months, could not adjust themselves to zoo environment for many years, and, in spite of the fact that they, as well as their mates, were in perfect physical condition, during this period they only gave birth to stillborn and abnormal cubs. I reminded my opponents of how unmanageable Mara had been when she arrived at the location and how soon she had changed when George gave her the love and attention she had been missing and how his treatment of her had brought out her endearing character. Finally I recalled how Girl had fretted at the coast when she was separated from Boy and indeed could not be used for filming until she was reunited with her brother. But all my arguments were silenced by the hammerings of the carpenters who were busy making crates for the lions' departures.

One morning I found two boxes in the compound where the younger cubs were kept. Cuddling together in the farthest corners of the compound, obviously terrified, the members of each litter

Ugas greets George

Henrietta reproaches Ugas

Love affair between Henrietta and Ugas

clung to each other; this was their only reassurance as people rushed around offering them meat to induce them to enter the crates. In the late afternoon the cubs had still not moved but watched with evident terror the arrival of a truck. It had come to transport them to the Nairobi airport. Four cubs were picked out according to the requirement of the zoo and carried away, struggling. The remainder were left to their bewilderment until later they, too, were split up and dispatched to other zoos.

I fail to understand how anyone who had spent ten months with these intelligent and sensitive animals could treat them as if they had no feelings and sort them out like packets of tea in a grocer's shop to sell to various buyers. I thought sadly that when these unfortunate cubs found themselves deprived of love and of all familiar surroundings, to which would be added the shock of traveling conditions and of quarantine regulations, they would probably become suspicious or unfriendly; then people would term them unpredictable and dangerous beasts, but no criticism would be made of the people who were responsible for turning lovable animals into fierce lions—an image of the King of Beasts which the ignorant public accepts.

Watching the departure of Henrietta was a heartbreaking experience. She was my favorite and had endeared herself to all of us by her good-natured and grand sense of humor. She could always be relied upon to act tricky scenes in which other lionesses had failed. Being a born comedienne, she had given everybody endless fun with her clowning. A trick she often put on for visitors was to get entangled in the ropes attached to an old tire which she would then fling onto her shoulders like a rucksack, after which she paraded up and down until her audience was weak with laughter. Such a deep bond of affection had developed among all of us for Henrietta that it seemed unbearable to think of her returning to confinement at the Entebbe Orphanage. We had fought for her freedom more vigorously than for that of any of the others, so it was a shock when one afternoon I arrived at her compound to see a caged car placed against the gate to take her away. She jumped eagerly into the familiar Land-Rover, obviously thinking that she was off for another romp in the plains. Through the wire she licked my hand trustingly for the last time. When I watched the car disappearing from the Simba Camp, taking her to lifelong imprisonment, I felt as if I had witnessed an execution.

The worst scene of all was the separation of a lioness from her cubs, whom she had borne only three weeks earlier. The little ones could barely crawl, and when they lost their balance, as they did constantly, they miaowed for help until Mom licked them affectionately and restored them to happiness. It was sheer cruelty to deprive such young animals of their mother and for purely commercial reasons: I quote Sally Carrighar:

Harry F. Harlow at the University of Wisconsin, with Margaret K. Harlow, has an extensive project to study the development of sub-human primates, especially the influence in their lives of love and affection. Harlow is unusual as a biologist in making a frank statement that he hopes his findings may have some relationship to the subject of human behavior.

In order to have a large colony of the monkey subjects for the investigations, ten years ago fifty-five infant monkeys were removed from their mothers as soon as born and were placed in a nursery where the conditions seemed so ideal—from the standpoint of feeding, supervision and health protection—that one could wish many children might have as auspicious a start. The only thing they lacked was contact with an adult monkey. They could play with their infant companions during certain hours and interesting observations were made about the form that their play took as these monkeys matured. So far they seemed quite normal.

Meanwhile another batch of monkeys, ninety of them, were similarly reared away from their own mothers but with manikin mothers that were something like large-sized dolls with terrycloth bodies artificially warmed. The bottles from which the infants were fed even had nipples which protruded from some of the manikins' breasts. The babies developed great attachment to these substitute mothers, and something was learned about the importance to infants of softness and warmth.

These so-hygienic young monkeys also appeared to thrive; more of them may have lived to grow up than would have if they had been raised under normal conditions. The fact was gratifying, since it was hoped to form them into a breeding colony, from which there would be a continuous supply of infant monkeys for further tests. To the astonishment and dismay of the scientist, the ninety motherless young never reached a stage where they wanted mature sexual relations. None of the males and only one female has ever been willing to copulate. Of the monkeys reared with the manikin mothers the record is better, but only slightly: of the ninety, four have become parents. And this too is significant: of the females that did bear children, none treated her offspring well. They either ignored them or abused them so badly that the young had to be taken away from them.

There have been other surprising and sad developments as the experimental monkeys matured. They have shown many signs of extreme neuroticism and even psychosis. Most of them spend their time sitting passively staring out into space, not interested in other monkeys or anything else. Some of them tensely wind themselves into tortured positions, and others tear at their flesh with their teeth. Harlow reports that these are all symptoms found in human adults confined in institutions for the insane.

These results were totally unexpected, and even now it is difficult to explain why an early and close physical contact with mothers is so essential. Normally, that kind of contact does not last very long—only a few months in rhesus monkeys. After that time the young "begin to get on the mother's nerves." And that is the stage at which impatience can lend an impetus to the start of the training program, a stage at which being treated with some irritation does not have any adverse effect on the growing monkey. It is a natural period in the animals' development and they go on from it to mature and almost without exception to form heterosexual relationships.

In the wilds, of course, a newborn animal deprived of its mother's care would not often survive. It is not known what happens to infants that are able to live but whose mothers have given them too little attention or for too short a time. Perhaps in adult years these infants become the "lone wolves" known in many species. Men who are familiar with animals —hunters, naturalists, trappers—have long assumed that the animals' solitude when they are grown is due to a lack of mothering at some time in their youth.

In the case of monkeys like those of the Harlows, who can say whether the more important lack was the physical contact with living mothers or the failure of emotional reassurance? If warmth of feeling exists at all in these animals as adults, perhaps it cannot be expressed because they never learned the way to communicate an emotion. A social sharing precedes sexual sharing, and if there has not been a normal give-and-take between an infant and mother, the social instinct may never have been aroused. In the results of the Harlows' experiments some animal psychologists see a similarity to the hundreds of known situations in which human children have failed to develop normal social attitudes when they were deprived of maternal care, or had inadequate maternal affection during some of their early months. When those children did not actually die, as many did, they, like the Harlows' animals, have become withdrawn, sometimes antisocial, or have failed to establish families of their own in their adult life. Now the possibility is proposed: that a deficiency in the mother-child relationship actually means that no "imprinting" process occurred.*

* *Wild Heritage,* pp. 78-80, © 1965 Sally Carrighar, Houghton Mifflin Company, Boston.

3

*I Decide to Return Pippa
to the Wild*

DURING THESE TRYING WEEKS, Pippa was my comfort; it was wonderful to see how rapidly she developed her wild instincts, although this made her increasingly difficult to handle. She seemed to live only for the hours when I could take her to the plains, where she could romp about and be happy; while it was marvelous to watch her enjoying her freedom, it was less fun trying to bring her back to confinement. To give her the maximum exercise at home I not only enlarged her compound but also stretched a long steel cable between two trees to which her leash could be attached by a smoothly running ring. Pippa enjoyed this new run along the cable for a few days but soon came to dislike its limited liberty. Seeing her struggling along the wire or running frantically up and down inside the compound, I became convinced that a prolonged confinement would damage her character. So even though Pippa was only fifteen months old and far too young to fend for herself, I decided to take her as soon as possible to the Meru Reserve and remain there with her until she could be returned to her natural wild life.

I discussed my plan with two friends who had reared cheetahs in the past; both assured me that Pippa would always remain dependent on me because, once a cheetah has established such an intimate contact with a human being as to accept hand feeding and even to take the person's hand into its mouth, it will never leave its friend for good, even if it sometimes goes off on its own for some days. Despite these discouraging remarks, I intended to give Pippa at least a chance of living a natural life. To prepare her for this I had her inoculated against distemper and wrote to the Dunkeys for their consent to set Pippa free. I was much relieved when I received their reply:

Yes, we would both like to hear of Pippa going back to her wild state again. It would be just what should be for her; we would all then feel that we had been able to save her life and give her back to the wild where she should be, and I do hope you will be able to do this and not be too sad when she is gone. I still miss her very much and know it will be the same for you. I am so pleased to hear that you have managed to get two of the lions [Boy and Girl] back to their life; I feel so sad when I see them locked up in cages. I couldn't take my children to the zoo here; it upsets me too much to see the poor things in this cold and wet, and the children also feel upset and do not want to go there.

We went to Isiolo to collect our camping kit. There we learned that recently the Shifta's activities had increased to such an extent that it would be unwise to bring back the boxes containing our valuables from the film location where they were. So we employed two caretakers to guard our house and furniture and then returned to Naro Moru; here we rented part of a house to store our belongings during the time we should spend rehabilitating our animals.

It rained and rained, and this made it very difficult to set up our two camps in the Meru Reserve. Since cheetahs and lions do not live happily together, it would be impossible for them to share the same camp. We resolved the problem by establishing two camps at a distance of sixteen miles from each other; in this way the animals would be kept apart, while we could remain in close contact. George and I had engaged a young assistant who, in order to cope with the necessary preparations, was obliged to travel several times over the 180 mud-soaked miles that lie between Naro Moru and the Meru Reserve. Finally, all was ready for the move. George went first in his cage-equipped Land-Rover, with Boy and Girl, and I followed a few days later with Pippa. The slippery roads caused much delay, then I ran into a police check-post where, to my great surprise, I learned that I was not in possession of a valid driving license. By the time I had explained that all the documents concerning my car were dealt with by my chartered accountant at Nairobi, and after I had written a letter to the firm asking them to cope with this matter, several hours had elapsed, so we arrived at our destination in the late afternoon.

There we were welcomed by the Assistant Park Warden, Joseph Mburugu, who generously offered to help us in any way he could. He was an Imenti-Meru and was in charge of the Reserve while the Park Warden was on leave. Taking immediate advantage of his kindness, I asked for labor to clear a new campsite as the one my assistant had prepared was too far from the river for carrying water to the camp and too close to the road for privacy. He promised to send men the next morning, and after he had left we settled down for the night. Although we were exhausted, we did not sleep much but listened to the whuffings of a lion who circled our camp until dawn.

The labor gang turned up early, and a busy day started. Putting Pippa on her leash, we went off to look for a new site. While struggling through the shoulder-high grass, I noticed that Pippa was very nervous, especially when we approached the river. At first she stuck close to me, then she refused to go farther, so I secured her to a shady tree nearby. We selected a good camping site under a large acacia.

Soon the place was bustling with noisy Africans clearing the ground and erecting tents. Pippa was not pleased at being left out of the fun and "chirped" her protest through all the hammering and yelling until I let her loose. My fear that she might bolt proved unjustified; to my surprise, she settled among the busy men, utterly ignoring them.

The new campsite was below a gentle slope and thus concealed from the road which led to Leopard Rock, the headquarters of the Reserve, four miles away. The distance from the camp to the river was about 150 yards. To guarantee a safe supply of water, if elephants or other game should claim priority to its access, Joseph provided us with enough pipelines to pump the water into camp, a luxury I had never had in all my twenty-eight years of safari experience. He also offered a Game Scout to escort me on my walks with Pippa.

The Game Scout was an old friend of ours, a kindhearted, loyal Igembe-Meru, with a genuine love of animals. He was also one of the best trackers we had ever come across. By profession he was a carpenter, but he had worked for many years under George collect-

Pippa with George and Joy

ing information for the Game Department. Later, he was in charge of Elsa's goat larder until her death in 1961. His heart was as large as his flow of never-ending chatter, and he was always in trouble with newly-wed or bolting wives. When I now inquired about his matrimonial affairs, he grinned and confessed, with a twinkle, that he needed just a little more money to pay the bride-price for yet another wife. I do not speak Swahili well, though I have managed to get along for twenty-eight years with the Africans, but now, when our old friend jabbered excitedly, it took some guessing to realize that what sounded to me like "Local" was his pronunciation of Leopard Rock and that this was where he wanted me to meet his bride. As his name, Toithanguru, was as unpronounceable to me as the English language was to him, I nicknamed him Local.

We pitched the staff tents at a short distance from mine and the young assistant's, which were close to a kitchen shelter, a store tent, and Pippa's compound. Finally, all was fenced in by eight-foot-high wire to protect us against unwanted visitors, whether Shifta or four-legged.

Thanks to constant patrols by the Home Guard and the Police, the Shifta had not troubled the Reserve for several months though they were active outside its boundaries, which to the north adjoined the N. F. D. The Park Warden chose the site of my camp, partly on security grounds because of its nearness to Leopard Rock, partly because the surrounding plains were excellent cheetah country. Sparsely covered with trees and scrub, they offered open views in all directions; they were made still more attractive to Pippa by many termite hills which stood like reddish pinnacles among the luscious greenery.

That afternoon on our first walk across the plains, Pippa was quick to recognize the vantage point these termite hills provided. She leapt onto every one in sight, and from it watched the Grant's gazelles and waterbucks, elands, kongonis, oryx antelopes, and baboons. She also never missed a tree with a rough bark, and we had to keep a careful watch lest she should disappear into the foliage. Screening the surroundings from her lofty position, she kept us waiting for a long time before she leapt to the ground to give chase to a flock of guinea fowl which she provoked into flight. Next she was distracted by a buck and, before we could stop her, dashed after him, and we lost sight of both in the high grass. When she returned she rubbed her head against my knee, purring, but stopped abruptly

Pippa climbing tree

Pippa on termite hill

when a bird offered the chance of another chase. I had never seen Pippa so playful or so energetic, and her happiness was infectious. At sunset, as we returned to the camp, she had a game with two kongoni antelopes before she decided to follow us home and settle down for her meal. To give her complete freedom I took off her harness and only at night shut her up in her compound in order to protect her from predators until she would be able to defend herself. To provide her with something familiar in her new home I had brought her wooden hut, which we reassembled inside her enclosure. This proved an excellent idea, and from now on, every morning, at first light, I heard her jumping onto its roof where she remained until we took her for a walk.

Cheetahs and lions will always take advantage of any elevation, be it a hill, a rock, a tree, an anthill, or a car, and there is a case on record of a pride of lions which took over an abandoned house in Tanzania on the roof and veranda of which they were often seen. Elevations offer not only a strategic advantage but are above the tsetse fly belt and often catch a breeze. The roof of the wooden hut was Pippa's substitute for such summits, and she made the most of it.

Next morning I was awakened by the hunger rumblings of elephants. Obviously, we had pitched our camp close to one of their drinking places. Sniffing at our scent with raised trunks, two of these giants stood close to the tents; ten more were on the far side of the river. Pippa sat erect on her hut watching these new friends as eagerly as we did until the herd joined up and walked down river. Later Pippa disappeared. We searched in a large circle around the camp until I became alarmed by the shrieking of baboons coming from the direction in which the elephants had gone. I dashed off by car but saw only two buffaloes emerging from the river bush from which the noise had come. After this we continued the search on foot until lunchtime, when George arrived. He had been outside the Game Reserve to make a kill and brought some meat for Pippa. The arrangement to kill outside the Reserve had been agreed on with the Park authorities and was to hold good until Boy and Girl could kill for themselves.

George had made his camp at the foot of Mugwongo Hill, in the center of the Reserve. The nearest river was three miles away, but there was a large swamp near the base of the hill. This attracted many of the animals which roamed across the savanna where the bush was denser than around the camp. It was an ideal spot: the game felt safer from predators when they went to drink at the swamp than they would have done in dense river bush, and therefore they congregated in great herds here; also, Boy and Girl were in less danger in the open from possible attacks from their own kind. The rocky surface of the hill offered superb lookouts and lairs, and as the local lions were known to reside here only occasionally, Boy had a good chance to become "King of the Castle."

George shared his camp with an assistant, a cook, and a lion boy who had helped with Boy and Girl since their arrival at the film unit. As I had been eager to see how they would settle in, we had decided that I should visit George the next day, and this I did. At midday the lull was broken by the piercing shrieks of baboons. Fearing for Pippa's life, I dropped my knife and fork, grabbed my sunglasses and helmet, and ran in the direction of the noise, thereby causing panic among the monkeys. The entire camp had followed me, and the appearance of so many people made the monkeys flee in ear-splitting frenzy, which naturally did not help us to find a frightened cheetah. We made a thorough search through the high grass, inspecting every bush and investigating all trees beneath which we thought she might have found refuge from the baboons. We searched all through the afternoon until finally it became too dark to continue on foot and George had to return to his camp. Fearing that poor Pippa might be in trouble, I continued looking for her by car, driving slowly along the road, calling and stopping repeatedly until at 9 P.M. I returned home, defeated.

Soon afterward I heard an unmistakable purr and a moment later felt the head of a very thirsty and hungry Pippa brush against my knee. After she had drunk nonstop for a long time I gave her all the meat George had intended as a three-day ration: she gulped it down, stretched out, and fell asleep.

I would have given a lot to know about Pippa's adventures, but I had to content myself with the fact that she had not been injured, for which I was most grateful. How much she would have to learn before she would be able to live on her own. The law of the bush is harsh and does not allow for any mistakes. One of the greatest dangers here were the baboons. However amusing these clowning monkeys can be, they are notorious for savage attacks on single animals,

Pippa in camp

which they can tear to pieces with their formidable canines. Since Pippa chased anything moving, these troops, which had their territories along the river but scattered everywhere in its vicinity, were now our greatest problem. Pippa must quickly be taught that these tantalizing "jack-in-the-boxes," who so temptingly popped their heads out of the high grass, were her most dangerous foes. For one thing, their ability to shin up the smooth stems of a doum palm into safety, which Pippa could not do, gave them a great advantage.

Another problem was getting her used to drinking from the river: up to now she always had been given water from a bowl or had drunk from shallow rain puddles. Though the river here was in many places narrow enough for her to jump across it, it was alive with fish, pythons and crocodiles, and, in the deeper pools, hippos. The dense vegetation growing along its banks gave shelter to buffaloes, elephants, lions, antelopes, monkeys, and an occasional leopard, the creature most feared by all wild animals. To get access to the water through the thick undergrowth we had to follow game tracks leading to drinking places, but though these provided convenient gaps, they were covered with the spoor of the animals which frequented these pools, and the scent they had left behind terrified Pippa. The only way to get her used to drinking from the river was to take her for a long walk, then, when she was thirsty, lead her to a drinking place and sit with her until she had quenched her thirst.

We were at an altitude of about two thousand feet and the climate was warm. Most animals keep under cover during the heat of the day, so we decided to take Pippa out for her exercise early in the morning and again from teatime to dusk. During these walks we covered as much terrain as we could so as to get her acquainted with her new home.

Her education started with a walk to a low ridge from which she could see our camp and also overlook the surrounding plain and observe any approaching predators. Often we lost her in the high grass, then, looking around, found her hiding nearby, ready to dart off as soon as we spotted her. Giraffes intrigued her greatly. She has sharp eyesight and, even if these stately sentinels appeared far away on the horizon, she would start off at once for the chase, later to return panting but obviously pleased at having put such large creatures into action. When it got hot and she was tired, we rested under a tree until she dozed off.

Pippa and Local

I now arranged for Local to stay with her to make sure that she would not get into trouble while I visited George. When I sneaked off she lifted her head sleepily but made no attempt to follow me: this looked promising, as I wanted her to be as much as possible away from camp.

The track to George's camp led through attractive country along swamps and hilly plains with patches of doum palms everywhere. The doum palms are very useful in arid regions because they always indicate ground water, however deep one may have to dig for it. I crossed wooded ground where elephants and rhinos had left their mark by rubbing against the rough bark of large trees until it was smoothly polished. Finally I reached the Rojoweru River, one of the five major streams of the Reserve; it was from this that George had to get the water for his camp, three miles away. After crossing the river, Mugwongo Hill with its twin top, by far the largest of all outcrops in the area, came into view.

Partly because it was a landmark at the center of the Reserve, and partly because of the quantities of game in the area, an airstrip had been cleared at its base for the use of tourists and for poaching control. I realized that this airstrip would come in very handy should George ever be in need of help. How soon this was to be, neither of us could then have imagined.

I found George and his assistant sitting gloomily inside their tents, both feeling very depressed because Boy had not moved since the previous day and was obviously ill. I went to visit him and saw Girl lying close to her brother. She was licking his head affectionately, plainly trying to comfort him. His breathing was very fast. George took his temperature—not an easy thing to do with Girl guarding Boy so closely and suspicious of every move George made, but finally he succeeded in pushing the thermometer into Boy's rectum; when removed, it showed 104.4°. The normal temperature of a lion is about 100°. We thought that Boy must have been infected by a tick and was suffering from the dread tick fever from which Elsa died, or that he had developed trypanosomiasis as a result of being bitten by tsetse flies. In either case he needed treatment urgently. I suggested that a blood smear should be taken from Boy's ear which George's assistant could take to the Nairobi Veterinary Laboratory, from which he would return with the necessary medicines.

Meanwhile I made radio contact with the Vet at Meru and asked him to come immediately with a field microscope in case Boy's illness needed treatment before the assistant could get back from Nairobi. Both Vets considered that Boy was suffering from trypanosomiasis. This can be cured by berenil injections, which George administered without much difficulty during the next days. Boy seemed hardly aware when George pushed the needle into his thigh. The drug worked very effectively and soon Boy was well again. How differently individual wild cats react to tsetse bites is shown by the fact that Boy became infected as soon as he arrived in the Reserve, while neither Girl nor Pippa ever contracted this disease.

When I returned home in the late afternoon I saw a cobra in the annex to my tent and killed it. I then looked for Pippa and found her with Local at the same spot at which I had left them in the morning. Sleepily, she followed us for a stroll and only showed interest when she almost stepped into a flock of guinea fowl, which, giving their grating call, took to flight. Joseph had kindly allowed me to shoot an occasional game bird in order to teach Pippa how to hunt, and so now I asked Local to kill one. The bird dropped almost on top of Pippa, still flapping. Having no clue as to how to tackle it, she watched it with a bewildered expression and poked at it with her paw until we wrung its neck. We then removed the pellets to prevent her from getting lead poisoning and gave it to her. Though she was hungry, she only ate half of it.

Next morning I went on with Pippa's education by taking her to the tree where she had rested with Local the day before. I hoped that this time she would remain there by herself during the heat of the day. But after I had settled her by the tree, she three times stubbornly followed me; then I gave up and took her to the river to a drinking pool where I offered her the remains of the guinea fowl. When at last she seemed to have fallen asleep I withdrew quietly only to see her following me equally quietly back to camp.

If Pippa had disliked being confined at Naro Moru, at her new home she really hated it. However, since she was still too inexperienced to cope with the dangers of the night, I had to harden my heart and trick her into her compound at sundown, and of course this was just the time when all her senses were keyed up for hunting.

That night three lions circled our camp whose whuffs and gruntings I heard until early dawn. I do not know how Pippa reacted to them, but with the first glimmer of light I heard her thumping on

Pippa and Joy

*Pippa climbing
down tree*

her hut and saw her staring in the direction in which the lions had disappeared. When, later, I wanted her to come for a walk she refused to join me and sneaked off into the high grass close to camp, from where, even at teatime, she was reluctant to follow us to the river for a drink.

When night came still more lions kept us awake; we heard their bodies swishing through the grass outside the fence. I expected to find Pippa even more timid in the morning, and so I was surprised when I saw her chasing after waterbucks and finally lost her about a mile from camp. At teatime she came back, thirsty and tired, but as soon as she had quenched her thirst at the river (she was still very nervous about drinking its water), she was off chasing some Grant's gazelles.

During the next days Pippa sneaked away whenever we wanted to take her for a walk and made it plain that she preferred to explore the bush without us. Finally, one night she failed to return. We spent the whole of the following day looking in every likely place but found no trace of her. Continuing our search next day I was much alarmed to hear frequent outbursts from the baboons which might well have meant that Pippa was in trouble. When on the third day we had still not come upon a trace of her, I was near panic. Walking up the ridge in the late afternoon, scanning the plains below through my binoculars, I almost walked into a sleeping lion who was resting close to a small tree the lower branches of which overhung a rocky platform which was obviously his lair. He was as surprised to see me as I was to see him but behaved with more restraint than I did. I yelled while, glancing back repeatedly, he rumbled off sedately. Soon he disappeared into the high grass and I had a chance to investigate his lair.

I was much relieved to find no trace of Pippa among the remains of his last kill, but his presence added to my anxiety as his lay-up was much too close for safety; indeed, he could watch Pippa's every move, and ours, when we were in camp. We named this bush Lion Villa and soon discovered that it was frequently used by this young lion. His roar, which ended in a succession of quick whuffs, made us give him the nickname of Simba Haraka—the lion in a hurry. This endeared him to me as my own nickname among the Africans has always been Memsahib Haraka—the lady in a hurry.

After dark I went on with my search by car and drove slowly, calling to Pippa, but I met only a few elephants. Later, sitting in my canvas bath under the stars, I listened to the howl of a hyena. This caused my fear for Pippa to increase, and I spent a sleepless night.

Out again at dawn, I inspected the fluffy remains of a hyena kill. There was nothing sinister about them, but I still felt very anxious. Local tried to reassure me by saying that Pippa was surely alive and well and probably enjoying herself with a mate. When we returned to camp, how great was my relief to find her placidly sitting there, her belly full. As soon as I approached her I noticed a strong smell, and though she hardly glanced at the meat I gave her she struck at me when I tried to de-tick her and behaved in an unusually wild manner. Was Local right: had she been with a male?

While I was still trying to make friends with her, a car arrived bringing Joseph and some of the Meru Councilors. Everyone admired Pippa but she kept aloof, looked through her visitors, and finally walked away. After the party had left I took her for a walk along the road, where we met an elephant. Pippa promptly stalked him: approaching most cunningly, she took him by surprise and swiped at his hind leg. Trumpeting his protest, the giant cantered off with Pippa following determinedly until both disappeared. She did not return that night.

4

The New Campsite

NEXT DAY there was still no sign of Pippa, and I discussed the situation with Joseph. We agreed that the thick undergrowth along the river harbored far too many baboons, and that this, together with the nearness of the road, were handicaps to her rehabilitation, so we decided to look for a better camping site. The nearest open water was at a swamp some five miles distant; we drove there. Feeding the swamp was a narrow rivulet called Mulika. Only a few doum palms and single bushes grew along its banks, so that any animal while drinking could see whether a dangerous beast were approaching. After a mile the stream left the swamp and ran parallel to a ridge which led to open plains. Here we saw herds of elands, Grant's gazelles and oryxes, zebras, and elephants. It was ideal cheetah country, and Joseph said he had recently watched a pair of cheetahs and a single male close to the place which we now chose as our new campsite. Since it was only an hour's walk from our present camp, we thought we would take Pippa there on her walks so that she would get used to the area before moving into it.

We decided to start introducing her to the place at once; but Pippa had different ideas. She kept away from camp for three days. We searched fruitlessly, then a Game Scout brought news that Pippa had been seen at dawn playing with jackals on the airstrip near Leopard Rock. When I arrived there she was very friendly but soon ran off to the plains, where she chased Grant's gazelles until the sun became too hot. Then, with the meat I had brought I enticed her into the car and took her back to camp. She remained there until late afternoon, when she walked off into the bush and did not return. During the next few days we had plenty of exercise and much anxiety trying to trace her spoor.

We searched within a radius of five miles around the camp, thereby getting to know the area intimately. There was a large rock which was obviously popular among lions and leopards, whose pugmarks we found around it. From its top we had a superb view of the plains, the nearby river, and the surrounding bush. We met rhinos, buffaloes, and elephants, as well as smaller animals.

On the fifth day, while I was watching an elephant through my binoculars, I detected a cheetah sitting on a tree stump some four hundred yards away. Hardly believing my luck, I called "Pippa," at which the cheetah turned its head and looked at us. As quickly as we could we scrambled toward the place, carefully maneuvering around the elephant until we were near enough to identify the cheetah, which had watched our every move. But before I could look through my field glasses it vanished. Though I was not sure it was Pippa, it seemed unlikely that a wild cheetah should have allowed us to approach so close. On the other hand, if it were Pippa, why should she have run away? Following the spoor to the river, we almost collided with five waterbucks which broke out at full speed from the undergrowth and came in our direction but swerved when they saw us. It seemed likely that they were bolting from the cheetah. Encouraged by their behavior, we continued our search; I called repeatedly but only a few vervet monkeys responded. Thinking that if the cheetah I had seen had been Pippa she would by now have returned to camp, we walked home, but we waited in vain for her.

Early next morning I went back to the place where I had seen the cheetah and sat in ambush for several hours near a small lagoon which seemed to be a much-frequented drinking place. Except for the rustling of the doum-palm fronds in whose shade I sat, the stillness was unbroken. I tried to imagine what Pippa might be doing if she were in this beautiful place, which looked to me like a real cheetah paradise. If already she were able to kill and no longer needed my protection, why should she return to the camp where by night a wired compound curbed her freedom and by day visitors annoyed her? I was more fond of her than I liked to admit, but why should she love me? I had come comparatively late into her life, and she had

had no choice in the abrupt change of her foster parents, and also, however much I had tried to compensate her for her loneliness and frustrations at Naro Moru, I could give her little in comparison to the natural life of the bush which was now offered her. The question I asked myself with anxiety was, could she already look after herself? I was also worried lest she wander across the river and sit outside the boundary of the Reserve, where recently Shifta activities had been reported. To combat these a platoon of Kenya Rifles was operating in the area and Pippa might well get into trouble if she met the soldiers.

After spending the whole day near the lagoon I had to return home alone, but when we searched the area next morning we found the clawmarks of a cheetah who had climbed the tree near the rock and, farther on, spoor leading across the river where the animal had rested in a palm thicket close to the water. Again I sat in ambush all day, but all I saw were five elephants toppling a doum palm to get at the nuts growing high up on its crown, and later two waterbucks which passed close to my hide-out, evidently bolting from some danger higher up the river. Investigating the place from which they had come, I found fresh cheetah droppings, but no Pippa.

Another three days passed in futile search, then, late one afternoon, a messenger arrived to tell me that Pippa was back at Leopard Rock. Arriving there just before dark, I found her near the garage among a crowd of Africans. Chirping like a bird, she ran to me and jumped into the car. She was ravenous and ate all the meat I had brought with me. I was alarmed to see how thin she was. She looked very small and had a wet, cold nose, a sure symptom of illness. When we returned to our camp she just ate and ate as I took ticks off her. Then I noticed that her hind legs were stiff and her gums pale.

Next morning I sent a radio message to the Vet at Meru asking him to come with a field microscope; meanwhile I kept Pippa quiet and fed her as much meat and milk as she would take and comforted her; she responded affectionately.

I also sent Local to investigate her spoor, which he found linked up with the recent cheetah track we had seen near the lagoon. This proved that it was Pippa we had been following. Since she was obviously starving it was strange that she had not returned to our camp but had walked in the opposite direction to Leopard Rock. When, later in the day, she chased some birds and climbed a tree just for the fun of it, I felt relieved but was nevertheless glad when the Vet arrived. After examining a blood smear and taking Pippa's temperature, which registered 101.2°, he diagnosed *Babesia canis,* the tick fever which affects dogs. This was interesting inasmuch as it showed another affinity between the cheetah and the dog. Elsa had died of *Babesia felis,* which infects only cats. The Vet had brought some phenamidine isethionate with him to treat the illness, but as Pippa was only mildly infected he advised us to wait for a few days in the hope that she would build up an immunity. Meanwhile, we were to keep her confined and carefully watch her temperature and other symptoms. I took her temperature morning and evening for the following five days. It varied between 100° and 101°—which is normal for a cheetah.

She had a ravenous appetite; it was now that I first noticed her craving for the orange-yellow zebra fat and also for mud. I was amazed when I saw her satisfy her need for mud at every puddle. I asked George if this were not unusual, but he assured me that cheetahs eat mud either to get a supplement of minerals or to stimulate their digestion. Pippa was more affectionate toward me than she had ever been till now and followed me everywhere, but she growled at the assistant and at the Africans. As her condition improved, her restlessness increased, and after a few days keeping her confined became a trial to both of us. I took her on the leash for short walks but had great difficulty in coaxing her back to camp, as wherever we went there were animals that aroused her interest. Discovering that her determination to chase them was thwarted, she began once more to strike at us with her sharp claws, as she had done at Naro Moru. There I had been able to wait until it was dark till she felt like moving. But here I could not take the risk and had to get her home while it was daylight. A further problem came from the few elephants who were grazing around the camp at the time. Pippa always watched them tensely, and I could imagine what a tantalizing scent each fanning of their ears brought her.

When, after six days' confinement, she seemed fit again, I gave her a great zebra feast and let her loose. At once she found some ostriches to chase and then spent the day near the river. In the evening she followed us back to camp for more meat; at 5 A.M., purring loudly, she came to my bed, then she disappeared.

For the next three days we tried to find her whereabouts until some Game Scouts sent a message to say that they had seen two cheetahs sitting under a tree close to Leopard Rock. The Scouts were in a truck; when they stopped the smaller of the two cheetahs walked up to them but soon went after the larger of the pair, which bolted. We drove to the place and screened it by walking parallel at short distances. Suddenly, my assistant almost stepped on the two cheetahs, who fled instantly. He had, however, time enough to notice that one cheetah was darker in color than Pippa. Tracking spoor was impossible on the rocky ground; that and the high grass defeated us, so we had to drive home.

It was long after dark when I heard Pippa's purr. Before I could get up she walked into my tent and licked me affectionately. I noticed that her belly was full and that there were some bloodstains below her vagina and her rump, and that her hindquarters were wet from licking Otherwise, her coat was unusually silky. Having no meat, I offered her milk and three eggs. Usually she liked these but now she ignored them, and after a short time she left.

I followed her and was surprised that she paused several times to wait for me and even ambushed me; each time when I reached her she purred and licked me. Finally, after climbing up a tree and looking about alertly, she was off. Listening in the stillness, I wondered if she had only come the four miles from Leopard Rock to tell me that she had seen us searching for her in the afternoon but, as she had found a boy friend who was suspicious of us, she couldn't stay, she just wanted me to know that she was very happy. On my way home I remembered Elsa's behaving in a similar fashion in a similar situation.

At dawn we followed Pippa's spoor and found her halfway up the ridge chasing a greater bustard. From this she was diverted to stalking guinea fowl which led her up to three elephants; by the time the giants moved away we lost her and did not see her again for several days.

I had been invited to show the Councilors at Meru the film George and I had made of Elsa and also to give a talk on rehabilitation and other methods of wild animal conservation. I drove there with Joseph, who introduced me to an audience of some four hundred people seated in the newly built Council Hall. Everyone was excited to know that Elsa had lived in the Meru Reserve, and all showed enthusiasm for our work and wanted to co-operate.

I was particularly interested in the development of this Reserve because it was here and in the adjoining N. F. D. that George, as Game Warden, had for twenty-five years looked after the wild life of the region. He had visited this area more frequently than any other part of the vast expanse that was in his care because here poaching was at its worst. Knowing this bit of country so intimately, we had always hoped that it would one day be turned into a Game Reserve. The combination of its ecologic conditions was excellent and with its varied fauna it could become a true Garden of Eden. No other East African Game Park has so many permanent rivers and swamps, so great a variety of vegetation and scenery, such differing altitudes (they vary from a thousand to forty-five hundred feet). As a result the wild animals have no need to go outside its boundaries during their migration or even during a severe drought. Another advantage is that the area is heavily infested with tsetse fly, harmless to most wild animals but fatal to livestock. This means that it can be of little use for grazing, though rice might be grown.

Therefore, when the Councilors agreed, in 1956, to turn four hundred square miles into the Meru Game Reserve we both felt very happy. We were all the more attached to the place because it was here that we had rehabilitated Elsa and lived on and off for two years in the area with her and her cubs. Later, when the books I wrote about her and her family earned royalties, these supported the Reserve on many occasions, but in spite of this and of the fine efforts made by various people to develop the area there were many difficulties still to be overcome. So Joseph and I were very happy that the Councilors had shown so great an interest in the Reserve.

Next morning we found Pippa's spoor near the swamp where Joseph and I had chosen a new home for her. We returned to camp to collect meat and prepared to spend the day there. Suddenly Pippa emerged sleepily from a bush close to a grove of trees. Considering that she had had no food from me for six days, she was in good condition but wolfed down the meat we had brought while we settled for our picnic lunch.

How lucky it was that Pippa had herself discovered the home we had picked. I thought what a good thing it would be if we were not obliged to move camp and could come just as visitors to see her. She seemed to be of the same opinion, for when I started the engine to return home Pippa made it plain that she wished to remain at the swamp.

Early next morning we returned and found her still there. She was very glad to see us and followed us for a walk, climbing every termite hill and tree in reach to scan the ground for yellow-necks, which at this early hour perched provokingly on stones. When it became hot I settled at the grove, laying out my sketching kit on a low camp bed. Meanwhile Pippa ate the meat I had brought for her. Later Joseph joined us. He was very fond of Pippa, and she liked him and allowed him to play with her. We decided not to move the camp for the time being and, should Pippa settle near the swamp, gradually to reduce our feeding visits till she could do without our help.

Pippa could not have chosen a better headquarters than this grove of trees, from which she could overlook a vast stretch of country. During the next days we visited her regularly and developed a routine. As soon as we found her we took her for a walk. Either we would explore the Mulika, which wound its course through the rocky ground and marshy patches and passed within a few hundred yards of the grove, or we would cross it and walk to the sandy plains beyond, which contrasted with the bush-covered hills and stony escarpment that lay near our camp. Wherever we went there were enough trees and termite hills to give Pippa a lookout for Grant's gazelles, zebras, oryxes, and the never absent yellow-necks.

During the heat of the day we rested in the grove. I sketched Pippa eating her breakfast while the men went fishing in the deeper pools of the Mulika, where they caught a delicious kind of catfish. Pippa showed great interest in the catch and sniffed at the cold fish, but it was the oddity of the kill rather than its flavor which aroused her curiosity. As soon as it got cooler we went for another walk until the sun was low, and then, leaving Pippa eating her dinner, we drove home. Since she certainly knew the way to camp but never followed us we decided, after five days, to stop our visits for a short time and see what she would do.

Pippa showing her affection

Joy feeding Pippa

Pippa drinking at Mulika

5

Poachers, Shifta, and a Change of Campsite

NEXT DAY Joseph was to lead an anti-poaching patrol along the Ura River and agreed to let me come too. The Tana is the largest river in Kenya—about three hundred yards wide at our starting point, where the Ura runs into it. Our presence alarmed a school of hippos which protested with loud snorts and blew jets at us before their bulky, glistening bodies submerged. Joseph showed me a burned-down fishing lodge and a wrecked boat which the Shifta had destroyed some months ago, thereby hoping to stop navigation on the Tana, which was the boundary of the Reserve.

We crept quietly through dense undergrowth along the banks of this lovely river, passing many places we had explored with Elsa. Her camp had been a few miles upstream and every inch held poignant memories for me. Suddenly I fell over a fallen tree and hurt my ribs. Though I tried to ignore the pain, movement became increasingly painful, but as there was nothing I could do I went on until we sighted a poacher on the opposite bank aiming at a hidden target with his bow and arrow. To prevent the release of the arrow Joseph shot into the air while two Game Scouts plunged across the river. Then Joseph followed them and they all disappeared into the thick undergrowth. Listening intently, the rest of the party kept very still for what seemed an endless time, then the three men returned, wading belly-deep through the water, holding their rifles above their heads.

They told us that while the Scouts were chasing the bolting

Joseph and two Scouts wading through the Ura

poacher they were charged by a rhino. This was obviously the beast at which the poacher had been aiming his arrow. Quickly the men shinned up a tree, where they remained besieged by the rhino for long enough to allow the poacher to make his escape. By the time Joseph arrived, both rhino and poacher were gone. Soon after this we saw three more poachers setting traps for crocodiles on the far bank: they too bolted before the Game Scouts were able to get across the river. The thick vegetation along its banks was a great help to poachers, who knew where to slip through it and disappear. When, later, we found more traps, recent campfires, and finally human footprints inside the thorny fence around Elsa's grave, Joseph gave orders to patrol the area for a week.

I wanted to know how Pippa was getting on, but in the interest of her education and also of my aching ribs I decided to wait another twenty-four hours before visiting her; then, taking zebra meat with us, we set out and found her at the grove, very hungry. She came to me but ignored the assistant and Local, and when later the men shot her a bird as a farewell gift she paid no attention to them. We did not return for two days, then we found Pippa again waiting for us and very thin. Obviously she was not hunting and was relying on us to feed her. I hated starving her, but it was for her good and the only way to get her to go wild. Even if it might take some time before she was able to kill for herself, she was learning bush law much more quickly this way than if she were living at the camp, to which, however, she could easily walk if she felt hungry.

Next morning I awoke to the sound of heavy firing. Alarmed, we drove to see if Pippa was all right. As usual, we found her waiting for us. While I was feeding her, Joseph passed on his way to George to warn both of us that during the night the Shifta had attacked the village of Lare, outside the boundary of the Reserve. There had been casualties on both sides. The Security Forces had captured a lot of ammunition, two rifles, and one hatchet and were now following some two hundred fleeing terrorists into the Ndaia forest. Joseph advised us to keep no lights burning after dark, then he went on to see George. I did not think we had much to fear from the Shifta, who were mainly after food and firearms, of which we had so small a supply that we were hardly worth attacking. Lare was a different matter, a fleshpot in the fertile hills, and the firearms held by the nearby police post were no doubt worth the risk of a fight. In the

Pippa surveying the plain

circumstances we decided to visit Pippa daily. I loved these hours with her, and though she was never as demonstratively affectionate as lions are, I knew that she was happy and content when she lay close to me, purring, as I sketched her.

Unfortunately, at every breath my ribs reminded me that they were cracked. Finally I could bear the pain no longer, so I chartered a Flying-Doctor plane and went to Nairobi. Here I was kept in the hospital for five days. As soon as I was fit again I visited the Animal Orphanage to see Ugas. He belonged to the National Parks and for this reason had lived there since the filming of *Born Free* had been completed. He recognized me instantly and, rubbing his soft nose against my hand through the wire, groaned despairingly. While he paced restlessly up and down the enclosure, the keeper told me that the orphanage had recently received more lions than it could accommodate and hinted that we might now have a chance of getting Ugas; this was the more likely because he was developing into such a dangerous character that nobody liked to go near him. Our good-natured Ugas was certainly only reacting to his circumstances, and which of us would not become bad-tempered under similar conditions? As soon as I returned to Meru, George and I asked to be allowed to rehabilitate Ugas and soon received permission to do so.

During my absence my assistant and Local had looked after Pippa and told me proudly how she had excelled herself by putting a jackal in its place. Watching it approach her meat, she had rushed at it, causing it to dodge behind the car; then, chasing it around, she had hurled it into the air and made it run for its life, though she could easily have killed it. Unfortunately, all this happened too quickly for them to take photographs.

At the beginning of July my assistant had to leave to take a job he had been offered some time previously. I was sorry to lose his company, but so long as I had Local to guard us against any possible danger I was no longer in real need of an assistant. Except for the activities of the Shifta, which had constantly to be controlled outside the boundaries of the Reserve, our days passed very peacefully. While we were at the grove with Pippa we listened to the noisy weaver birds which, making use of our presence as a protection against predators, had recently begun to build their nests in the nearby trees. We heard the high-pitched bark of zebras. We watched buffaloes and elephants standing belly-deep in the swamp, stirring up flocks of egrets hidden among the reeds. This was the time of year when giraffes drop their foals, who look gloriously out of proportion with their enormous shoulders and knees, short necks and far-too-large heads crowned at this early age with two hairy tufts that later would develop into horny stumps.

Joseph often joined us and I found the cheerful confidence with which he tackled all problems very stimulating. Shortly he was due to start on a two-year training course for Wardens at Mweka College in Tanzania. As soon as the Warden returned from leave he would be off.

Pippa had recently developed a bleeding patch around one of her molars as well as scaling of her pads. I wondered whether I was giving her the right food. If cheetahs really need a lot of feathers and roughage, her diet might be deficient for she got hardly any of these from the meat which George usually brought for her, nor did she eat the guts or feathers of the game birds we occasionally shot. She preferred the fatty tissues of the quills. I increased the dose of Abidec in her milk and hoped this might help her to recover quickly. She still did not know what to do with the birds we gave her until we opened them up for her to eat.

Again she disappeared for two days, and eventually we found her near Leopard Rock, very thin. I enticed her inside my car with meat, and though this was her ration for several days, she finished the lot before I had covered the five miles back to her grove. This was the first time she had left the swamp since she had made her home there thirty-eight days earlier. I wondered why she had moved until, near Leopard Rock, I found the answer in the fresh spoor of a male cheetah.

Meanwhile, the Warden had returned. He suggested that we should buy a Land-Rover for the Reserve out of Elsa's royalties. To make the purchase we both flew to Nairobi. I used this opportunity to consult a Vet about Pippa's sore gums, for which he prescribed lederkyn tablets. He also advised treating the scaling of her pads with terra cortril. To prevent her from licking off this drug he suggested using it as a spray which would dry instantly. When I got back I had to use all my cunning to succeed in squirting the icy liquid on Pippa's toes. She greatly resented the procedure and tried to outwit me by tucking her foot under her body or bolting whenever she saw me with the hated spray. In the last resort, she pushed it out of my hand

71

and covered it with dust. I succeeded in my task, however, and soon she was fit again. Watching her as she chased kongonis and ostriches, I thought that she had come a long way since the days when she played hide-and-seek around rosebushes with the Dunkey children. Today she did not hesitate to swipe at the legs of an elephant. The only creatures she treated with respect were crocodiles, and by the cautious way she jumped across the stream I could judge how scared she was of them. She teased me whenever I tried to photograph her jumping over the water: she would sniff around until I lost patience and moved on, then she promptly jumped. If I wanted to take a picture of her balancing on the slender branches of a doum palm, she would sit aloof, apparently unaware that below I was focusing the movie camera on her, but as soon as I gave up, in exasperation, she would perform incredible acrobatics and, *en passant,* take a swipe at my legs to make me feel a still greater fool.

Her next absence lasted for eight days. Searching for her, we came upon so many lion spoor close to the grove, and also trees crashed down by elephant, that I began to wonder whether she might be looking for a safer home. When she returned from the plains beyond the swamp she was hungry, but otherwise in excellent condition.

Elephants had recently caused so much damage in the maize shambas in the foothills of the Jombeni range that the farmers now demanded that they be shot. In the hope of avoiding this the Warden decided to try to drive the marauders back into the safety of the Reserve by spraying them from his aircraft with "man-scented" maize flour. He invited me to join him when he made his ingenious experiment. Before taking off in the two-seater Piper Cruiser he handed me a few small paper bags filled with crushed maize into which little bits of dirty African clothing had been mixed. After flying over Pippa's domain we crossed wide swamps teeming with animals and then threaded our way into the hills. Here we observed several herds of elephants which, hearing the vibration of the low-flying plane, crashed, panic-stricken, through the bush. Circling quickly over the scattering giants, the Warden succeeded in maneuvering them into running in the direction of the Game Reserve. Then he speeded them on their way by dropping the smelly maize over them.

That evening the Warden came to supper to discuss various projects he planned for the Reserve for which he wanted the help of the

Pippa

Elsa Wild Animal Appeal. The camp was lit up by a pressure lamp. He suggested that I should erect a palm-frond screen in front of my tent to conceal the light, thinking that without such a precaution I might be an easy target for Shifta. When, reluctantly, I had erected the screen I well understood the mental effect which walls can have on prisoners. Used as I was to having an open space around me, I much preferred spending my evening sitting outside the screen in the dark, feeling myself part of the surrounding world rather than enclosed in a kind of lighted cell.

Pippa spent only four days near the grove, then she again went off. Two days later she met our search party halfway between the swamp and camp but soon absented herself once more for three days, and finally she disappeared until the ninth of August.

Unfortunately, I had arranged to fly that morning to Nairobi to see a doctor because I was suffering from kidney pains. I could not postpone the trip, so I left Pippa in the care of Local and flew off. Again I visited the Animal Orphanage at Nairobi to find out when we could collect Ugas. I also hoped that some cheetah experts there would be able to explain why, after apparently being happy on her own for three months, Pippa had suddenly returned to civilization. I was told that cheetah cubs run for two years with their mother, who during this time teaches them to kill. I rather doubted this theory because Pippa appeared to be so independent. I told the experts that she had already shown interest in a male. According to them this was very premature since a cheetah female, as a rule, begins mating only when she is two and a half years old.

Pippa's apparent inability to kill at her present age my doctor explained to me by a comparison with a premature baby. He said that the sucking action of a baby depends on the co-ordination of fifty-six muscles which develop only during the seventh month of pregnancy, and consequently any embryo born prior to that date is unable to suckle. This might explain why Pippa was so helpless even when presented with a guinea fowl: no doubt her hunting instinct was still dormant. But no one could offer any theory to account for her behavior in keeping away from camp for three months at an age when she "should have remained with her Mom" or why she had now returned. Since she had broken the "accepted rules" of cheetah behavior, I decided to let her have the choice as to how to live her

Pippa snatching hat from Local

Local offering fish to Pippa

life. I hoped that, this way, she would be happy and that I would learn new facts about cheetah behavior in the wild.

During my three days' absence Pippa stayed in the camp but disappeared the morning before my arrival. Next day she turned up at Leopard Rock and I enticed her into my car with a rabbit. It had been given me by the experts at the Orphanage as a treat for her. And a treat it was. The roughage of the carcass provided her with an essential ingredient of her natural diet. This had been completely lacking since the Warden had forbidden me to shoot an occasional guinea fowl and I had been forced to feed her solely on meat. After having eaten the rabbit to its last hair, Pippa tapped my legs—her way of asking me to take her for a walk. Realizing now that her hunting instinct was still dormant, I watched her with more understanding as she rolled in the dust while a herd of Grant's gazelles approached. She ignored the leading ram as he pranced nearer and nearer, step by step, tossing his beautiful head and snorting provokingly until he was almost on top of her. Then she sat up, and this was enough for the gazelles to bolt as fast as they could run. She did not chase them but continued her dust bath.

Meanwhile, George had had an exciting time with his two lions. Girl had already made her first kill—a Thomson's gazelle—when she was seventeen months old, exactly at the time the hunting instinct develops in lions. After having adapted herself to a wild life during the last five months, she had now killed, within eleven days, a baboon, an eland, and a zebra, which George watched her doing expertly. The interesting fact was that Boy had not attempted to join his sister either in the hunts or in the killings but had always remained at home, though he was quick enough to be the first to eat the kills. The behavior of both confirmed our observations on Elsa's cubs, including the fact that lionesses change their deciduous teeth when about twelve months old, while the males grow their permanent teeth two or three months later. This evidence seemed to indicate that lionesses develop much more quickly than the males.

During those days several visitors came to our camp whom Pippa either ignored or left by walking off. She accepted only Local and me, and though she usually reacted affectionately to us she was now sometimes aggressive, chewing up the groundsheet in my tent or biting at my legs. Obviously she was frustrated and looking for an outlet. As soon as it got dark she always left the camp. I could well understand her reluctance to stay in camp at night, for the Haraka lion had recently been prowling around and one night he paced up and down between the staff's compound and mine for more than an hour, whuffing so loudly and so close that I expected him to come into my tent at any moment. Eventually some lions responded to his whuffs and attracted him away from us.

On the twentieth of October I was wakened at midnight by the vibration of a car; in it were George and Ugas. Both were tired after a nine-hour drive, and while we celebrated Ugas's arrival with hot coffee to warm George up, he told me that Ugas was here only for three days on probation and, should he give trouble because of his allegedly dangerous character, he would be sent to Whipsnade Zoo. Having told me this, George changed coffee for whisky and, with a twinkle in his eye, remarked that Ugas's future was in no danger for he was the same good-natured creature we had always known him to be. Already he was rubbing his head against the wired car to lick my hand, although he had every reason to be ill-tempered after the long, bumpy drive. Later they both went on to George's camp.

About this time the Director of the National Parks, Mervyn Cowie, flew in to look at the Reserve which we all hoped might soon be taken over by the National Parks. The day was marred by the drowning of a giraffe: the animal had been spotted in the early morning bogged in a swamp, and when we arrived with ropes, jacks, and winch it was already beyond help. Reticulated giraffes are among my favorite animals, and when we found it lying on its side with its muzzle submerged in water, obviously having been unable to raise its head high enough to breathe,* I felt as though I were witnessing the death of a friend.

It was now very hot and especially oppressive around the camp because of its sheltered position. This brought on a return of my kidney trouble. I was carrying so much surplus fluid that I looked like a Michelin tire advertisement. Since Pippa did not seem happy here,

---

* *"High Blood Pressure for a Long Neck.* Because the giraffe's neck is so long, the animal needs an extremely high blood pressure so that blood may reach the towering head. But what happens when the giraffe lowers its head seven feet below the heart's level to take a drink? What prevents brain hemorrhage? Scientists, keenly interested in the giraffe's heart and blood system, have found that this living skyscraper is marvelously designed to cope with the problem. The Creator equipped it with an automatic valve to control the blood supply, so that there is neither brain hemorrhage upon lowering the head nor sudden draining of the blood when the head is quickly raised."—*Awake,* Jan. 8, 1966 (published by Watchtower Bible and Tract Society of New York, Inc.).

I discussed the situation with the Park Warden and he suggested that we should move into Kenmare Lodge, where we would be more comfortable living in one of the bungalows. We should also be in less danger from the Shifta, as he intended to install a platoon of General Service Unit close by to control the bandits around the Reserve. It would be advantageous for Pippa, too, since the main cheetah population of the park lived in that area and she would find company of her own kind. Finally, he mentioned that he hoped I would help to improve the present state of the Lodge, which had deteriorated since the manager had left.

Kenmare was originally built by Lady Kenmare as a private lodge with a manager in charge. It was an attractive place with palm-log bungalows nestling around the main building, which contained a spacious dining-cum-sitting room, with a large veranda. From here visitors overlooked the Rojoweru, one of the five chief rivers of the Reserve which passed below through picturesque rocks and had deep pools alive with fish and crocodiles. A swimming pool in front of the Lodge was overshadowed by acacia-thorn trees and surrounded by a carefully weeded lawn and bright-colored flower beds. Recently the Lodge had been for sale; at my suggestion it had been bought with American money which my friend, Alouise Boker, had collected in order to give the buildings to the Meru Council. Until the future of the Reserve was decided the place was kept as a lodge where visitors found everything provided, except food. Across the river is an airstrip connected with the Lodge by a cement causeway. This leads to one of the main roads of the Park; Kenmare itself is a cul-de-sac.

Looking forward to a more comfortable home, we packed up for our eighteen-mile drive. I watched Pippa as we sat in the moonlight on our last evening in the camp. How happy she seemed to be and how wonderfully she had responded to her free life. Now I began to worry about taking her to a lodge, for there she would inevitably turn into a tourist attraction and all she had achieved might be lost. So next morning I called on the Warden and got him to agree that we should camp within two miles of Kenmare and not move into the Lodge. We soon found an ideal camping site by the little Vasorongi stream at a point at which a fallen log made a perfect bridge to the plain beyond and where a few large trees provided shade. A few hundred yards upstream the Mulika joins the Vasorongi, but on its long way from Pippa's swamp it had dried up in the present hot season. Judging by the many footprints along its sandy bed and densely covered banks, it was a popular resting place for many animals. Two miles downstream the Vasorongi runs into the Rojoweru River, which bounds the plain we could see stretching away in the distance.

The only drawback to this otherwise perfect campsite was the proximity of the road which connected Leopard Rock and Kenmare: it passed within three hundred yards of us, but by pitching our tents with their backs to the road I hoped to maintain privacy. Later I enforced it by putting up two signboards: EXPERIMENTAL CAMP—NO ENTRY. Our tents were set up under two magnificent tamarinds, whose polished trunks reminded us that we were not the only ones who found them useful. Pippa climbed them and watched us from her lofty seat while we erected a small compound near my tent for her protection at night, until she became acquainted with her new environment. When all was ready, she jumped down and, making her way across the tree bridge, disappeared into the plain beyond the stream. Following her, we found her lying along a branch high up in an acacia, her head resting on her front paws as she watched a few kongonis. The sun was setting and I was anxious to get her into the compound, but when I succeeded in making her enter the enclosure she was out again in an instant, having climbed over the wire. Later she settled for the night near my bed but disappeared at dawn. Tracking her spoor for over a mile, we found her sitting on an anthill close to Kenmare Lodge, from which she was observing the goats we had brought there as an emergency meat supply and which were herded by Local's eldest wife.

I diverted her interest by calling her and walking quickly in the opposite direction along a game path which was patterned with the spoor of various animals. Intrigued by their scent, Pippa sniffed and followed me slowly until the path led to a well-used drinking place on our stream. Before reaching it we crossed a limestone deposit which broke over a small cliff down to the water. Pippa explored the place and, jumping gracefully across the bubbling water from islet to islet, landed among the bulrushes: she seemed to be in her element. Finally, she flung herself beside me under the shade of a tamarind and purred contentedly. Her happiness was catching. We sat for some time in silence until a hammerkop appeared. Our arrival had obviously interrupted his fishing. Quite still, but cocking

Pippa, Joy, and Local

Pippa, Joy, Joseph, and Local

Pippa on doum palm

Pippa jumping stream

his hammer-shaped head, he was watching a little pool, then suddenly, with lightning speed, he picked a tiny fish out of it, stepped light-footedly across some boulders, and repeated the operation. Meanwhile, a Goliath heron had arrived and he, too, started fishing. If the hammerkop was grotesque in shape and the smallest of the storks, the Goliath, with its slate-blue plumage and elegant build, was the most beautiful and the largest of the herons found here. Later, a flock of sand grouse landed at the water's edge for a long drink; they were joined by some pigeons who had a quick sand bath before quenching their thirst. Pippa watched them all through half-closed eyes. She was feeling far too comfortable to give chase.

Man is usually credited with being the only creature that is conscious of his reactions, and at this moment I was indeed acutely aware of the happiness and peace within myself. But, I wondered, can we be sure that animals are never aware of their own responses? Why assume that Pippa did not know that she too was happy?

Later, we strolled downstream toward the Rojoweru. I have loved this beautiful river ever since we camped with Elsa on its banks. Like most of the rivers of the Meru Game Reserve, it has its source in the Jombeni hills. It runs through the most varied scenery from the forested slopes into the plain below. In some places there are cataracts and narrow gorges; in others it flows slowly over sandy ground, then, at the next bend, turns into rapids. Walls of beautiful lianas and creepers, the deep red stems of raffia palms, their glossy fronds overhanging crocodile-infested pools, the thick foliage of fig trees, contrast with lacy acacias under whose shade elephants doze during the midday heat—all these are a part of the riverside scenery. In the late afternoons we and Elsa had often watched herds of drinking buffaloes or followed the cautious movements of lesser kudus and bushbucks, ever on the alert for the lions, which we frequently put up.

The only way to move about in the denser, thorny bush was to follow the game tracks, which we did, until we reached the mouth of our stream. Here its water runs underneath a tunnel of limestone before it flows into one of the Rojoweru's deep pools. Seeing the many spoor and fresh hippo droppings among the palm seedlings, I understood why Pippa kept nervously behind me. The neverceasing rustle of the doum-palm fronds above us, now and then broken by the shriek of a hornbill or the timid voice of a vervet monkey, made Pippa still more tense. Finally, when I saw the track of a python, as thick as an arm, in the sand, I left the river and returned to the open plain, and Pippa relaxed.

We reached home just in time to see the Warden circling low in his little plane over our camp and dropping a small parcel which got caught in the top branches of the tamarind. Local struggled up the tree to get it, but he was outstripped by Pippa, who swiftly leaped up into the branches and looked as though she were laughing at Local's clumsy efforts to untangle the parcel.

But the day's fun was not yet over, for when we took Pippa for another walk we found fresh cheetah spoor. They were much larger than hers and obviously belonged to a male; she sniffed excitedly at them. When it got dark we hurried home but almost collided with eight elephants who suddenly emerged from the bush, moving in the same direction as we were and cutting us off from camp. There was nothing to do but to run ahead of them to cross the stream before they did. Pippa enjoyed our race thoroughly, running to and fro between us and the elephants. Just in time, we managed to reach the safety of the camp.

When, later, the moon turned the nearby bushes into shades of silver gray, Pippa sat close to me and, resting her head against me, purred. Again I thought of how little it takes to make one happy so long as one has someone to share one's feelings with. How dependent I had become on Pippa's company I realized only when she got up and vanished into the dark, leaving me alone with my thoughts and the immensity of the African night. Had she gone to follow up the cheetah spoor we had seen that afternoon?

The next I saw of her was in the early morning, chasing waterbucks in the plain. She must have been hungry since our meat supply had run out two days earlier, so I was relieved when George arrived in the late afternoon with a small buck. He had had to drive a very long way to make the kill because his usual hunting grounds outside the Reserve had recently become a battlefield between the Shifta and Police. In order to educate Pippa to tackle a kill, we gave her the complete carcass. This was the first time she had to open it herself. She started with the hindquarters, then crunched the ribs, always her favorite part, and finally ate the liver. Then she settled near the kill to guard the remains for the night, but I quickly dragged them in front of my tent so that no lion or hyena should interfere.

Recently I had acquired a refrigerator, operated by kerosene. It had become a "must" as in this hot climate Pippa's meat lasted only two days, and we could not afford to waste it. Next morning, after storing the remains in the refrigerator, I tried to entice Pippa to come for a walk, but she moved to the little palm-log cabin in which the refrigerator was kept and there continued her guarding operation. When she got bored she found an old football—a toy from the filming days at Naro Meru. It had never been used since we came here, and its pressure was low but ideal for Pippa to grip it between her teeth. Proudly carrying the ball around, she asked for a game. So Local, the cook, and I tossed the ball between us and kept Pippa busy trying to catch it until it rolled into the stream. She dashed after it but, anxious not to wet her paws, waited until the current moved it near the bank and she could catch it with her teeth. She then brought it back, placed it before my feet, and asked me to continue the game. I was rather startled to see Pippa act as such a perfect retriever and, wanting to know whether she would repeat this action, threw the ball back into the water. Instantly she went after it and this time poked it carefully with her feet into position until she could grip it, then she ran back and placed it again at my feet. For the next few weeks the game became almost a ritual. On a rainy morning she would even drop the wet ball onto my bed in her effort to get me up and make me play with her. Soon she discovered a new method of getting the ball out of the water more easily. This was by letting it float downstream until it reached a little bridge we had built near the kitchen; here she could pick it up easily. Sometimes she trembled so much with excitement that the ball, as she held it between her teeth, shook with the vibrations. It was fascinating that Pippa, classified as a cat, should have such a strong retrieving instinct, yet another characteristic held in common with the dog.

Although the ball game had become a passion with her, Pippa spent more and more time away from camp. At first this was only during the daytime, but soon she disappeared for nights too. I knew that she was never far off, but I worried because she was eating very little and always seemed restless. One day she even became aggressive and, chewing at the groundsheet of my tent, growled fiercely at my approach. I diverted her attention, and then enticed her for a walk. When it got dark she stayed behind and remained away all night.

Pippa in Land Rover

Pippa retrieving football

Pippa triumphant

I had arranged to meet George the next morning, halfway to Elsa's camp. On the way I passed Kenmare Lodge and drove in to look at our little herd of goats. As soon as I stopped the car Pippa appeared and, seeing the goats grazing in the distance, rushed like lightning among the animals. Running and shouting, we rounded up the bleating goats and managed to confine them in their compound. By this time Pippa was chasing the chickens belonging to the Game Scouts at the Lodge. They, instead of rescuing the terrified birds, stood giggling and perhaps calculating the amount of compensation they could ask for every dead bird. But Pippa had no wish to kill; she wanted to play and, although I had not fed her for four days, she only held a protesting chicken for a short time between her paws, then let it go unharmed, and rolled playfully in the sand. I tried to coax her into my car, but she leapt onto its roof and, balancing herself awkwardly, remained so poised till, halfway back to camp, she jumped off and disappeared.

I was already late and knew that George was waiting for me in the bush, so after asking Local to collect some meat from camp and, with it, induce Pippa to come home, I drove on. We had often visited Elsa's camp since she had died. On many occasions I felt a strange sensation as if she were present, and however depressed I might have been, soon a wonderful sense of peace and harmony came over me and smoothed things out. George was worried about poor Ugas, who, for the last few days, had had an irritation in one eye. While we were discussing Ugas's trouble we were interrupted by some rustling in the bush not far away. Following the sound, we missed a pride of six lions by seconds. Their pugmarks and the freshly flattened grass gave evidence of their hurried retreat at our approach. Strolling along the river, we watched a pair of hadada ibis feeding two young in a nest in a tree. These beautiful birds are fairly common here, but it was the first time we saw them on a nest.

My return to camp at teatime coincided with Pippa's. Jerking her head at me, she asked for her afternoon walk; during it, she often listened to noises in the bush but never investigated the source of her interest. This was explained when Local, on our return to camp, told me that he had seen a lion close by. Knowing how frightened Pippa was of lions, I was surprised that she disappeared for the night and took this as another step in her rturn to the wild, where she could evade this enemy in a natural way instead of relying on my protection. During the next three days she only came in for feeding visits, but, however short these were, she never missed her retrieving game. I felt sorry for poor Pippa: she had so little fun compared to a wild cheetah and was always alone with only us as substitutes for her own kind.

CHAPTER

6

I Get into Trouble

ON THE TWENTY-THIRD of September, George sent a message to say that Ugas had a high temperature—104°—and his eye was getting worse, and would I take some blood smears to a Vet at Nairobi as he did not want to leave Ugas alone. Meanwhile he would inject him with berenil as he suspected an infection by tsetse fly. So off I went, leaving Pippa in the charge of Local. The Vet found no trypano-somiasis but a surplus of white blood corpuscles in the blood smear, and suspecting that a septic focus was responsible for the high tem-perature, he suggested penicillin. I radioed his advice to George, knowing that he had penicillin in his first-aid kit.

On my return five days later I found the camp deserted except for the cook: everybody was around Kenmare searching for Pippa. I drove toward Kenmare calling for her, and she soon turned up, fit, but very thin. Local told me that during my absence she had been away from camp with other cheetahs for most of the time. Following her spoor, he had come to the Gambo plain (Gambo is Swahili for "across the river"), where he saw that she had joined a male. Both their spoor led to the stream. Here he found two more cheetah spoor, and evidence that yet another pair had been around Kenmare, and that Pippa had tried to join them. During these days she had only twice accepted food.

All these escapades accounted for Pippa's thinness. I had no diffi-culty in getting her into the car and back to camp, thanks to a bait of meat. Here she ate an enormous meal, finally relaxed close to me, purring loudly, and seemed very glad to see me home again. None-theless, she disappeared once more as soon as it got dark. During the night she twice reappeared and rubbed her head affectionately against mine through the mosquito net.

The following night I noticed a catlike animal on the tree bridge which vanished as soon as I turned the flashlight on it. Next morning I saw cheetah spoor, but if they were Pippa's why had she bolted—from the familiar light or from me? For two hours we searched in vain for more spoor, then, on our return, found a very hungry Pippa waiting in the camp. We also found George's assistant with the news that Ugas's eye was getting alarmingly worse. I suggested that the assistant should drive immediately to Meru and from there telephone to Nairobi for a Vet who would fly at once to George's camp and be prepared to operate on the eye if necessary.

The assistant went on to Meru and I drove to George. Poor Ugas —his eye was almost white and seemed to hurt him a great deal, but I was relieved to find him, for the first time in the last four days, without a high temperature. Although the blood smear had not shown any infection, Ugas had obviously had a trypanosomiasis in-fection which George had cured with berenil injections. When the Vet arrived he suggested more penicillin and cortisone injections to clear up the white film across the eye, but he warned George that these powerful drugs might upset Ugas and make him irritable, a well-known side-effect of cortisone treatment.

Knowing how conservative Pippa was in her habits, I hurried back to camp to take her for her afternoon walk. Although she had eaten an enormous meal during my absence and could hardly move, she followed me and soon became excited about something in the bush, listening repeatedly in the same direction. As darkness fell she dis-appeared. She was always most careful to conceal her whereabouts and never left the camp if she could be observed. When later George's assistant passed by on his return from Meru, he told me that he had seen the spoor of two cheetahs about two miles up the road. Obvi-ously, Pippa had at last found better company than ourselves, so I was surprised to see her turn up on the following afternoon for her re-trieving game. Afterwards we went for a walk, during which we saw an otter. This was the first otter I had met in the wild, and I was far more excited than Pippa as I watched the animal move among the reeds close to the stream, its sleek fur shining in the sun.

Later, Pippa became excited at finding fresh cheetah spoor along the road, superimposed on the track of a truck which had passed only half an hour earlier. She sniffed at the spoor in great agitation but followed me home for a large meal before disappearing in the direction of Kenmare. During the next three days she disappeared at dark and finally stayed away for two full days. All her spoor led to the vicinity of Kenmare, where she was spotted one evening by a Game Scout. Following his report, we went there and, on our way, met three cheetahs who bolted instantly. Soon Pippa appeared from the opposite direction. We led her to the cheetah spoor but she ignored them and followed us to camp for a quick meal and was off again. It was a beautiful full-moon night, and I felt lonely.

This did not mean that I had not enough to do; on the contrary. The time I spent with Pippa was my relaxation from paper-work, typing my ever-increasing correspondence with the members of the Elsa Committee, headquartered in Nairobi, the Elsa Trustees, headquartered in London, the Government and the Game Department of Kenya. We were trying to help various animal-conservation projects, among which the development of Meru Park had priority. We were greatly handicapped by Shifta who not only prevented tourists from visiting the Park but also held down most of the available local Police, General Service Unit, and Game Scouts, who were needed to defend the boundaries of the Reserve from raids and were therefore unavailable for poacher patrols and other constructive work within the Park.

How close the Shifta were I only realized when, the following day, Local's wife arrived asking what she should do with our goats as, from the Lodge, she could hear the Shifta chopping trees downstream. Before I was able to tell her to lock the goats in their enclosure and provide grass and water for two days, several Police cars passed by on their way to Kenmare. They told us there was a rumor that a Shifta gang, some hundred and forty strong, had escaped from a battle two days ago and were now on their way to the Tana River.

Soon more police trucks arrived, and one of their Land-Rovers stopped in my camp with orders to arrest me. My surprise was equal to my shock, as my conscience was unaware of any crime. But I was told that I had committed two offenses: not having paid my fine when I was found to be driving without a valid license; the second, that I had ignored repeated warrants ordering me to appear in Court. I explained that six months ago, when I had been found not to have a valid license, I had, in the presence of the Officer in Charge of Nanyuki Police Station, written to my chartered accountant at Nairobi and asked him to settle the matter. I added that I had never received any warrant. I did not want to leave camp now when the Shifta were operating so close to it, but the men said they would have to force me into their car if I would not go willingly to Meru Police Headquarters, from which they promised to bring me back that evening.

So, without being allowed to change my clothes or to have lunch, I squeezed into the Police Land-Rover and set off. After driving thirty miles we reached the turn-off to Maua, the small village where the Police were stationed. It is three miles off the road to Meru; to my surprise, they went to Maua. When I asked why we were not proceeding to Meru, they told me that they wanted first to collect a few things from their substation. But as soon as we arrived there the Land-Rover was exchanged for a beat-up truck. I was told that the only alternative to this form of transportation was to walk the fifty miles to Meru.

I said that as I had no hat I would become ill if I were exposed for hours to the midday sun. It was then agreed to place me in the front seat between the driver and a Police escort. We started off but soon stopped to pick up more passengers, who pressed into the overloaded truck.

These stops were frequently repeated, and it was lucky for me that they were. I knew that George's assistant was on a shopping trip at Meru and due to return today. So when, at a pick-up stop, I recognized his car approaching, I signaled to him; he, realizing from the strange conditions in which he saw me traveling that something peculiar must have happened, turned his car and followed us to Meru. There we halted in front of the Police Headquarters. I asked to get out and stretch my legs but was ordered to remain inside as I was to go on another fifty miles to Nanyuki, where I was to be put in jail until my case could be heard.

I was stunned. After some quick thinking, I said that I had to "spend a penny." This I could not be refused, though the escort followed close behind me. Once inside the Police building, I went straight to the Office of the Superintendent, whom I knew. After I had explained the situation to him he apologized and suggested that I should deposit a bond of five hundred shillings with him until I was told officially when I was to attend the Magistrate's Court in Nanyuki. Meanwhile, I could return home. Before I did so, I telephoned to Nairobi for a lawyer to defend me.

At last George's assistant and I were on our way home, but first we were delayed by engine trouble; next the lights gave out, and finally a heavy cloudburst made the road exceedingly slippery. Under these circumstances we could not drive down the steep escarpment to the Meru Reserve, and so we went on to Maua hoping to get a bed at the Methodist Mission, whose doctor I knew. Arriving in the late evening at his house, I was surprised to hear a noisy party going on inside this normally quiet place. I then learned that my doctor friend had left and that his successor not only ran the hospital but also taught the African staff music: the "noisy" party was in fact a lesson. With all the local drums, homemade flutes, xylophones, imported guitars and concertinas, accompanied by singers in excellent voice, it was indeed a gay lesson which got noisier the longer it went on. Although the place was full to capacity, the doctor would not hear of letting us go elsewhere and insisted on giving me his room and himself moved into the kitchen.

Next morning, as soon as there was enough light to see the road in the drizzling rain, we went on and arrived for a late breakfast. I was relieved to find my camp as I had left it, and Pippa gave me a warm welcome. I had brought seven pounds of meat for her from Meru which she gulped down as though it were a mere hors d'oeuvre. When I took her for her afternoon walk she led me through very thick bush to a pile of branches, the ends of which had been neatly cut by pangas. Under the heap we found the remains of a recently killed giraffe. It was unlikely that poachers would come so close to Kenmare and to my camp—only people really desperate for food would risk such a large kill in our vicinity—so we concluded that the Shifta must have had a feast here and taken great trouble to cover all the remains so that no vultures would give them away.

Again, Pippa stayed away for the night; for company I had an elephant who spent a long time feeding just across the stream. Although I yelled and turned my flashlight on him, he took no notice and continued tearing leaves from a bush. Since he had the whole of the Meru Reserve to feed on, he must have found some special titbit in that bush, for he repeated his visits for the next few nights and kept me sleepless.

At last I was notified that my case was to come up on the eighteenth of August. George accompanied me, to give me moral support. After driving the whole day on 180 miles of bad roads to Nanyuki, we dined with the lawyer who had come from Nairobi to defend me. He advised me to plead guilty as, by some mistake, the license fee had not been paid since May. Apart from this, he said, I had not committed any offense and should not worry.

When we entered the Courtroom it was packed with Africans who regarded a "case" as fine entertainment free of charge. As soon as the Magistrate arrived I sensed trouble. He charged me with two offenses: one, driving without a valid license, to which I pleaded guilty; two, contempt of Court, by refusing, in a rude letter, to attend the Court, and to this I refused to plead guilty. My lawyer apologized on my behalf for this letter and explained that it had been written by the Park Warden, who, being an Honorary Police Officer, had replied on my behalf to a warrant which had been sent to him in August. The style of his letter had antagonized the Magistrate, who was in no sympathetic mood, and this did not improve when my lawyer stated that I had not been given the minimum legal notice of ten days, but only nine days, to attend Court and argued that, in consequence, this charge, at any rate, was invalid.

There was a hush. It was the first time I had attended a Court, let alone been in the Box. I listened, fascinated, to the heated debate between the Indian Magistrate, the African Prosecutor, and the Irish lawyer over myself, an Austrian by birth. The argument centered around the proper interpretation of the legal term "ten days from the day of Offense" and whether or not this included the day on which the offense was committed. Several thick "books of words" were studied. Finally, the Magistrate admitted that the Police had been in error and that he would therefore only charge me a fine of thirty shillings for the car license.

As we left the Court we were offered the daily newspaper where bold letters on the front page covered the news that the *Born Free* film had been chosen for the 1966 Royal Command Performance and that Her Majesty the Queen would attend the World Première in London on the fourteenth of March.

We left Nanyuki in high spirits which even the heavy rain could not dampen and arrived at the camp long after dark in a drenching storm. Pippa soon appeared, gave me an affectionate welcome, allowed George to pat her, and spent the night at home.

During the following days the rain continued and soon all rivers were in flood. Pippa was terrified of the muddy torrrents which concealed crocodiles and hippos, but she splashed about in every rain puddle, licking the mud with gusto and so getting her daily ration of minerals.

She was about twenty months old when I first saw her seriously stalking a kongoni calf. The young antelope was well protected within its herd, but Pippa managed cleverly to separate it from its mother, circling the calf closer and closer until she was no more than a foot away from it. At that, the mother charged, butting her head at Pippa and swiping at her with her horns; Pippa dodged the attack until the rest of the herd joined in, then, when she found herself surrounded by bucking kongonis, she decided to abandon the sporting way of getting a meal and returned home with us for a well-served dinner.

Of course it was easy for Pippa to know when meat was in the refrigerator or when the assistant passed our camp on his way to shoot a kill outside the Reserve. But one day she seemed to sense a fresh supply when none of us knew that the assistant had gone to shoot meat for her. All day she refused to leave the camp and only in the late afternoon went a short distance up the road and stayed put. She sat there patiently, looking along the road as if waiting for something to turn up. Soon the car appeared and, sure enough, there was a kill for her inside it.

We had often observed similar inexplicable instances of foreknowledge with Elsa. I have described them in the books I have written about her. If they were due to extrasensory perception or to telepathy, why did nothing of the sort ever happen when Elsa and her cubs and Pippa had disappeared and we were searching with great anxiety for them?

Pippa now left my camp for three days, and when we at last found her spoor they were together with the pugmarks of a male. Might he have been responsible for the ineffectiveness of telepathy between Pippa and me? She might have been too preoccupied to think of me. Her return to camp seemed to be dictated by hunger, for she gulped the meat down so quickly that she promptly brought it up, but she instantly ate it again. We had often seen wild cheetahs behaving in this way, and it may have given ground to the generally accepted fallacy that cheetahs regurgitate meat for their young.

Meanwhile, the weather had deteriorated so much that all movement by foot, car, or even plane had become very nearly impossible. This was awkward because poor Ugas was once again in great pain from his eye, which, after a short improvement, had now become almost blind. With great difficulty we succeeded in flying three visiting Vets from the United States, England, and Germany to George's camp. They diagnosed two ulcers growing on the cornea for which no surgery was needed and which penicillin would cure. Accordingly, George again gave Ugas injections.

During the early November days the bushes on the plains were often loaded with migrating house martins taking a short rest on their long flight from Europe. The birds clustered so densely together that I could hardly distinguish their bodies until Pippa made a rush at them and stirred them up into a cloud. I was interested, too, in swarms of large beetles which, attracted by a buzzing sound, we found flying round and round a bush almost like a swarm of bees. Local informed me that they were carrion eaters. I had often watched carrion-eating beetles at their feasts, but I had never before seen them in swarms and wondered if this had anything to do with the rains. Local, usually most knowledgeable about anything we saw on our walks, did not know the answer. But several times he saved me from walking into a rhino or buffalo by drawing my attention to the hissing of invisible but alarmed tickbirds who were feeding on the animals and provided a warning system for their host and for us. Local often showed courage when a buffalo emerged unexpectedly from the grass in front of us and would quickly chase it off with well-aimed stones, but he was helpless when faced with a harmless monitor; the mere sight of these large, green-mottled lizards gave him the jitters and made him run for his life. He was also scared of chameleons, a fear he shared with most Africans, who will not touch these innocuous creatures. But, strangely enough, he would kill any snail at sight. When I asked him why he did this, he replied: "Because they have a house." I failed to see the logic of his explanation but made him promise not to destroy these useful creatures which enjoy their lives as he does his. Usually we walked in silence, hoping to see some of the many animals which had left their spoor along the game paths. Even when nothing exciting happened during our walks I often felt sublimely happy. On our return to camp I liked to prolong my sundowner long after dark so that I could watch the stars appear. Listening to the stillness, sometimes broken by a distant lion whuff, I often wondered why I could never find the same peace of mind when living among people as I experienced here. Was it the closeness to wild life that gave me such a sense of immensity that everything else seemed unimportant, or could it be that we often deceive ourselves about the people we love by projecting our ideals onto them, only to discover later what their real selves are like, and then blame them for disappointing us? If some of us come to find animals more attractive than people, is it because we cannot project human qualities onto them and so can never mutually deceive or disappoint?

To make camping more comfortable we built, with Local's help, a small palm-log hut which I used as a studio and dining room. To give it a homely touch, I pinned photographs of Elsa's family and Pippa on its porous walls and erected a few shelves to hold books and crockery. We spread a groundsheet across the floor to keep the scorpions, which like to hide in sheltered places, under control.

Though our mutual interests were few and conversation was difficult because of our limited knowledge of each other's language, I was lucky to have a nice, good-natured man like Local to help me with Pippa.

One afternoon we were walking through very thick bush, Pippa following at some distance, when I heard the rumbling of an elephant close by. Local grabbed me by the shoulder and whispered: "Run." We both rushed back along the path by which we had come until we reached open ground, where we were joined by Pippa. Local told me, breathlessly, that I had walked straight into three lions on a waterbuck kill which they must have just brought down as his legs were still kicking into the air. He demonstrated the situation very convincingly by measuring the distance from us at which one dark-maned lion had sat at the kill, one younger, blond-maned lion a little farther away, and a lioness close to the path, not farther than some six yards from me. How lucky it was that the growling of the lions, which I had mistaken for the rumbling of an elephant, had warned him just in time to prevent an accident. Good old Local, it took him some time to calm down. It made me feel a fool to have remained unaware of what had been going on, although I had been walking ahead of him. Pippa seemed quite unconcerned as she licked her paws, which made me wonder if we really had been so close to lions, from which, at their faintest sound, she usually bolted.

The light was failing and we returned home. Suddenly Pippa bounded off into the bush and soon I saw, near her familiar head, another cheetah's head appear above the grass. For a short while both ran in circles around each other until the wild cheetah sat down within about fifty yards of us. Pippa approached it carefully. It showed great interest in her but she ran away whenever it moved toward her, looking constantly at me as if to ask my advice. Local and I stood absolutely still. Gradually both cheetahs moved on to the road and sat down within six feet of each other. After a few minutes Pippa rushed to the wild cheetah, which quickly got up, only to be clasped by Pippa around the rump. The response was a growl, and she retreated hurriedly. This was the first time I had a full view of the animal, which was much larger than Pippa, and either a male with a very full belly or a pregnant female—I could not identify the sex in the diffused light. Both now walked around and around each other for about fifteen minutes, Pippa always taking the initiative, even though she seemed nervous. Finally the wild cheetah left the road and disappeared behind a bush. By now it was almost dark and, even when looking through my field glasses, I could hardly follow what went on. All I noted was that Pippa seemed very undecided, looking first at the cheetah and then at me. Both were listening intently as though another cheetah might be hiding in the grass. Just then I heard a car approaching and sent Local to stop it. Meanwhile both cheetahs returned to the road, the wild one settling down not more than ten yards from me; Pippa moved toward me. Slowly I stepped backward to the car, hoping that she would remain with her new friend, but both followed me, the wild cheetah keeping to its "safety belt" of ten yards, while Pippa passed me and walked determinedly toward the Land-Rover. I rushed ahead of her and jumped into it, telling the driver not to turn the lights on but to take Local and me back to camp, which was about half a mile away.

My hope that I had succeeded in leaving Pippa in the company of her wild companion was dashed when she appeared shortly afterward and demanded her dinner. Fearing that being fed might spoil this chance for her to behave as a wild cheetah, I ignored her. After a short time she went off, leaving me feeling a brute. Around midnight I was awakened by her soft purr. Now she got her way, and after feasting on fresh kongoni meat she disappeared again only to return at dawn for more food. As soon as it was light enough for spooring we returned, together with Pippa, to the scene of last evening's incident. Here we found the pugmarks of two cheetahs in addition to Pippa's. Afterward she walked back to camp with us but left as soon as she heard the vibration of the car which was bringing George to camp. She stayed away for two days.

When I had told him the news I suggested that we should investigate Local's lion kill, for in George's company I felt I'd be safe if the lions were still in the vicinity. Together with Local, we approached the place with great caution and were relieved to see no vultures on the trees, which usually indicate that the lions are still on their kill. We had expected to discover these greedy birds fighting over the remains of the carcass, and plenty of jackal and hyena spoor around, but we found nothing except the spoor of an elephant, which proved that my hearing belly rumbles had been correct; otherwise the place had not been disturbed, except for a log with two branches sticking up into the air which Local had obviously mistaken for the kicking legs of a waterbuck. We teased him about his vivid imagination. He seemed hurt that we doubted him and insisted that even if there were by now no evidence to prove his story, he really had seen three lions on a kill. We had to leave it at that and returned home.

CHAPTER

7

Taga

ON THE TWENTY-SECOND of November I had to go with George's assistant to Nairobi for a few days. On our return we stopped at Meru, where we heard of a baby leopard that was being reared by the Fathers of the Catholic Mission at Tigania, which we had to pass on our way home. Of course, we called at the Mission.

Father Botta, who was in charge of the tiny leopard, was known to be a great animal lover, and he was certainly doing his best to help the little cub, but as he had plenty of other work to do as well he could not give it the constant company it needed at its age. The cub, deserted by its mother when it was about two days old, had been found on a rock a fortnight earlier during heavy rain. Since then it had been fed on cow's milk, but it had developed heavy blood scouring which Father Botta was at a loss to cure. As I had several medicines in camp to treat scouring, he agreed that I should take the cub with me and nurse it until it recovered. I felt sorry to deprive the kind Father of his pet, which he obviously loved, but as I had more time, as well as better facilities, to help it, he entrusted the cub to me. Providing us with enough milk for the journey, he promised to visit us soon, and we left with the little leopard on my lap.

Passing through a village, I bought a blanket and a baby-feeding bottle, as well as cod-liver oil to supplement the Nestle's Ideal Milk and glucose which I had in camp. Most of the way the cub sucked my fingers while I stroked its very fine, silky fur. The rosettes, at this early age, were so close together that its coat looked almost black except for some yellow fluff along the neck and head. The largest part of the little animal were its paws, already equipped with well-developed, sharp-pointed claws. As far as I could make out it was a female, and I decided to call her Taga—short for Tigania. She had only opened her eyes when she was ten days old, and her vision was still blurred by a bluish film. In spite of this, Taga had a most appealing expression.

I wondered how Pippa would react to this newcomer to "her" camp. Would she mother the baby or treat her as a rival? In the bush, like most wild animals, cheetahs are even more scared of leopards than of lions, because the leopard's light build—it weighs only some 120 to 150 pounds—its lightning speed, its superb ability to climb trees, and its nocturnal habits give this cat many advantages over other predators. For their part many experienced hunters regard leopards as the most dangerous of all the wild animals of Africa. Looking at the helpless and endearing creature I was holding in my arms, I could hardly credit her with this reputation and felt already deeply attracted to this future terror of the bush, but I realized I would have to be very tactful in giving her affection and security without provoking Pippa's jealousy. Luckily, she was not in camp when we arrived so we were able to concentrate on setting up Taga's home. Pippa's wired-in traveling crate made an ideal bedroom for the cub in which she could sleep close to me at night. For her day playground we erected an enclosure; inside it Taga could move safely until Pippa was prepared to accept her and they could play together. Local, the cook, and the labor boy started work enthusiastically, for they had taken an instant liking to Taga in spite of the awe they ordinarily feel for all dangerous animals. But who, indeed, could resist this fluffy cub crawling between our feet and often tumbling over these animated "rocks"?

I fed Taga every two hours with one part of unsweetened Nestle's Ideal Milk diluted with two parts of water, to which I added one drop of Abidec vitamin, three drops of cod-liver oil, a little salt, and some sulfaguanidine against the scouring. Watching Taga massaging the bottle to get more milk, as if it were her mother's belly, I decided to attach a little board close to the neck of the feeding bottle which would give her a better substitute for her mother's belly than the slippery bottle provided.

Pippa did not turn up that evening so I kept the cub on my lap

Taga with her tin of milk and being bottle-fed

while I was having a sundowner outside the studio. It was getting dark when suddenly I saw a cobra wriggling under the table toward my feet. Holding Taga in one hand, I snatched the stick I always kept ready for such occasions and killed the snake just before it could strike. I was rather alarmed by this incident, not so much for my own safety, which I could ensure, as for Taga's. Obviously, while she was in such a defenseless state, I would need to be on the lookout for snakes. At 10 P.M. I gave her her last meal, then I placed her next to my bed, inside her sleeping crate, which I had lined with grass to keep her used to natural conditions. I covered it with a blanket and we went to sleep.

At 6 A.M. I was awakened by Pippa's purr. For half an hour she took no notice of the covered box, but then when she discovered Taga she sniffed at her and purred. Quickly I brought her milk and played with her until she settled placidly outside the tent and watched me feeding Taga. This seemed a promising start to their relationship. I was still more relieved when Pippa took up her usual routine and, after she had had her meal, disappeared for the day.

I spent the morning in the studio dealing with correspondence, while I held Taga on my lap to keep her warm. She sucked my finger whenever I stopped typing; she called "Wa-wa-wa" when she was comfortable and made a high-pitched miaow when she was distressed. Later she crawled unsteadily around and ventured outside the studio, then she found her way inside her sleeping crate, which I had placed nearby, and went to sleep in it. When Pippa returned at teatime she sniffed at Taga through the wire, but the only response she got to her friendly purr was a snarl from the cub.

To make up for this rebuff I took Pippa for a walk and took pains to be particularly affectionate, but whenever I touched her she ran away growling and finally disappeared. Assuming that she did not like the leopard scent on my clothes, I decided to change them whenever I was with her until she got used to Taga. On our way home we saw Pippa in the twilight, chasing after a jackal; she was almost on top of him when both disappeared from our sight. Later, when I heard repeated jackal barks, I wondered whether Pippa had made a kill. I never knew, as she kept away for two days.

Meanwhile, little Taga won all our hearts. Even the cook, who was no animal fan, offered to baby-sit whenever I was out of the camp, and dozed next to her while she explored her enclosure and made herself a cozy lair beneath the foliage of a little bush. Taga always looked for hiding places to rest in, and as she poked into all the dark corners I had to search the studio for scorpions. The little leopard was born house-trained and always went a short distance away to relieve herself. One night I heard her whimpering and struggling up the wire of her box. Going to her rescue, I found it drenched. After this, I always listened to the slightest sound which might indicate her wish to be taken out. When she had done her job, she always turned around and around inside her crate to flatten the grass for her bed and then fell asleep again.

A few days later I became worried because she was always constipated unless she had been given a laxative. My massaging of her belly in the hope of stimulating her digestion had no effect, and I only learned, much too late, that I should have wiped her anus with a damp cloth, and that no animal at so early an age can defecate unless the mother licks its anus.

Each morning, after feeding her, I de-ticked Taga. It was unbelievable how many ticks she collected; I could remove them only with forceps. Otherwise she was amazingly clean and often licked herself.

Taga was a great tease. She always made me laugh when, snuggling on my lap after her meals, her belly round like a balloon and lying on her back, she paddled her legs while looking up at me with her bluish eyes, obviously smiling. But even at this early age her claws were razor-sharp and left scratches that became septic. I tried to tuck them back but this only made her paddle more actively. If dreams are to be regarded as subconscious reactions to suppressed emotions, I wondered what Taga could be suppressing when, in her sleep, she sometimes paddled madly as if fighting for her life. Soon she became so active that one of us had to baby-sit all the time to prevent her from getting into trouble.

Of all the wild animals I have reared, Taga was by far the quickest in her reactions as well as in her development. After being in camp only one day she knew her way around and never got lost. Before she could walk properly she already climbed the wire of her pen, if I approached it. When she was twenty days old I noticed that her top incisors were breaking through. After two more days the bottom incisors appeared, and after another two days the canines could be seen. At thirty-four days the lower molars were visible, and when she was forty-two days old her deciduous teeth were complete.

At the age of three weeks her pinkish nose and paws turned black, while the yellow fluff on her head and neck became more noticeable. By this time she was already holding on to anything she wanted with incredible strength; she dug her tiny but very sharp teeth and claws into my hand so that I had to give way, even though I was wearing elbow-long khaki gloves. Undoubtedly she was aware of her power to get what she wanted, but she also knew how to compensate for a scratch by being so affectionate and charming that none of us could long be cross with her.

At the beginning Pippa was amazingly tolerant of Taga and often tried to rub noses with her through the wire. But animals are as moody as people, and if, one day, she was friendly to the cub, the next she bolted at her scent; and she could be very jealous, too, though she showed this in a dignified way, by ignoring me rather than taking it out on her rival. I kept the two animals separated until I was sure of Pippa's reaction. Luckily, it was not very long before I was able to keep Taga on my lap while Pippa rested, purring, close to us and I stroked both simultaneously.

Our life seemed perfect. The birds and animals around the camp had also by now accepted our presence, and I could watch a pair of agama lizards sunning themselves on Pippa's tree bridge, the bright turquoise-colored male bobbing his orange head up and down at the slightest sign of danger while the brownish mottled female, who was smaller, dashed for safety into the hollow tree stump where they lived. They liked ants and small pieces of meat and came quite close to get these delicacies. Very colorful, too, were a pair of beautiful sunbirds—extremely rare in this part of Kenya. They built their nest of feathers and leaves, with a proper roof above the entrance hole, and they attached the nest by a stalk of grass to a bush overhanging the stream. Under this bush there was also the home of a monitor lizard which I had often heard at night rustling in the grass close to my tent. Though monitors frequently dine on eggs, the monitor was much less of a danger to the sunbirds than a redheaded weaver. I had never seen this bird near camp until the morning he attacked the sunbirds so ferociously that they left their nest and built a new one, also overhanging the stream, farther away. I expected the weaver to occupy the abandoned nest, but, having driven the sunbirds off, he left as suddenly as he had appeared. We had often seen colonies of weavers building their nests on bushes ov-

Joy with Taga and Pippa

Taga with her "animated rocks"

erhanging water, probably to protect them from such predators as genet cats. But clever though this was, I wondered how the fledglings escaped drowning after their first parachute outing, which was likely to land them in the water below. Perhaps some weavers may have been aware of this danger, for a few chose the trees under which we camped to build in, presumably considering our presence a protection.

Next breeding season, our beautiful sunbirds also built their nest above my tent. At the time they were the only birds nesting on the large tamarind, and I was awakened every day by their happy chatter until the female started to incubate. Then one morning they gave cries of alarm: the redheaded weaver had returned and was once more attacking them. For many hours he darted furiously at the female and at the nest, which she defended most courageously. Finally, the weaver left and all was quiet again. But my hopes that the sunbird had won her battle were destroyed when, later, the redheaded weaver returned, bringing a whole flock of blackheaded weavers with him. Eventually, the tamarind tree was swarming with these canary-yellow invaders all starting to build nests around the frantic sunbirds. My working table was underneath the tree, but typing was out of the question, not only because of the din but because I was almost as upset about the attack on the poor sunbirds as they were. Flinging stones at the weavers, I kept them away for a day, but early next morning I had to leave the camp for a short while and returned to a deadly silence. There was no sign of the weavers or of the sunbirds. All I saw was the sunbirds' nest on the ground with a broken egg beside it. It seemed that the weavers had only made a pretense of nesting to scare the sunbirds off, for now, victorious, they had left their unfinished nests hanging like grass rings from the tree. This war between the redheaded weavers and the sunbirds puzzled me. The weavers did not live close by, so no territorial claim could be involved, nor could the nectar-feeding sunbirds interfere with the seed- and insect-eating weavers. Why, then, this urge to destroy?

Perhaps I should admit that I, too, had, no doubt equally unjustifiably, killed a snake nearly every day. Never had I experienced such an invasion of a camp by cobras, night adders, and boomslange. After dark I always kept my feet up on a chair so as not to impede the creatures. But even though I knew the snakes might only be looking for a sheltered place, I never trusted them and, besides, on account of Taga, I had to be especially prudent.

Her instinct for concealment had become so strong that often none of us could find her, and it was only by accident, when I spilled some water near a provision box in the spare tent, that I discovered her hide-out. Then suddenly two little paws appeared from behind the box, and Taga heaved herself onto its smooth metal surface and eagerly licked the mud which resulted from the spilled water. Afterward she quickly went back to her safe refuge. Having learned from Pippa that cheetahs need mud to keep fit, I assumed that leopards digest it too. So from now on I provided little mud puddles daily near Taga's favorite lair while pretending not to know she was there. Respecting her wish to hide, I only called her from a distance, and it was touching to see how she came racing toward us as long as we kept clear of her hide-out.

Whenever I treated her with sulfaguanidine her scouring ceased, but it reappeared as soon as I stopped dosing her. On the fifth of December, when our old friend the Vet—Dr. Toni Harthoorn—came to my camp on his way to George to look at Ugas, whose eye had deteriorated, I told him of Taga's trouble. Toni prescribed a diet of rice water, milk, and strepotriad tablets. Afer two days' coaxing Taga consented to swallow the tablets, which cured the scouring completely. Toni thought that her recent restlessness was probably due to teething and advised me to let her rub her gums against anything hard she could find. Nevertheless, I often found my fingers used as a grinding stone in addition to the wooden sticks I provided which she chewed into pulp. Later I was sent the photograph of a leopard cub of the same age as Taga which had been reared in a zoo. No doubt it had the same urge to rub its gums against hard objects, but a plastic collar, the size of a soup plate, made this impossible. If the cub, justifiably resenting such treatment, turned fierce it would certainly be charged with having a dangerous character, whereas the blame should fall on those who prevented it from satisfying a natural instinct. Taga suffered no frustrations and was given every chance of developing her natural habits.

She loved climbing up the wire of her compound, and we had to be on the watch to prevent her from getting over the top. Climbing chairs was more difficult, because she had to heave herself onto the seat, and when she had pulled her full belly into position sometimes

Taga and the cook

she fell back, only to repeat the effort until finally she managed to settle on the chair. When she had succeeded Taga smiled at us and gave her "wa-wa-wa" call of contentment. She was thirty-four days old before her toddling movements changed to energetic strides. At about the same time she also started leaping high into the air, thus cleverly preventing me from catching her. This trick became a favorite game between us which she always won.

Animals, including man, sometimes react to the accustomed setup rather than to the object they are looking for. As a rule, I fed Taga on a chair outside the studio. If she wanted food and the chair was not there she climbed up the palm-frond walls of the studio and waited. She seemed to know she was fed above ground level, so that was where she should be when she was hungry. Likewise, if her crate had been removed she would fall asleep on the bare ground, on the spot where it usually stood. I myself often react in this way; for instance, I look for an object in its proper place even though I should know I have put it somewhere else. Surely this shows that automatically conditioned reflexes are not a prerogative of animal behavior, as many people claim.

Taga's round, baby head had lately grown more elongated; her ears instead of being set low (an endearing trait in young animals) were now near to the top of her skull, and the skin behind her ears had turned black, so that she looked a proper little leopard. Yet, although she was growing fast, seemed generally fit, and had plenty of exercise, exploring her territory or climbing up the wire of her enclosure, she could never produce feces unless helped with liquid paraffin. When she was tired she often snuggled up to Pippa, who lay so close to the compound that only the wire separated their bodies. Watching the two licking each other affectionately, Pippa purring and Taga reaching out her tiny paws to her through the wire, touched me deeply.

Since Elsa had become world-famous, my life had changed greatly. To cope with all the publicity, I had deliberately fenced off my emotional reactions. Of course I was fond of Pippa, but it was the arrival of Taga, so obviously in need of protection, that got below my guard. She, like Elsa, had come to me at a very vulnerable age and drew heavily on my maternal instinct. Pippa I had first got to know when she had passed cub age. The relationship between us was therefore more that of good companions.

Taga climbs chair and smiles at us

Pippa was away from camp between the seventh and the eighth of December. This was nothing unusual, but her coat was exceptionally silky and her behavior uncommonly aloof, and I began to wonder if she had been with a male. I made a note of these dates and, counting ninety-three days for a gestation period, marked the ninth of March as the day of a possible birth.

I still took her for long walks, during which she played hide-and-seek with me, nibbled at my hands, and swiped at my knees playfully, but on our return to camp she behaved unpredictably, either passing Taga without a glance or rushing at her aggressively, though on another occasion she would sniff at her through the wire in a friendly fashion or snuggle up as closely as possible to her.

One afternoon Father Botta came to visit Taga, with a party touring the Park. All made a great fuss over Pippa, who singled out the youngest of several children, a tot of four years; nosing her and swiping at her legs, she took great delight in this new friend. The little girl was equally attracted to Pippa: neither showed any fear and both enjoyed the other's company. Later the party came to my camp. Taga, too, was drawn to the child, who responded as she had to Pippa, and paid no attention to the anxious looks of the parents. This incident seemed to disprove the theory that man's fear of wild animals is innate and to show that it develops only after human beings have been taught that wild animals are dangerous. A close investigation of accidents involving so-called dangerous beasts often proves that these have occurred only after the human being has provoked the animal and that it has acted simply in self-defense. Father Botta was so pleased with the way in which Taga had developed that he offered to let me keep her until I was able to return her to her wild life.

Later in the evening I saw a beautiful dark cheetah which I recognized as Pippa's friend. It ran off in the direction in which she had disappeared earlier in the day. Pippa did not turn up for forty-eight hours, and when she came back she stayed only for a quick meal, then went off for two more days, after which she turned up just for a meal and again disappeared. When I saw the spoor of a male cheetah leading in the same direction, I knew beyond doubt that Pippa had found a mate.

Her frequent absences gave me more opportunity to concentrate on Taga. The little leopard's eyes were now clear of the blue film which she had had as a baby, but she still retained a pronounced squint which seemed to handicap her in focusing. Hoping to improve her vision, I made a paper ball, tied it firmly together with string, and hung it above her box. Taga loved this new toy and, after a few unsuccessful attempts, never missed the mobile target wherever I located it. I also hung up a small hessian bag filled with paper into which she hooked her claws and then swung around; it was, I thought, a good exercise to strengthen her tendons. Next she discovered the wastepaper basket and tore up its contents with so much gusto that my camp resembled a snowfield of litter. Exploring the beer crate and making the bottles clatter was also fun. The only thing I did not like about Taga were her very sharp claws, and I could not teach her to sheathe them when we played. I tried to blunt them with a nail file but soon gave up as the nails grew, within a day, to even sharper points. In the end I always carried sulfanilamide powder with me to dress my many scratches. Apart from this, Taga was irresistible and I loved looking into her intelligent eyes, which could be so laughing and happy but also, when angry, so murderously hard.

I wanted to free her of the many ticks she collected daily; they worried me because, as a rule, they occur in such profusion only on sick animals. Yet, except for her digestive and teething troubles, Taga seemed fit enough. I wished to stimulate her digestion, and soon found out that she defected more easily if I took her to the spot where she had previously produced droppings. This reminded me of the habits of dik-dik (antelope) and rhino which, for different reasons, also use the same place until the pile of their droppings gets too high.

On the twenty-first of December Taga had little appetite and was rubbing her gums; I put this down to teething trouble. Later, George's assistant called and, having himself reared a baby leopard, advised me to start Taga on minced meat. This she took greedily; indeed, she liked the new diet so well that I gave her another helping in the evening, after which she slept throughout the whole night. The next day she was listless and refused food, although she did lick lots of mud. She was six weeks old that day, and her last molars broke through. I dipped my finger into glucose and made her suck it, hoping that this would make her thirsty and accept milk. But she only opened her mouth, gasped, and refused to drink. Within the last two days she had become alarmingly thin, but again I attributed this to teething. I tried to comfort her, stroking and cuddling her whenever she came out of her hiding place, and after dark I took her into my bed. She cuddled against my neck, following every movement I made so as to keep close to me; meanwhile, ticks and fleas crawled over me! All night she held and sucked my fingers or patted my eyes softly and licked my face, making tiny noises. This was so different from her normal chatter that I suddenly realized she must be desperately ill.

Listening to her movements, fearing they might suddenly stop, I prayed for her life. As soon as dawn turned the sky crimson, Pippa appeared. She settled close to us, watching intently. When I got up, leaving Taga safe inside the mosquito net, Pippa bowled me over and then rushed off across the stream. This morning, for the first time, Taga produced solid feces without having had a laxative. Hoping it might be the result of eating meat, I tried to give her some more, but this only upset her. So I arrranged to go with her to Meru to see the Vet there, an African who had previously helped me when Pippa had been ill with tick fever. Knowing Taga's affection for the cook, I took him along so that he could hold her on his lap while I was driving the eighty miles along very bad roads, but at each jolt poor Taga struggled to me. It was difficult to steer under these conditions, and, although I was most anxious to reach the Vet as quickly as possible, I had often to stop to comfort her. At last we arrived at Meru. It was 11 A.M. The Vet took a blood smear: the blood did not coagulate but ran like water. Judging by Taga's anemic condition— her gums had gone white—he diagnosed *Babesia felis*, the tick fever of which Elsa had died. Seeing my distress, he reassured me, saying that he could cure Taga as the illness was only in its first phase. While waiting for the result of the blood test I sat with Taga on the lawn outside the surgery. She was now too weak to stand on her hind legs and lay limp in my lap, but she watched alertly every move the Vet made. He tried without success to make her swallow diluted glucose by squirting it into her mouth with a syringe. I took her temperature, which was almost normal—102.1°. The Vet assured me that Taga would recover thanks to the powerful drug phenamidine and left us to prepare the injection.

I looked at Taga and stroked her silky fur. She held my fingers in a very strong grasp. Then the Vet returned with the injection containing 1 cc. of phenamidine, 5%, based on the assumption that Taga's body weight was six pounds. This seemed to me a very large dose—I believed she now weighed no more than four pounds at most—but the Vet insisted on this measure. I shall never forget Taga's eyes as she looked searchingly at the Vet while he injected her. They seemed to hold all her life in them. Soon she was deeply asleep. Her heart was beating fast and she was breathing rapidly. The Vet prepared more injections for me to give her at my camp over the next two days and then closed his office for the luncheon break. Looking at Taga, I thought that to drive her in her present state over the bumpy road was inconceivable, so I suggested that I should wait for two hours and see how she reacted to the treatment. During this time I met Father Botta, who, watching Taga breathing so fast, wondered, as I did, how her heart could stand up to it. Waiting anxiously for the Vet's return, I decided to spend the night at Meru so as to give Taga a complete rest.

I called at a friend's house, and while he made arrangements for us to spend the night there I sat in his cool office with Taga in my arms. Suddenly she made a small sound, stretched out in a spasm, and fell limp. We rushed to the Vet, who injected her with some substance which might counteract the action of the phenamidine, but Taga was already beyond help. I left her body with the Vet to carry out a post-mortem and drove home. It was the twenty-third of December. I dreaded Christmas Day.

CHAPTER

8

Extinction or Survival?

WHEN I ARRIVED in camp I removed everything which had made up Taga's little world. To add to my desolation, Pippa was absent. The next morning a Game Scout reported that she had been seen near Kenmare. We searched for several hours without success, then we went to look for a Christmas tree, as I had invited George and his assistant as well as a young Indian, Arun Sharma, who was doing voluntary work in the Reserve, and three friends from Nairobi, for Christmas Eve dinner. While preparing the Christmas tree I visualized Taga's laughing eyes looking out for mischief. What fun she would have had with all the glittering tinsel I hung on the thorns of a small balanitis tree. If her personality had dominated us while she was alive, her spirit seemed almost more present now that she was dead. Wretched as I felt, I was glad when finally the guests arrived and I was obliged to entertain them. They had brought some delicious fish which they had caught that afternoon and a chicken from Nairobi, together with wine and the traditional plum pudding. The party started well. I lighted the candles on the Christmas tree and presented the gifts—including sugar, cigarettes, and money for our African staff. I was determined that everyone should have a good time, and I was grateful that nobody mentioned Taga.

After my guests had left I fell against the corner of a wooden box and injured my ribs. Luckily, George had remained behind, and he picked me up, for I was unable to move without help. The next morning, as I was still immobilized, Local searched for Pippa on his own but did not find her. Later in the afternoon three visitors came: Dr. and Mrs. Jean Russell and Dr. Paul Martin of the University of Arizona, in Tucson. They were touring Africa to find out why many animal species which had become extinct in America still roamed the African plains; being especially interested in elephants, they had called to discuss our experiences with these creatures.* While we were talking I admired a silver bracelet of unusual design that Mrs. Russell was wearing and asked if it were of Navaho origin. She was surprised that I should know where it had come from, so I explained that I had become interested in the various Red Indian tribes during my travels in the United States and had collected a few pieces of their jewelry as well as some books about their customs. Mrs. Russell told me that the bracelet was a genuine, sand-cast Navaho piece and said that she was so fond of it that she had worn it every day for the last ten years.

Suddenly we heard a rustle, and Pippa appeared. I was amazed that she should come into camp while there were so many visitors around; no doubt it was because she was very hungry, for after she had eaten a hearty meal she promptly disappeared.

Although I had tried not to show my distress about Taga's death, Mrs. Russell must have sensed it, for the next evening, while I sat in the dark thinking of Taga, a car arrived with a note from her and the precious Navaho bracelet, which she said she wanted me to keep. I was deeply moved; from now on it was "Taga's bracelet," and whenever I was asked by some official body to help wild animals, I wore it. Little did I then guess that within two years I should be giving a luncheon broadcast on animal conservation in New York with Mona Dayton, to whom President Johnson had given an award for being the best schoolteacher of the year in the United States. During our conversation she looked as if mesmerized at "Taga's bracelet" and finally asked me how it had come into my possession. When I told her the story she explained that she was a great friend of Mrs. Russell's and had helped her to get the bracelet from an Indian she knew on one of the Arizona reservations, and so she had been amazed to see someone else wearing it.

The following morning Pippa arrived. Before she settled for her meal, she sniffed for a long time at all the places where Taga used to

---

* Later, Dr. Martin's researches were published in *Pleistocene Extinctions*, by P. S. Martin and H. E. Wright, Jr.

play. As I was still unable to bend down, Local brushed and de-ticked Pippa, which bewildered her. Later he took her for a walk, but she kept looking back expecting me to follow, then she heard a car approach and bolted across the stream. I had sent for the doctor at Maua; he diagnosed fractured ribs and said they needed more rest than I was giving them. So, willy-nilly, I had to stay put for a few days, during which time Pippa often came to camp.

Local had asked for leave to go to see one of his children, who was seriously ill. After two days he returned with the sad news that the child had died. He accepted this stoically as the will of Mungu (God) and seemed surprisingly detached, until he took Pippa for a walk, then, while he was playing with her, I saw him wiping his eyes and kissing Pippa, which he had never done before. Obviously, the grief over his child's death went deeper than he allowed himself to show, and I found it significant that he could find relief by sharing his emotion with Pippa.

When it got dark she kept on hiding from us and finally pretended to chase a giraffe, a tactful way of disappearing for the night. During the following days she seldom came to camp, and even when we met her in the bush sometimes she avoided us by sinking most effectively into the grass. Knowing her to be close, we searched the surrounding area systematically and discovered her often within a yard of us, pressed to the ground and frozen, her coat blending to perfection with the straw-colored grass. Sometimes we did not find her, though we knew that she was around. Freezing is the best form of concealment, and all animals practice it when cornered. For instance, I had recently found a night adder on the road; its body seemed to be broken, except for the extended head, which stuck up into the air. Puzzled by this, I threw a stone near it, then several more, and walked up to within three feet of it; still the night adder remained immobile. Then I threw a last stone which hit the snake, which only then shot off.

On another occasion I surprised a ground squirrel standing on its hind legs and holding one front paw suspended in the air. Seeing me, it froze instantly. I timed it; for fifty minutes it remained absolutely motionless in this uncomfortable pose, then I lost patience and withdrew. Other animals go even further and sham death. I well remember a young Verreaux eagle owl, the largest of its kind in Africa, lying apparently lifeless on the ground with an injured eye.

As her body was still warm, I picked her up and, carefully avoiding the powerful talons, carried her to the car and drove home. When we arrived the bird seemed to be dead, but we were not absolutely sure so we put her in a large crate and shot a hare, which we placed next to her. After a few hours we came back to find the owl still "dead," but of the hare, only a few tufts of fluff were left. We then provided the owl with a pigeon and left her again. A little later we approached the crate very carefully from the back and saw the owl heartily tearing at the pigeon, but as soon as she noticed us she again promptly shammed "dead." This game went on for three weeks—in fact, until the owl was well enough to be released. Then there were the two ground hornbills, as large as turkeys and similar in appearance, who escaped from captivity by shamming death so perfectly after their capture that they were left alone long enough to give them time to disappear. While writing these lines, I notice a little gecko clinging to the studio wall within two feet of me and keeping so still that it is hardly perceptible except for its dark eyes. Geckos have another defense as well as freezing: they can adapt their color to their surroundings, as chameleons and agamas can.

All these animals were wild and had good reason to avoid a human being, but even Pippa, who was my friend, could quickly revert to her natural ways when she preferred to be alone. Although I took this as a sign of her going wild, I always worried in case a snake or some injury might be responsible for her absence. The uncertainty of what might have happened to her was a constant strain, but I could do nothing to relieve it except to look daily for fresh spoor.

I was very glad when she turned up on the evening of the thirty-first of December and gave me her company for New Year's Eve. While she rested, relaxed, near me I wondered when she would have cubs and how she would behave. Would she bring them into camp or even give birth to them here, or would she revert completely to the wild? If this happened she would be the first man-reared cheetah to produce wild cubs. Also, by offering me a unique opportunity of finding out more about the habits of wild cheetahs, she might perhaps help to solve the problem of why cheetahs breed so badly in captivity.

A few days later Local asked for leave. He came back with a new wife, the fifth, as far as I know. Sensible as this was after his recent bereavement, I wondered how he managed, at his age, to get such a good-looking girl to marry him. I hoped she would remain with him: his last three wives had bolted, leaving him broke. He told me that he had given two hundred shillings in cash as well as a steer for the girl—a gentle hint about a wedding present which I agreed to give him—but in three months' time. We both laughed and then took Pippa for a stroll to the Rojoweru.

She too was glad to see Local back again and skipped around him, purring, until we reached the river. There we surprised a hippo cow with such a tiny calf that it was still a very pale color. Alarmed by our approach, both struggled up some shallow rapids, the mother pushing the little one between the rocks, until they submerged in a pool. While we were watching them another hippo surfaced within three yards of us. Opening its cavernous mouth, he ogled us intently as he passed slowly by. The bank here was level with the river, and I watched the hippo apprehensively, but Pippa had the cheek to growl at him until he sank back into the water. Watching all this was still another hippo concealed under palm fronds on the opposite bank. Although Pippa was usually very nervous near the river because of crocodiles, today she showed no fear; on the contrary, she sat close to the water, growling fiercely at the slightest ripple, let alone the protruding eyes of the hippos. She must often have met these bulky beasts when they were feeding by night on the plain, but she showed no respect for them, nor for that matter did elephants impress her. She kept growling at the hippo at such close range that eventually I thought it wiser to leave the river. On the way home she chased a flock of guinea fowl and finally spun around and around on one spot as though she had St. Vitus's dance. When I approached I saw that she was playing with a tiny chick which she had already injured. I wrung its neck and forced her to eat it, hoping to teach her the purpose of a kill.

Later in the evening I had my bath as usual in the open, behind my tent. Sitting in the square canvas tub, I always enjoyed watching the stars and sometimes saw the dark shape of an elephant feeding across the stream. It was a grand way to relax. But tonight I had an uneasy feeling that I was being watched and, turning my flashlight around, saw a lion about fifty yards away sitting near my car. I dressed hurriedly and told the men to remain inside their tent.

Next morning I was awakened by Pippa's purr, then she bumped her head against mine through the mosquito net before she settled down next to my bed. This was the first time since Taga had shared our life that Pippa had again come inside the tent. After getting up we investigated the ground around the car and found the pugmarks of a large lion. Later we saw the spoor of two lions and one lioness along the road leading toward Kenmare. Pippa kept away all day and that night; no doubt she wished to avoid them. Besides, it was full moon, which always made her restless.

Heavy thuddings on Pippa's little hut, which stood within ten yards of the back of my tent, woke me up in the middle of the night. When in camp she always used this as her lookout, and I knew the sound she made when she jumped onto it. But these thuds were much heavier. For some time I listened tensely to the noise, then I heard the movements of a heavy animal and a large lion appeared at the entrance of my tent. Terrified, I yelled, but he just stood and looked at me. After a minute he turned around slowly and walked a few steps toward the stream, looking back at me, then he returned to Pippa's hut. I called for Local. By the time he emerged from his tent the lion had gone to the kitchen shelter, which was between the men's tent and the studio. Local turned his flashlight on him, but again he just stood still, blinking into the glare. No wild lion would behave like that, and suddenly it dawned on me that it must be Ugas, who had been missing for four days from George's camp. I assumed that he was looking for a mate and had followed the lions whose spoor we had seen on the road. Probably it was also Ugas who had surprised me in the bath last evening, for he now walked to the car and sat in the exact spot at which yesterday's lion had sat. Finally, the lion strolled off into the dark.

I dressed quickly and told the cook and the men to lock themselves inside my studio (the only place with a door in the camp) and stay there until my return. I then took some meat and, with Local, went to my car, calling "Ugas, Ugas." Soon the lion appeared and walked up to the Land-Rover—there was no doubt now that he was good old Ugas. I dropped the meat, hoping this would keep him close to camp until I could return with George. I then drove on along a narrow, rough track, in preference to the good road, as the latter passed Kenmare and I did not want to alarm the Game Scouts at the Lodge at that time of the night.

After a few miles the track led into densely wooded bush and wound its way among trees which made it impossible to see more than a few yards ahead. The ground was covered with fresh elephant droppings and their unmistakable smell filled the air. I was frightened, for if these colossi suddenly blocked my way there would be nothing I could do. I grew still more frightened when the track petered out and I had to find my bearings by the distant, double-peaked Mugwongo Hill toward which I bulldozed my way across ant-bear holes and boulders until I reached George's camp. Always a good sleeper, it took some time before he drowsily grasped the purpose of my midnight call. Then he had to repair his Land-Rover before he could follow me home; by the time we arrived in my camp it was 4 A.M. Thank God, Ugas was still close and, hearing George's familiar voice, came bounding from the bush to greet him. Fond as I was of Ugas, I was relieved to see him jump into the caged car to eat the meat bait we had placed inside it. Securing the doors firmly behind him, George drove the lovesick lion back to his camp. I was sorry for Ugas because, good-natured as he was, he was never allowed a chance to flirt with Girl, who was jealously guarded by Boy.

What were we going to do with Ugas? He needed a mate and it was obviously for this purpose that he had followed the wild lionesses until he came to my camp. By that time he must have been hungry and, recognizing my car, not to mention me in my bath, he had quite naturally walked into my tent hoping to get some food. Certainly he had no bad intentions, but, finding a lion in my tent, how was I to know that it was only Ugas?

George thought the solution would be to accept a litter of three lionesses and one lion, all four months old, which had been offered him recently for rehabilitation. This "kindergarten" would keep Ugas company until the females were old enough to form his harem. Accordingly, he sent his assistant to collect the cubs, which arrived a few days later.

CHAPTER

9

The First Litter

NOW THAT PIPPA evidently considered it safe to return to my camp, she came and pounced hungrily on the carcass of a goat. I knew that feeding her regularly would retard her going wild, but I did not want to starve her during her pregnancy.

On our walks together, when I watched her sniffing at stones or bushes and following determinedly some scent through shoulder-high grass too tall for her to look above, I realized how much I missed by not having her sense of smell. For a predator scent is the most important of the senses; it always seems to be more highly developed than sight and hearing, however good these may be. Anything downwind might escape Pippa's notice as long as it kept still. (Once I was even able to guide three tiny francolin chicks, sitting downwind, into safety while Pippa followed the brave mother bird fluttering out of her reach in the opposite direction to divert attention from her young.)

People sometimes say that cheetahs lack intelligence. We are inclined to judge an animal's intelligence by human standards, which is a great mistake. Each species has evolved its own peculiar form of intelligence, the one best suited for survival. The fact that under similar circumstances animals often behave differently from us does not imply that they are unintelligent, but that their reactions are governed by senses of which we are unaware, because we are limited to our five senses. For instance, we are only beginning to recognize the existence of telepathic communication between human beings. But Elsa, and also Pippa, have given enough evidence to show that animals can make much more reliable use of telepathy than man can. Considering that some of the reptiles are known to have survived almost unchanged for two hundred million years and marine mammals for sixty million years, while the history of man can only be traced back two million years, it would be of immense value to learn more about the senses which animals possess and which at the present time are still beyond our perception. If we can do this then we may perhaps be able to survive without exterminating other species and finally also ourselves.

Pippa always got exactly what she wanted and what was best for her, and she often used great tact to get her way without upsetting me. However self-willed, aloof, or independent she sometimes appeared, she was still very much in need of help, and though she did not demonstrate her feelings except for an affectionate nibble at my hand, or a purr, we knew that we had each other's affection.

The Shifta were now constantly raiding the neighborhood of the Reserve and controlling them had become too much of a commitment for the local Police and Game Scouts, so a General Service Unit platoon was installed at Kenmare. Their arrival was a mixed blessing for us. Of course, their presence increased our security, but the constant coming and going of trucks filled with noisy troops upset our peace. Two days after their arrival nineteen Shifta were killed close to the boundary of the Park. This battle and the vicinity of the platoon provided endless gossip for my staff.

It is unbelievable how chatty African men can be. It always took me some time to break the flow of Local's talk during our walks even on occasions when it was essential to keep quiet if we hoped to see animals. But, once back at camp, he made up for his enforced silence and filled the evening by repeating stories of the day's events, each time adding some embroidery to the facts.

We had been searching for Pippa, one day, and when the sun was getting low had walked in silence along a narrow game path leading through dense thornbush to the river. I went ahead but was concentrating on the ground, looking for spoor, when I suddenly found myself almost alongside two rhino horns which looked like sticks among the branches of a bush that concealed the rest of the animal's body. The second it took for the rhino to turn around and face me gave me a chance to run, but on the narrow path the great beast gained speed as he charged after me, and I almost collided with Local, who was frantically loading his rifle. In the nick of time he shot into the air. This made the rhino swerve, then he started spinning around and around as if to use up his unreleased momentum, and this gave us the chance to run until we reached open ground and were safe.

Breathless, we burst out laughing. One word stumbling over the next, Local stammered excitedly: "Have I not been a man? What would have happened if I had not shot? I think you would have been killed first because you were much nearer to the rhino, and did you see the second beast behind, which was also coming for us until I fired?" I was most grateful to Local and congratulated him on his courage and presence of mind. On our way home, when the light was already fading, he spotted a herd of elephant with three young calves concealed in the gray bush which I would never have seen. Knowing my fear of elephants, he tried to reassure me by saying that he regarded these giants as far less dangerous than rhinos, which always made him cold with fear. When he said this I understood why he was so proud of having stood his ground with the rhino, and I listened patiently to his various versions of our adventure until we reached camp, where he lived on this story for many days to come.

It was now the dry season, when lots of tourists visit the Park, and sometimes call at my camp in spite of the warning notices. I sympathize with their wish to see Pippa, but I was here to help her to go wild, and consequently I declined to show her off to strangers. Recently she had shown resentment when I touched her or de-ticked her. This was especially noticeable when the male was near. After her last stay in camp she had taken great care to conceal her whereabouts until we found her spoor linked up with those of her mate.

Now she was absent for several days. I spent the evenings listening for her familiar sound but everything was still, too still sometimes. When, after five days, she turned up she was not hungry, she looked well fed, and she rubbed her head affectionately against me before flinging herself onto the ground, purring loudly. She seemed very happy. I felt that she might be telling me that she had been together with her mate but that she was also glad to share some of her time with me. While stroking her, I felt for her enlarged nipples, which she resented. I was surprised to find she had as many as thirteen, and surprised also that the number was uneven. Later she settled near my bed and, listening to the somber hooting of an owl, we fell asleep.

Next day I made a birthday cake for George. I always marvel at the way in which the Africans can cook on just three stones—the usual custom when camping. As for myself, I don't claim to be a good cook even in less primitive conditions, so on this occasion I concealed the rather poor result of my efforts under thick layers of icing, adding for good measure a few cherry decorations, which made the cake at least look presentable. Pippa spent the day in camp watching me engaged in my unusual occupation.

When it got dark I drove to Kenmare to collect a goat for her. To my surprise, I found Dr. Grzimek and his daughter-in-law there. They had come to look at the Reserve with the intention of helping to raise funds for its development. I had met Dr. Grzimek on various occasions concerned with the conservation of wild life, to which he continually contributed funds which he raised in Germany. I invited them both to my camp, and we spent the evening together, with Pippa lying close to us. As Director of the Frankfurt Zoo, Dr. Grzimek was especially appreciative of Pippa's way of life and asked me to keep him informed of the progress of her rehabilitation; he also asked me to send him details about the birth of her cubs.

He was interested to learn that the Park Warden had recently left for South Africa, there to collect three pairs of white rhinos in the hope of getting them to settle and breed in the Reserve. Rhinos in Africa and Asia are alarmingly on the decline, mainly because in Asia it is believed that their horns contain an aphrodisiac, though in fact the horns consist of compressed hair; nevertheless the illegal trade in these prized trophies goes on and threatens the survival of the rhino. Of the two species living in Africa, only the black rhino is found in Kenya, while the surviving white rhino is now confined to South Africa. Its name is a misnomer since its coloring is exactly the same shade as that of any other rhino; "white" is a mutilation of the original description, "wide-mouthed rhino."

On the following morning I took the Grzimeks over to George, not only to celebrate his birthday but also to discuss his work with the lions. As Dr. Grzimek had instigated and financed, with German funds, most of the research on wild animal behavior done in the Serengeti National Park in Tanzania, he was very much interested, and we spent a stimulating morning together. Before he left the

Reserve I showed him parts of it which impressed him sufficiently to make him promise his help. This would relieve us of a financial responsibility, for up to now it was mostly out of Elsa's royalties that the Park had been kept up.

When I returned to camp Pippa greeted me and wanted to play, but I felt hot and dizzy and, taking my temperature, found it was up to 104°—another attack of this cursed malaria. I was unwell for some days. One night I heard the breathing and snorting of two big animals close by; I called Local, and he identified them as two rhinos. When they came uncomfortably near he fired a shot into the air to which they paid no attention, and for another hour we listened to puffings and to the breaking of branches. In the morning we found their battlefield some sixty yards from camp; here the grass was trampled flat and the earth churned up. Obviously they liked the place, since on the following night they turned up again and came so close that we could see them with our flashlights. Focusing the beam right on their eyes, and yelling and shooting above their heads, made no impression on the pair; oblivious of our demonstrations, they continued their fight—or was it love play The fact that they came twice to the same place made me inclined to think they were on their honeymoon; nevertheless, I was relieved when they left for good.

Pippa kept me company during most of these days, nibbling at my hand and skipping around the tent to entice me out for walks. She now demanded two big meals daily, but unless I was holding the bones for her to gnaw the meat off them she was a wasteful eater. Unlike lions, who hold their food in position to get the best of it, cheetahs gnaw or tear off a large chunk without using their paws.

Pippa had lately found an ideal lair in which to spend the days; it was at the junction of the now dry Mulika and the stream, close to camp. Concealed and shaded by dense bush, she was here protected on all sides except for a narrow gap leading to the water.

She was so secretive about this retreat that I wondered if she had chosen the place for her future nursery. Her wish to hide, her reluctance to move more than necessary, her fierce resentment when I touched her belly, and her increased appetite were obvious signs of her pregnancy, which I reckoned was by now one and a half months advanced. Though she kept close to camp, she concealed her whereabouts most cunningly and, taking great pains to fool us, avoided our company. For the first time I felt banned from her world, but, respecting her wish, I remained in the background. On the twenty-fifth of February, for the first time, I felt movements inside her belly.

On that day I received an invitation from Columbia Pictures to attend the World Première of our film *Born Free* in London on the fourteenth of March, and it had been arranged that I should be presented to the Queen. Ordinarily I would have been overjoyed to accept this honor, but in the circumstances I felt worried: I did not want to leave Pippa alone at the time when she would be having her cubs. Finally I decided to accept the invitation, provided everything went well with Pippa until the day of my departure. The next step was to ask George's assistant to move into my camp as soon as possible so that he could look after Pippa during my absence. Though she knew him well and had always liked him, in her present state she might take exception to an outsider and I wished to give her time to get used to him. The day he joined us coincided with the first downpour of the rainy season. Pippa was away and when she turned up the next morning seemed not to mind an additional tent and gave the assistant a friendly sniff. During the following days she appeared so much at ease with him that I thought it safe to leave her in his care and fly to London. We arranged that he should keep me informed and send me a cable when the cubs were born, as well as writing a detailed account of all that happened.

In London I was plunged into a turmoil of activities, including preparations for a trip to the United States, where I was asked to help with the promotion of the film premières which were to start a few days after the London opening. When the evening of the Royal Command Performance came, all who had been involved in the making of it were extremely anxious. The film was an enormous success, but for me it was even more than a success: it was a triumphant tribute to Elsa.

Little did I then know that, perhaps at the very moment in which the Scots Guards heralded the Queen's arrival with all the traditional splendor and I was being presented to Her Majesty, alone, deep in Kenya's bush, Pippa was giving birth to three free-born cheetahs. This was the culmination of all that *Born Free* meant to me.

I had had no news except a cable on the thirteenth of March: "No birth, Pippa well." Meanwhile, the assistant wrote in his diary that Pippa had come daily for brief visits up till this date. On the thirteenth she arrived at dawn, had an enormous meal of zebra (her favorite meat), and, in spite of her highly advanced pregnancy, was very playful. After staying for two hours she crossed the stream and made for an anthill where she often rested. In the early afternoon she returned and ate again but refused to be handled. By then it was evident that her hour was near; she had difficulty in walking, her vagina was enlarged, and he saw movements in that part of her belly and concluded that she would give birth that evening or the following morning. Pippa left again about 7 P.M., crossing the stream when it was too dark to follow her. She then stayed away for six days. In spite of prolonged searches he had no clue as to her whereabouts, though on the nineteenth he saw her mate near the stream. On the afternoon of the twentieth Pippa turned up; her figure was normal, but she was thin and hungry. After eating the best part of a goat, she played affectionately with the assistant, and he noticed that twelve of her nipples had been suckled while the thirteenth was dry. She stayed in camp for half an hour, then walked across the road into thick bush where I had often seen her go before I left for London. The assistant and Local tried to follow her but she resented this. She sat and would not move until both had turned back. An instant later she was gone. All the next day she kept away, but they saw her mate walking in the direction where the assistant believed that Pippa had her cubs. The following afternoon she returned, coming from the same spot where she had last disappeared, ate a large meal, and, after making sure no one was following her, went off again toward the bush.

On the twenty-second of March I received a cable informing me that Pippa had given birth to cubs, probably three. I had arranged to fly that afternoon to Austria, but I canceled the trip and managed to get an evening plane to Nairobi. Next morning, on my arrival, I chartered a small plane and, after dropping a note to George as we flew over his camp, was at my camp by lunchtime. The Nairobi airfield had been fairly wet, but here the rains must have been very heavy indeed and I found the men working hard to repair the soggy camp. I did not expect to see the cubs during the three days I was to stay, before flying to the United States, but I hoped to see Pippa. All the first afternoon went by without her turning up. My disappointment was lessened by George's arrival, and I spent the time giving him all the London news. This cheered him up in his distress about poor Ugas, whose eye had suddenly become alarmingly bloodshot and swollen. We passed the evening discussing the details of the recent happenings, but although the assistant kept assuring me that all was well with Pippa, I had a sleepless night, listening anxiously for any sound of her. When at last she appeared at dawn she ignored me and went straight to some buffalo meat. While she gulped it down as fast as she could, I sat close to her and felt very happy at seeing her so fit and so obviously in a hurry to return to her cubs.

As soon as she had finished her meal and had had a long drink from the stream we walked to the road. Here she sat down, purring loudly, and when I stroked her she licked my arm and face while watching to see if anyone were following us. We then moved on, struggling through dense bush for half an hour, Pippa waiting three times for me while I picked thorns out of my sandals. At last we reached an open plain in the middle of which grew a thornbush: it was an *Acacia mollifera,* commonly known as "wait a bit thorn" because of its backward-curving thorns which, hooking viciously into one's clothing and flesh, cause one to halt instantly. Suddenly I heard a sound like a stick breaking; we stopped and listened: the sound was repeated. Pippa moved very quickly to the bush, then waited for me to catch up with her before she disappeared into its thick foliage. I now saw three cubs in the center of the bush, which was about eight yards in diameter. Close to the cubs the ground was clear of larger sticks, and a few depressions in the sand showed where the family had been resting. By now Pippa had crawled through the thorns and placed herself between her young and me. The little cubs squatted on shaky legs; they looked at me, snarling, spitting, and repeating the same snapping sound we had heard before.

One cub was smaller than the others, but all were very lively for ten days, and their eyes were already open. They were about twelve inches long, much larger than Taga had been at fourteen days, but she could almost walk by then whereas these cubs only just managed to keep their front legs up in an attempt to crawl. The upper half of their bodies was covered with a longish, gray fluff reaching from tail to head which left their eyes and faces sleek. The lower part of their bodies was short-haired, darker than Pippa's coat, and very densely spotted. The demarcation line between the long fur and the short was clearly defined.

Pippa's first litter at 10 days

When, after about ten minutes, the cubs settled down, Pippa put herself in a position to be suckled; the little cubs moved clumsily to her teats, the biggest pushed the others aside, but in the end all fed contentedly. At that moment an eight-inch-long millipede, as thick as my thumb, appeared and moved toward the cubs. Pippa sat up instantly, spat at the intruder, then relaxed and watched the millipede moving among the cubs; it even crept under her tail before it disappeared. I was surprised, knowing that a millipede's sting can bring out a nasty rash on human skin, but, doubtless like ants, they do not sting cheetahs. The cubs went on purring continuously during this incident; their purr was much higher-pitched than Pippa's and was most endearing. I watched the scene for an hour, during which time the cubs often stopped feeding to change position while Pippa licked their anuses and other parts of their bodies until they dozed off; I had never seen her eyes so soft. When she looked at me I felt that, although she was now the mother of wild cubs, our relationship had not altered.

I withdrew quietly, wondering whether this thornbush was the place where Pippa had given birth. I investigated the two nearest bushes without finding any signs of their having been used, but, to my horror, under one of them I saw a large gray cobra coiled up. As I had no means of killing it I could only hope that it would not harm the cheetahs. The next bushes which might have been suitable for a nursery were some three hundred yards away, perhaps too far for Pippa to carry her young. I therefore assumed that the bush where the family now was, had been their birthplace. It was strategically well chosen because, from within, Pippa could see any danger approaching from a long way off. The only disadvantage was the distance from the stream, but if she had selected the river bush for her nursery the many animals coming there to drink would certainly have endangered the cubs, and flooding during the present rains could have meant disaster. Pippa had taken me to her lair in a very roundabout way: in a straight line, it was no more than a ten-minute walk from camp.

Next day she did not turn up. I felt worried about the cobra, so in the afternoon I went with the assistant and Local along the narrow game path which led straight to the nursery. We had walked in silence about half the distance when Pippa suddenly appeared and, blocking our way, made it plain that she disapproved of our going farther. I asked the two men to retire and remained with her until they were out of sight. She then took me by a long detour back to camp. I wondered whether she was doing this to conceal the short cut to her lair. After eating a good meal she started back by the same long way we had come. I followed her for about four hundred yards, when suddenly she leapt off into the bush and disappeared. Taking the hint, I returned to camp. The following morning there was again no sign of Pippa and, taking into account her behavior on the previous day, I was reluctant to disturb her at her lair, but since it was my last day in camp in the afternoon I set off alone to see the family. As I approached I announced myself repeatedly in a low voice. Arriving at the thornbush, I found Pippa resting and her cubs fast asleep. She looked calmly at me as I settled down outside the bush and took many photographs. After a while the cubs woke up and, in their efforts to crawl to Pippa, toppled over and landed on the ground, mingling in a soft mass of legs, tails, and full bellies. She licked them affectionately, to which the cubs responded with high-pitched purrings. They were a little steadier on their legs today and even tried to climb between the branches of the bush.

In the hour and a half during which I watched the family, Pippa left her young twice and sat in the shade of the shrub where I had seen the cobra, leaving the cubs to my care. Needless to say, I did not go inside the bush, let alone touch the young cheetahs. When, after a short time, I strolled over to Pippa and patted her, she took my hand gently in her mouth, licked me and purred, and seemed as happy as I was. A little later she returned to her young and made ready to be suckled, but only one cub made a halfhearted attempt to do so and then soon joined the others, who went on playing and crawling over their mother until they got tired and fell asleep. Suddenly Pippa became alert. She sat up, listening for a brief moment, and then bounded off through the high grass and disappeared into the far bush. Judging by her expression, I assumed that she had sensed her mate, so, not wishing to be in the way when he arrived, I went home.

CHAPTER

10

Pippa Mates Again

THE ATMOSPHERE was oppressive, and I anxiously watched heavy clouds building up a threatening wall across the sky. I hoped the weather would not interfere with my plans. Next morning my chartered airplane was to arrive and take me to Nairobi, where I was to catch the plane for London and then fly on to the United States. But from the early evening onward such a downpour set in that by morning all my hopes of reaching Nairobi had literally fallen into the water. Prepared for a muddy drive, the assistant and I set off in my Land-Rover and, after a lot of digging out, reached the airstrip at Leopard Rock. It was a lake. All we could do was to radio-call the Nairobi airport and ask them to book me for a later plane to London. We were then told that the Nairobi airfield itself was under water and all international flights were postponed.

We set off, plowing along in the tough Land-Rover, skidding and slipping through the mud. Reaching Nairobi in the late evening, I had time for a quick clean-up before boarding the night plane to London. There I had good luck: I had forgotten that it was the day of the change to summer time—this one hour gained made it possible for me to catch the connection to Washington.

The next few weeks of constant traveling, interviews, receptions, banquets, radio and TV sessions were in extraordinary contrast to Pippa's world.

My anxiety about her and her cubs was lessened by the frequent letters I received from the assistant, who reported that all was going splendidly and that I should not cut my tour short unless he were to cable. As his news continued to be excellent, I stayed away for a month, during which time I traveled the United States from east to west and came back via Austria, Germany, and Switzerland. (All this was in connection with a promotion campaign for *Born Free.*)

On my arrival in camp on the fourth of May I was met by gloom. The cubs had not been seen for some time. Only Pippa had turned up at Leopard Rock, from where she had been driven back to camp; she had remained in its vicinity until three days ago. Since then there had been no sign of her. Instantly I went to look for her, but since she had been gone for three days there was no spoor, and my searches were fruitless.

Later I drove to George's camp, where I had a shock, for I found poor Ugas with only one eye. The treatment of his two ulcers had been successful and the eye had almost cleared when he ran into a long thorn which pierced the retina. Agonizing pain drove him almost mad until our friends the Harthoorns flew in and removed the fatally injured eye. The operation had been performed only a few days previously, the stitches still irritated Ugas, and two days earlier in his attempt to rub the itching eye against something hard he had broken out of his temporary enclosure. It was essential to get him under control before he added another injury to the wound, so after helping George to repair the compound we enticed Ugas back into it with a bait of meat.

When at sunset I returned to my camp I found a Game Scout from Kenmare there with news that Pippa had been seen near the Lodge. This was the last place I liked her to be, so I drove over at once and bought a chicken at the Lodge with which I hoped to induce her to enter the Land-Rover.

After I had called for a while she appeared. As she stood in the twilight she looked very small and lost; glancing nervously into the bush, she seemed undecided what to do next. What, I wondered, had happened to her cubs?

Eventually she purred, licked my hand, and leapt into the car, but she showed no interest in the chicken. After peering anxiously into the bush she eventually jumped out of the window and disappeared. By then it was almost dark, so I placed the chicken in the grass; observing this, Pippa reappeared and carried it away hurriedly. I could not see what was happening but hoped that she had taken it to her cubs. Expecting her to return to my camp next morning, I collected a goat from our herd at Kenmare and drove home.

Pippa came in at dawn, and before the men had had time to kill the goat she had it on the ground and dispatched it in a most efficient manner by enveloping its mouth in her jaw and suffocating it. After she had eaten almost the whole carcass I examined her teats; all were dry. Today the cubs would be seven weeks old: could they survive without milk? Pippa stayed in camp all morning, licking me and purring; usually these signs of affection would have made me very happy, but today they worried me. Why did she not go back to her cubs? Later she walked down river, and when Local and I joined her she made it very plain that she resented him. Unfortunately, he had to accompany me. Though we had hardly ever any need to fire, it was not safe to walk without a rifle, for a shot into the air might prevent disaster if we were to come upon a sleeping animal or one with young which, finding itself cornered, might charge in self-defense. So Local followed at some distance and kept on hiding in the river bush. When Pippa finally sat down I played with her until she went to the water for a drink, and then she discovered Local. Ordinarily she would have gone to him for a friendly tussle, but to-day she growled and was evidently upset at finding him close. She crossed the stream and disappeared on the far side. I was at a loss to understand her behavior. If the cubs were still around she would surely not desert them for such a long time; on the other hand, if she had lost them, why did she resent Local? I was also perturbed by the attitude of the assistant; previously we had got on very well together, but since my return I noticed a strange change in his behavior which I could not understand.

I had asked him to stay on in my camp to show me the places where Pippa had recently kept her cubs, but though we took her for long walks through areas where he believed her family might be, she always followed us home. On three occasions we found the spoor of one cub together with an adult, which raised my hopes that this might be her mate with one remaining cub, but Pippa behaved as if she had finally abandoned her family, and I had to resign myself to the sad fact that the poor cubs were lost.

During the next days Pippa followed me everywhere and was far more affectionate than she usually was. It seemed as though she were afraid of losing me, too. Just now the assistant took leave for two days; he went to Nairobi and never returned. Later he left the country. He was replaced by the young Indian, Arun Sharma. Pippa and Arun knew and liked each other, and whenever he came to my camp he made a point of making friends with her.

Again we found the spoor of a male cheetah on the Kenmare plains, and, judging by Pippa's now frequent absences, I believed this was her mate. Of course we tried to follow her movements, and though we rarely found Pippa we traced her spoor together with this male. When she returned to camp after these escapades she was not always interested in the meat I offered her but seemed to have called merely to say Hello. Was she in heat again? Certainly it would be best for her to start another litter. She lost no time and soon it became evident that she was in cub.

During one of our walks we found a puff adder killed by a ratel (honey badger). Judging by the spoor around, even this courageous, fierce animal had had a fight before killing the deadly snake. He had bitten it behind the head and, after opening the stomach, had eaten the entrails and left the rest untouched. This was one of the rare occasions I have seen of a mammal eating a reptile, and a puff adder at that. Next to the deadly mamba, I regard the puff adder as the most dangerous of the African snakes. However, I would like to add that the general fear of snakes is exaggerated, because statistics of people suffering from snake bite in East Africa prove that only 1 per cent are fatal. In the thirty years during which I have lived in Kenya, and this in spite of the fact that I spent most of my time on foot safaris, usually wearing sandals, the only casualty we have had from snake bite is one mule. I do not like snakes and give them a wide berth, or kill them if necessary, but I believe that, as a rule, we human beings give plenty of warning of our approach by our scent and our noisy movements, and that most snakes try to avoid us by moving away. Only the sluggish puff adder is too lazy to attempt to escape, and if one should have the bad luck to get close to one hidden in the grass, it will strike like lightning. Pippa was keenly aware of snakes and must often have sensed them in some curious way, for she never got into trouble, though she always kept her nose close to the ground.

About this time I was invited to a meeting in the Park between the Meru Councilors, officers of the Game Department and National Parks, the Elsa Committee, and the Park Warden to discuss the future of the Meru Game Reserve. Until now the Meru Council had tried their best to develop it, but lack of funds, and of experience, had kept the Park below the standard of others in the country, and we all hoped that this situation could be improved if the Councilors would agree to hand the Reserve over to the National Parks. The meeting was presided over by the recently appointed Director of National Parks, Perez Olindo, whom I had met a few years earlier while lecturing in the United States when he was studying at Michigan State University. Even then I was impressed by his sincerity. Perez is a Maragoli and his cheerful mind and quick thinking helped tremendously in convincing the Councilors of the advantages of the change. Though there were some tricky points to solve, the meeting ended in success. Of course it would take several months before all legal technicalities could be settled, but for the time being we were all satisfied. I, in particular, felt happy. The Elsa Wild Animal Appeal had supported this Reserve for the last three years, and we had agreed at this meeting to help for another two. Now we knew that this beautiful area would soon be able to compare with other National Parks and also, owing to its unique water supplies and ecological varieties, would develop into a major tourist attraction of Kenya.

To add to my happiness, Pippa turned up at Leopard Rock. She had been away for ten days (with the exception of her brief visit to the camp six days earlier); now, though she was hungry she looked well and had evidently been fed by her mate or was already able to kill for herself. She jumped eagerly into my car and we drove home. After having a good meal, she sniffed at all the familiar places and seemed overjoyed to be with us again, licking my hands and purring her best purr. Meanwhile, a Game Scout reported that a large, dark cheetah had just been seen near Kenmare. Pippa disappeared promptly after dark.

By now it was the first of June and I wondered when her new cubs might be due. Her frequent absences, often in the company of her mate, made calculating the gestation period difficult, but I guessed that by mid-August she might give birth again. I was therefore worried when the Park Warden told me that he needed Local for some months to do a special job and that he would be replaced by Guitu for this period. I would have preferred to have Local stay with us until Pippa's cubs had arrived and could only hope that his successor would also take to Pippa and that she would accept him as a friend.

Guitu was a good-looking Tharaka. This tribe lives on the boundary of the Reserve and is well known for poaching. Though Guitu assured me that he now ate only an occasional chicken, he had spent his life, except for the war years when he had been fighting in India, poaching. He told me about his travels and of the time when, a few years before, he had carefully watched George and me at Elsa's camp, evading us as best he could for fear that George might put him in jail for poaching. But now he said that he had been converted. He had also married and had turned into a dignified Game Scout, and now I benefited from his shady past for I found him to be almost as good a tracker as Local.

For the three days after Guitu's arrival Pippa came to camp only for short feeding visits, and she sniffed at him inquisitively. After four days she seemed to accept him and, on a walk, allowed him for the first time to touch her. She then led us toward a patch of forest near Kenmare and sat down, playing affectionately with both of us, even licking Guitu's legs. Nearby was a small, stony bank lined with large trees under one of which we had several times found the pugmarks of Pippa's mate. When we attempted to go to this tree Pippa blocked our way and remained sitting there, ignoring us. Since she had made it plain we were not wanted, we went home. For the next four days she kept away; tracing her spoor after her return, we found that she had come from the forest patch where we had left her. During the following days she ate as much as she could hold. Usually she restricted her stay in camp to her mealtime, but she spent the rest of the time in the vicinity. Occasionally she turned up for an afternoon stroll; more often we had to walk alone. She was now quite at ease with Guitu, and I knew that he was not the cause of her increasing absences from camp.

Three young pythons about eight feet long were now living down river at the limestone crossing. They were beautifully marked and lay motionless in the shallow water unless we came very close, when they shot off into the reeds. Pippa kept her distance. If we crossed the stream she jumped in long leaps from stone to stone, carefully avoiding wetting her paws. The pythons got quite used to our visits and remained at the same place until the rains flooded the stream; then they disappeared.

One afternoon a friend arrived just when we were starting off for a walk. I invited him to join us, with the result that Pippa vanished. So thereafter I made it a rule that no visitor was to come to the camp if Pippa were around—however lonely I might feel.

Some time before this I had arranged to take two friends from England around a few of the Game Parks of East Africa. I had carefully planned the dates to ensure that I would be back in good time for Pippa's second litter. My friends' arrival was now due. Young Arun was willing to look after Pippa and the camp during my absence. She always played with him whenever she came to camp, so I hoped all would go well. In case of trouble we arranged that he should contact me by radio, but as I received no SOS during my trip I stayed away for three weeks. It was the first holiday I had allowed myself for several years, though it was partly a busman's holiday because my object was to see how all the Parks had developed since I had last visited them. My friends had never been in East Africa and by their reactions I could judge the impact which these beautiful Parks and their wild animals were making on visitors. And this increasingly made me realize the problems which the constantly growing number of tourists would present.

Of course we are all very happy that more and more visitors are coming to see the animals and bringing much needed revenue to the various countries, but how is the atmosphere of Africa, which many of these people come to enjoy, to be preserved? What I am thinking of is the meaningful stillness of the bush broken by the calls and noises of wild animals. As soon as a creature has been spotted by one car, many other vehicles cluster around the animal, which by now accepts these four-wheeled monsters as a harmless part of its life. How can this steadily increasing flow of tourists be encouraged to come and at the same time be prevented from spoiling the Parks and turning them into litter-covered dust bowls? At present the situation is still under control. None of the existing lodges, which provide full catering service, has more than a hundred beds. The much cheaper bandas, to which people have to take their own food, are not very numerous, and the campsites, whose visitors have to be self-sufficient, are few.

How long, I wondered, will it be before the Parks become so overcrowded that they turn into open zoos? One way to prevent this from happening is to establish more Game Parks.

In Kenya there are at present only sufficient Parks to protect 50 per cent of the species, so for this reason alone more are urgently needed. In the circumstances I am quite determined that the Elsa Fund should be used primarily for these new Parks. Each time I return to my camp it is with an enhanced appreciation of its unspoiled surroundings. I realize how lucky I am to live (because of Pippa) in the Meru Park which, at present, is still virgin ground awaiting the development which will enable it to keep up to the standard of the other Parks.

Soon after my arrival Pippa turned up, purred loudly while I brushed her, licked my hand affectionately, and finally took the brush into her mouth and played with it. Her nipples were very large now, and so was her belly; indeed, it was so heavy that I assumed she would give birth within three weeks.

We went for a stroll, but after a time she remained behind and disappeared. Arun confirmed that this was now her custom. Though she had been in camp almost daily she had never stayed longer than she needed to eat her large ration of meat. She was certainly in excellent condition, and I was most grateful to young Arun for having looked after her so well. He then told about all that had happened. During my absence he had seen Pippa with her mate, had followed both for some distance, had watched her chasing a buffalo and, another time, a jackal. He had often found her spoor near the Mulika stream, together with that of a male; twice the pugmarks had led him to the tree where she had given birth to her first cubs, but recently he had found them close to the forest patch between the Kenmare Lodge and camp, where the spoor of her mate had also been seen.

For the next two days Pippa was absent. Her return coincided with Guitu's finding the pugmarks of her mate near Kenmare. After a good meal she walked down river toward two elephants; it looked as though she were deliberately using them to stop me from following her. When later in the afternoon I went out to find her, I saw her still in the same place. She came willingly for a walk and led me to the forest patch near Kenmare, where she soon vanished. This did not surprise me, because the ground was covered with the recent spoor of a male; I was amused to watch her sneaking through the high grass, her belly close to the ground, and sinking out of view as soon as she discovered that I could see her.

During the following weeks it became obvious that she only put up with us because we fed her, and she became more and more annoyed if I touched her. Sometimes she must have kept in hiding and watched us as we went out in search of her, then she would come quickly to camp and get her meal while we were absent. Her movements were now very heavy, and she never went far from camp, but it was only when lions were around that she stayed with us. I noticed tapeworm segments in her droppings which might, I thought, be the cause of her enormous appetite. I did not like to worm her so close to her delivery, but as it was bound to affect her condition I wrote to a Vet asking him to recommend a treatment which was safe for nursing animals. Meanwhile, I fed her with as much meat as she could hold. She was again away for two days which, according to her spoor, she spent in the plains beyond the forest patch. This had now become her favorite area and I assumed that she regarded it as a safe nursery.

On the seventeenth of August Pippa arrived in camp at 7 A.M. and after eating a large meal left for the plain across the road. A little later we saw her in the opposite direction down river on a tree trunk. By teatime she had come near camp again but remained sitting on an anthill watching our approach. As soon as we came near she ran away but, being hungry, walked parallel to us at a little distance back to camp to get her meat. She was in a most irritable mood and growled as soon as I talked to her. We therefore left her alone.

During the night an elephant came very close to my tent; I turned my flashlight on him, and silently he vanished. In the morning I found the signboard with the words "EXPERIMENTAL CAMP—NO ENTRY" broken to pieces as though to let me know who controlled entries here.

We traced Pippa's spoor, together with those of her mate, which led to the forest patch. The ground within this area was very stony and made it difficult to track spoor, and we returned defeated. When, during the next two days, we still were unable to find any trace of Pippa I became worried and drove over to George to ask for his help in tracking. He reminded me that when Pippa had her first litter she had kept away for a full eight days, whereas now she had been absent for only four days.

Then he showed me a cable from London asking both of us to go to Nairobi to meet the Chairman of the Elsa Committee and discuss an important contract. We were to telephone our decision to London by the twenty-third at the latest. Today was already the twenty-first. As my presence in Nairobi was essential, we decided that George should collect me early the next morning and with good luck we might return to camp the same day, a fourteen-hour drive there and back.

To appease my conscience, I started with Guitu at crack of dawn to search for Pippa. We had not gone far when we met a General Service Unit truck coming from Kenmare, and the driver told us that Pippa had been seen walking along the road toward my camp. Leaving Guitu to greet her, I quickly fetched the car, collected some meat, and returned just in time to see her coming into view. She looked very thin and small. I stroked her, hoping that her cubs were safe. But she made it plain that she was hungry and in no mood for petting; unfortunately, the meat was high, so she refused it. She also refused to jump into the car and be taken back to camp, where I could have given her a bowl of milk. So I drove home alone, hoping to have her meal ready by the time she and Guitu arrived on foot. But after I had left, Pippa turned to the river for a drink and then went back on her tracks toward the forest patch.

As Guitu was telling me this George arrived; we decided to put off the trip to Nairobi for a few hours and follow Pippa. George is an excellent tracker, and between him, Guitu, and myself we looked at every pebble, every freshly broken leaf or twig, scrutinized the area where we expected her to be inch by inch, and I called Pippa's name until I was hoarse; we failed to find any trace of her, and eventually we had to give up the search.

11

The Second Litter

WHEN, ON THE following afternoon, we returned from Nairobi, Guitu reported that Pippa had come to camp soon after we had left, had eaten most of a goat, and then had gone off. He had tried to follow her, but she had sat unmoving at his feet, so he had had to let her return alone to her cubs. This morning he had tracked her spoor beyond the forest patch but had not seen her; the afternoon search was fruitless.

Pippa appeared in camp at teatime on the following day. She was painfully thin, and I was surprised that in spite of my coaxing she ate very little. It was not long before she went back toward the bush. I followed with Guitu, taking my camera. As if she had expected this, Pippa guided us in a straight line over a distance of about two miles, straight to the place where we had looked for her before we went to Nairobi. Here she very cautiously approached a thornbush, listened, stopped, then walked around it, and only after looking several times in all directions did she creep inside its dense foliage.

And now I saw four cubs. They were very small; their eyes were still closed, and by the helpless manner in which they wriggled their way to Pippa's teats I judged them to be five days old. One cub was particularly tiny and shaky. It hardly moved and slept most of the time while the others suckled Pippa. I stood within nine feet of the family. Pippa looked at me very happily and contentedly. In her alarmingly thin condition, for which I partly blamed the tapeworm, I doubted if she could rear four cubs. The least I could do to help was to bring her meat and water daily and thus not only save her the long, hot walk of four miles to camp but also enable her to protect her cubs from predators by never leaving them.

I could not tear myself away from the family until the fading light forced us to go home; in camp I poured myself a drink and sat in the dark watching the stars get bigger and brighter. I could hardly believe what had happened today. I had been overwhelmed when Pippa took me to her first litter, when they were only ten days old; now her trust in showing me her new family while their eyes were still closed moved me very deeply. It also was of great significance: it is known that every animal, during the first days, weeks, or months, according to the species, displays no thought or intelligence and merely eats, digests, and sleeps. Anyone who adopts the creature during this vulnerable stage, which often terminates with the opening of the eyes, is automatically accepted and becomes the imprinting parent. This is the reason why newly born animals are so easy to tame. The fact that this aloof cheetah mother had shared her cubs with me while they were still blind made me determined to guard their wild heritage.

The love and trust shown me by Elsa and Pippa had opened a new world to me, one which is denied to most people. The more I became part of it, the more I became aware how dangerously we are separating ourselves from the wild life around us and how many people today seem to forget that we are only part of a world much bigger than the one we try to control. It is a monstrous thought that man is trying to coerce the eternal laws of nature instead of submitting to them. The human race is the most highly evolved and intellectually advanced of all the species, yet we are the only ones who ruthlessly violate the balance of nature by directing our achievements mainly to our own benefit. Although scientific research makes it plain that all life on earth depends on ecology (the interdependence of all organic matter), nevertheless we are doing our best to destroy anything which may look to us as if it competes with our own convenience. By doing this, we shall probably annihilate ourselves. What is the answer to this growing problem? We need to remember that many animal species have survived on earth for a much longer period than we will if we go on isolating ourselves from our fellow creatures. We should try to learn from the way in which wild animals cope, more successfully than we have done up to now, with problems such as territorial demarcations and birth control, to mention only two out of many. Strange as it may seem, our survival may well depend on how quickly we can readjust ourselves to the wild life around us and regain our basic values and the roots of life. Elsa and Pippa have helped to diminish our ignorance of the true character of wild animals as well as of their habits.

To make Pippa's life easier, Guitu and I started out next morning with a basket of meat, a can of water, and a bowl to drink from; I also carried a still as well as a movie camera, and field glasses. For the first mile we drove, then we walked in a straight line through the bush to where we had left Pippa yesterday. Within three hundred yards of the nursery I screened the surroundings through my binoculars for her mate, because I did not want to interfere with his visits to his family, then I called. There was no response. I went nearer and called again, but all was silent.

Leaving Guitu with the food some fifty yards behind, I walked slowly to the bush under which I now saw Pippa suckling her cubs. I was relieved that the small one was at a teat and nursing as avidly as the others. After pushing their tiny noses into Pippa's soft belly for half an hour, one after the other dropped off to sleep and their mother rolled over to the other side. I then showed her the meat and, reluctantly, after stopping twice to look at her young, she emerged from the bush. She was too thirsty to eat, but she refused to go the fifty yards to the place where I had placed the water, so I brought it to within a short distance of her bush. After she had drunk, I held the meat for her as she ate. This was to avoid leaving any scent on the ground which might attract predators. For the same reason I hung the basket on a branch; after Pippa had finished with her meal, I took great care to remove every morsel of food, and finally I carried it home in the basket. This became my rule.

I took some photographs. As soon as I came within "sight" of the blind cubs, three of them raised their heads toward me and spat; the weakling continued to sleep. It was incredible that, even at this early age, blind and hardly more than fluffy lumps of unconscious life, the cubs could already sense a danger which they could not see and of which they had no experience. Since they could already differentiate between the scent of their own kind and that of a different animal, this proved that the sense of smell develops before that of sight. The cubs spat and spat in my direction until Pippa put herself in position to be suckled again, then, purring and licking the cubs gently, she reassured them and we withdrew.

At teatime we returned with more meat—Pippa had eaten very little in the morning. Now she left the cubs and had a long drink, but she refused the meat. During the last eight days she had eaten only three quarters of a goat. After that she had merely nibbled at the remains. Was she ill? I dangled the meat enticingly in front of her, but all my tricks to encourage her to eat failed; she returned to the cubs and kept still to let them suckle her. Young though they were, they spanked each other vigorously to get the best teat. Until it got dark and we had to go home, Pippa never moved from her position. I only hoped that her mate was feeding her and that was the explanation of her poor appetite.

The following morning Guitu went ahead to search for the spoor of the cubs' father and I followed by car. This now became our routine as we did not wish to disturb the family should we see the male's pugmarks leading to them. Finding none today, we continued on foot. George had sent some zebra meat, and knowing how much Pippa relished it I hoped that she might eat well. But she hardly touched it, nor did she drink; instead, she spent the hour we remained there licking the cubs. They were crawling a little more steadily now, except for the tiny one, who did not suckle while we were watching. When in the afternoon we went back Pippa was again nursing the cubs, and only after they fell off would she come for a drink, then she drank non-stop for a long time. At last she ate a large meal, then she went for a stroll around her bush, but while she was doing so she kept a constant watch on the surroundings. I kept her company and was most touched when she repeatedly licked my arm as if to show her appreciation of my help, but she only allowed herself ten minutes for stretching her legs before returning to her family.

When, next morning, Guitu saw cheetah spoor along the road, we decided not to visit Pippa until the afternoon. On our arrival we found only the cubs; they were asleep. Pippa appeared about ten minutes later from the direction of the Rojoweru, which was the nearest source of water and was about a mile and a half away. Assuming that she had been for a drink, I was surprised when she thirstily lapped up all the water we had brought. Could it be that she had heard us coming and had turned back? The cubs seemed a little steadier, but they still could not support themselves on their four legs. Though Guitu and I only whispered, they raised their heads inquisitively. From now on, after my initial call, made from a distance to give warning of our approach, we always remained quiet during our visit to the family.

Next morning I saw cheetah spoor turning to the river in the opposite direction from that of the nursery. Guitu was supposed to have gone ahead tracking, but I did not find him at Pippa's turn-off so I traced his footprints to Kenmare Lodge, where I found him chatting with the wives of some of the Game Scouts. He was good-looking and popular with the girls, but at that moment he was less popular with me.

He and I now went on in silence to Pippa's nursery; we found her suckling her cubs. After they had had enough she had her fill of meat and water and then walked around her bush again to get some exercise. Meanwhile I watched the little ones rolling over each other and sometimes managing to stand on all four legs. As soon as their mother returned they rubbed their small noses against her and, standing on still shaky hind legs, patted and licked her face. They were nine days old.

When, at teatime, we came back, Pippa had moved the cubs some thirty yards to a shrub which provided hardly any shade, and all were panting from the heat. After taking a long drink she investigated the surroundings for a more suitable nursery, then she settled in the shade of a thorn tree. I took this as a hint and, intending to be helpful, picked up two of her cubs to carry them to her. Instantly she grabbed one by the scruff of its neck and carried it, dog-fashion, back to the shadeless bush. I had followed quickly with the other cub, which she immediately licked all over as though to cleanse it of my scent; then she placed herself in a position to be suckled. Meanwhile, I listened anxiously to the distant whuffings of two lions; their proximity made me worry for the safety of the family. After a time I offered Pippa meat. She rose to get it but then changed her mind and went back to the cubs as though to show that she was not going to leave them alone in my presence, and to make it even plainer that I had gone too far by interfering with her young, she placed herself between me and them, looked in the opposite direction, and ignored me. I left soon afterward.

That evening I was worried on account of the lions and also because I had injured Pippa's trust. I should have known better than to handle the cubs while they were still blind and defenseless. To add to my anxiety, six elephants spent the best part of the night across the stream, within only about fifty yards of me, browsing around their favorite bush. Turning my flashlight at the group caused them to stop feeding, but as soon as I went back to bed they returned. This game between us went on until dawn.

Early in the morning we found that Pippa had moved the cubs to a still more open bush where every bird of prey could spot them; she seemed unconcerned, and after drinking and eating a lot, allowed me to de-tick her.

Returning in the afternoon, we saw that she had moved the cubs for the third time, now, at last, to a more suitable bush. She was most friendly. Of course I was only too well aware that bringing her food daily was a mixed blessing, because our visits could upset her relationship with her mate as well as make her more dependent on my help than might be good for her family; still, at the moment it seemed to me to be the right course.

On returning to camp, I found the Park Warden together with the Vet (Dr. John King) and discussed this problem with them. Dr. King came often to the Park to check up on the acclimatization of the six white rhinos and was known for his remarkable knowledge of wild animals. He strongly advised me to continue feeding Pippa and to wait until the cubs were weaned before giving her the treatment against tapeworm. How long the weaning process would take, neither of us knew.

Our visit next morning turned out to be an important one: the cubs had opened their eyes. They were now eleven days old, and though their vision was still blurred by a bluish film, they looked straight at me with an earnest, inquisitive expression. It was extraordinary how suddenly their innocent, baby faces had changed, for now they resembled those of little old men. This was emphasized by the tear mark leading from the inner side of the eye to the corner of the mouth which, since the large, dark eyes were fully opened, looked like the deeply lined, wrinkled face of an old person. Their ears were still at the level of their eyes and pressed to the head, which made them seem even more like human beings, and enhanced their charm. They appeared quite bewildered by all the things they had now discovered. Already their movements had become more purposeful, and when they spanked each other they aimed as best they could to get their soft blows home. They were so active that Pippa had difficulty in licking their anuses. It became obvious to me that it was to keep these nurseries clean that she moved the cubs to different bushes. She had started the moves when they were nine days old and strong enough to stand the change.

Perhaps the exertion of discovering a visual world tired the cubs, for when we visited them the next day they were shaky and very sleepy. Pippa sat put with them during the two hours we remained there except once to go off for a quick drink, but I had to take the meat close to her cubs before she would eat a little. Recently she had put on some weight and her condition had improved so much that I thought it better from now on only to visit her in the mornings and thus give her mate more chance to see his family.

When we arrived twenty-four hours later I was horrified to find the little ones at the edge of the bush, exposed to any predators. There was no sign of Pippa. I used this opportunity to put my finger into the cubs' mouths to feel for teeth, but their gums were still smooth. Because of their fluffy underparts I was unable to distinguish their sex.

After some twenty minutes, Pippa turned up, her face and neck covered with blood. By the way she behaved I knew she had not been injured but was coming from a kill. She had a long drink, then guided us about three hundred yards to a small tree covered with vultures. She dashed among the scavengers that were on the ground, causing them to settle on the surrounding trees, thereby exposing the carcass of a duiker, which she had opened between its hind legs. Now she tore at its viscera, often looking at me as if to tell me how proud she was of her kill. When she could eat no more she rested, panting, looking up at the vultures which were circling in hundreds above us, waiting for their share. Being far too mean to waste Pippa's kill on them, I collected every scrap of the remains. She watched me calmly and did not interfere when Guitu carried all the pieces back to the basket; but when the first vultures flopped heavily to the ground she chased them off. As they were persistent and were still arriving in great numbers from every direction, I thought they must have informed every predator in the vicinity of Pippa's kill. So I asked Guitu to watch out for danger to the nursery while I took all that was left of the meat back to camp, hoping that this would cause the vultures to go off. When later I returned, I found Guitu

Her second litter at 12 days

perched high up in a tree, scanning the surroundings through my field glasses. He had spotted no predator but had seen Pippa move her young to yet another bush.

I sat down and watched the cubs. One was very inquisitive and stalked everything, including myself. My hand was on the ground; the cub sniffed at it cautiously, then placed its head in my palm and licked my fingers with its soft tongue while looking at me with large eyes. I did not dare stroke the cub for fear of taming it. Pippa watched us, purred, and also licked me.

During these days I saw large swarms of queleas. They are the smallest of the weaver birds but live in the largest of all bird colonies. Like locusts, they are most destructive to vegetation. I filmed some of their cloudlike swarms; one swarm took three minutes to fly past my camera before settling on a tree, which they soon left, stripped to the bare wood. Luckily, queleas did not invade the immediate neighborhood of the cheetah family, and Pippa was still able to find shady bushes to which she could move her cubs, which she did nearly every day. On two occasions I was able to film the transfer but had to be very quick as Pippa moved fast. She always carried a cub by its neck, dropping it at times to get a better grip, and in this fashion she covered distances of up to two hundred yards. To get stills, as well as moving pictures, given her pace, meant that I had to race ahead of her and even so hardly had time enough to set the camera. Before the cubs were three weeks old she had made nine moves; after that they could walk steadily. By the time they were six weeks old the family had had twenty-one nurseries.

The cubs grew rapidly and, probably because of this, slept most of the time. They were in wonderful condition, but Pippa needed feeding up as the nursing of four youngsters took a lot out of her. At the age of three weeks I first heard the cubs make a high-pitched chirp which I would have taken for the sound of a bird had I not seen them at it. They were calling Pippa, who appeared after ten minutes; the cubs then tumbled all over her and stood on their hind legs, embracing and licking her head. One was especially affectionate and finally cuddled cozily beneath her chin, engulfed between her chest and front legs. It defended its position in a comic way by spitting at the other cubs whenever they came close. The following morning we saw Pippa's mate walking toward the nursery,

Pippa carrying 17-day-old cub

Cubs at 18 days

Pippa and cubs, 17 days

Cubs at 29 days

and during the next four days we found his spoor along the road. Pippa was sometimes absent when we arrived. On two occasions she listened alertly while she was having her meal and then walked off into the plain, perhaps to join him. But I did not think he fed her, because she was always so hungry.

By then the family had moved some six hundred yards to a very thorny bush where the cubs would, I thought, be quite safe during her absences. They now played freely in Pippa's presence, but whenever we found them alone they sat rigidly put. To interfere as little as possible with the movements of the male, we made our visits during the luncheon hour because it was unlikely that any cheetah would be around during the hottest time of the day.

When the cubs were four weeks old I noticed the white tips of their canines breaking through. Two days later the teeth had grown so sharp that nursing must have become rather painful for poor Pippa.

By now the cubs had strong shoulders and long legs, and their movements were very graceful. They ventured some distance on their own, skipping between tufts of grass playing hide-and-seek, wrestling, and striking out with their front legs at each other. Finally they would race back, jump right into Pippa's face, tease her, and escape her cloutings by struggling up into the branches of their nursery bush. It was only now that I was able to determine their sex: only one cub was a male. Oddly enough, he was the smallest but he was the most affectionate and he always cuddled up to Pippa.

I was surprised when once she objected to my holding the meat for her and gave me a sharp nip, but I understood the reason when later I saw her mate perched on the top of a white anthill close to Kenmare. This limestone termite hill was a favorite salt lick and was visited by many animals. Next day we found the male's spoor nearby and there was no sign of Pippa. While waiting for her the cubs kept absolutely still and were so perfectly camouflaged by their gray-colored fluff that it was difficult to see them unless one knew they were there. At sunset I became worried for I did not like leaving the cubs alone in the dusk, the time when predators begin to hunt. I asked Guitu to remain with them while I went back to camp to see if Pippa might be there. I returned without her but with two flashlights, and we waited. Long after dark she appeared from the direction of the river; she was not thirsty but was very hungry. I did not want to

Pippa suckling cubs, 28 days

Cubs playing with Pippa

leave the meat behind, so we stayed with her until she had eaten. By then it was pitch-dark, and I felt far from easy as I walked for a mile through thick bush to reach the car. In particular I was afraid of elephants, because they move so quietly; but I had more reason to be wary of two lions whom we met along the road a few minutes after we had reached the car.

I worried all night about the safety of the cheetah family and early next morning set off to see them, but I found no trace of them. For three hours we tramped about, then it became too hot. On our way home we passed a small plain close to camp, and there we saw Pippa watching a Grant's gazelle. I drove up to her and offered her meat, but she had a full belly, did not look at our food, and, instead, nibbled playfully at my hand; as I was anxious to find the cubs, we followed Pippa. She walked very slowly toward her nursery, resting under almost every tree, obviously wishing us to leave her alone. When she realized that she could not get rid of us in that way she moved on and, trying to fool us, sniffed around each bush and pretended to look for the cubs, knowing, of course, that they were far away. By now it was very hot and we were thirsty and exhausted, but I was persistent, and so we dragged along until we had circled back to the thorny bush where we had left the family last night and where we had searched this morning. Here I almost stepped on the cubs; they matched the grass so perfectly that it was impossible to see them until they got up and ran to Pippa.

I had taken a small piece of meat with me, because I wished to see if they might like it, since they had recently shown interest by sniffing at Pippa's meat. The cubs spat at me, however, wrinkled their noses in disgust, and bolted. I left the meat and went off a short distance to give them time to investigate. When after some ten minutes I came back I found the meat untouched and the family gone. Again we searched for a long time without finding even a spoor. It seemed unbelievable that five animals could just vanish; certainly Pippa had won the round. In the afternoon we again searched thoroughly and finally found the family under a small bush. Though the cubs spat at first, they soon settled down but still made faces at the meat and obviously disliked it.

The following day we found them all together in the open sunning themselves. After a while Pippa came for a drink, then she quickly rushed after the cubs, who seemed to have disappeared. Within seconds we saw them racing through the grass, jumping over each other and swiping with their legs until they landed on the ground in a tussling ball, soon to leap off for another chase. Pippa had a hard time controlling them. She called in a sharp prr-prr quite different from her usual purr, which sounded like a broken rattle. The cubs did not always obey her, so she had to use another stratagem as well: dashing around them in a circle, thus provoking a chase and then gradually leading them to where she wanted them to be. When all of them were tired I gave the meat to Pippa. While she ate the cubs sniffed around and then, after a few cautious licks, tucked in, tearing off the flesh and spanking each other as they fought for a piece. Since they had disliked meat yesterday, I was surprised to see how greedily they now gulped it down. Eventually Pippa chased them off; perhaps she did this to prevent the cubs from eating too much at their first solid meal. They were five weeks old.

By now we needed to carry a large load, so I began to take Stanley, the labor boy, with us. Besides carrying the meat, he guarded the load, which made it easier for Guitu and myself to search for the cheetahs. Although Stanley was exceptionally thin, he was tough and a hard worker and often carried unbelievably heavy loads of firewood. He was also excellent at spotting animals and was completely fearless. All the same, I always took great care to leave him near a tree up which he could shin in case of trouble. The first time he came with us I left both men two hundred yards from the family before I went to see them, as I did not want Stanley to cause alarm. But the cheetahs had already seen us. They were very suspicious and bolted even from me. So I dropped the meat, and it was only after I had moved away that Pippa returned and carried it to her cubs, who were in hiding. Through my field glasses I watched them at their meal and, when they were satisfied, again approached them. This time I was tolerated, except by the little male, who spat and spat, defending his pride. I loved him for this and named him Dume, which means "male" in Swahili. I had not yet thought of names for the other cubs, except for one who was very light in color, whom we called Whity. The two other females were still undistinguishable. The cubs avoided coming close to us and Pippa was on the defensive, so we left early.

When, next morning, we found the pugmarks of Pippa's mate coming from the nursery, I wondered if Pippa's defensive attitude during

The cubs' first meal at 5 weeks

The cubs play with a bowl of water

our last visit had been due to his being near or whether Stanley were the cause. Leaving him still farther away this time, Guitu and I searched until dusk but did not find the family. This was the first time since the birth of the cubs that I had failed to see them for a whole day. I was worried, and so when George and the Park Warden called I asked their advice. The cheetahs had remained, since the birth of the cubs, about two miles from camp and were living as wild chee-tahs except for the fact that I fed them. Since the cubs were now eating meat and, besides suckling Pippa, would need water, unless I could get them to drink from a bowl they would have to walk a long way to the river, where they were bound to meet predators. Although they were lively enough, they were growing so fast that they never had an ounce of fat on them and each week needed more and more food. Feeding the family was interfering with their wild life, but by feeding them I would ensure the cubs' keeping in good condition until they were strong enough to look after them-selves. What should I do? George suggested that I keep the cubs at my camp over this period; the Warden and I thought it better to risk the danger of predators and let the cubs develop as wild ani-mals but with all the help I could give them in the bush on the feed-ing side.

Next day we took the carcass of a goat and gave it to the cubs; this was the first time they could get roughage as from a natural kill. They pounced on the carcass and, after Pippa had opened it, ate the liver, heart, and kidneys greedily, then nibbled at the cartilages of the ribs while Pippa crunched the rib bones and vertebrae. All ate a good portion of the skin by gnawing it sideways off the body. Mean-while I buried the water bowl at ground level to prevent it from tip-ping over and watched for the cubs' reaction. First they spat at it suspiciously, then they put a paw into the water and leapt away terrified by the ripples. Then Pippa came along and gave them a demonstration of how to drink; realizing now that this strange, mov-ing thing was not only harmless but good, they at last lapped and lapped and could not drink enough. Finally all four had their heads and feet in the water, fighting and splashing until they were drenched.

Pippa now moved her family every day farther from camp, and it became an arduous task to carry our heavy loads to her. If we had starved Pippa no doubt she would have come nearer to camp, but I did not want the family to live near to people and perhaps become tame.

I often admired the willingness with which Stanley carried the main bulk of our loads and yet grew more and more attached to the family. Certainly the cubs were very appealing. Except for their large eyes and enormous feet, they were already well-proportioned. They always looked elegant as they raced at top speed across the plain or climbed trees by hooking their claws into the rough bark, or played with elephant droppings. Pippa was an excellent mother and only showed occasional selfishness over food. I couldn't understand how she kept the cubs sitting put until she had had her fill. They were very obedient, and however hungry or thirsty they might be as they craned their necks watching her eat and however tantalizingly close I placed the food to them, they never dared to budge until Pippa permitted them to do so with a prr-prr.

It was in early October that I heard Pippa make a new sound. She was alone, and I gave her food and then went to look for the cubs. After she had eaten she called prr-prr and walked around sniffing for their scent. Obviously she had no idea of their whereabouts and was worried. Finally she repeatedly called a very soft ihn-ihn-ihn, so low that it was hardly audible. To this the cubs responded and emerged from a place which I had passed four times while looking for them. They rushed to the water bowl, fell into it, ate ravenously, and then played happily around, passing close to me and even nibbling at my legs. Their behavior seemed to depend on how Pippa was feeling. If she was relaxed they treated me as a pal, otherwise I got a spit.

The cubs had various sounds to express their moods. When they were happy they purred, when answering Pippa they gave a high-pitched chirp, but when frightened their voices became very shrill until they each sounded like the notes of a birdlike whistle. If they were fighting for food, they gave a long, gurgling squeal or, flattening their ears, snuffled threateningly.

We never managed to find the cubs without Pippa's help, and she did not always co-operate. One day we searched for fully two hours before we found the family sleeping under a bush. We had been close to it several times, and she must have heard me calling her but had not come forward. On another occasion she came to meet us from a distance and was very thirsty, but after she had drunk she sat firmly and would not guide us to the cubs. Next time this happened we did not give her any food and walked in the direction she had come from. Sniffing at the meat basket, she followed us from bush to bush, pretending to look for the cubs, but it was only when she realized that we were not going to feed her until we saw them that she led us to her young.

On the sixth of October we did not see the cheetahs. I was worried because next day I had to fly to Nairobi for a meeting. Guitu promised to do his best to find and feed them, and I left. When I returned he was absent. Stanley told me that as he had not found the family in the morning, at teatime Guitu had gone out again to search. When it got dark I went to look for him, but, being alone and without a rifle, I could not go far. I then drove to Kenmare in the hope of finding him there: no one had seen him. It was too dark at this hour to organize a search, so I returned home and spent a sleepless night fearing that he might have had an accident.

In the early morning I again drove to Kenmare to organize a search party. But only one Game Scout was there, the rest having gone the day before to Meru to shop. The Scout told me not to worry about Guitu as he knew the bush better than anyone else and, having a rifle, would be safe. Nevertheless, I insisted that the Scout should come with Stanley and me to help look for him. We found no trace of Guitu. I then drove to Leopard Rock headquarters to report his disappearance and ask for help. There I was told that he had joined the shopping party which had been expected back last evening but had not yet turned up.

When we reached camp we were greeted by Guitu with a blood-stained bandage round his head. His story was that he had run a thorn into his forehead while he was looking for the cheetahs and, since he could not remove it, went with the General Service Unit truck to see the doctor. He even produced a medical certificate, a piece of torn cardboard without an official stamp. By the style and spelling, I knew it was a fake, so I asked Guitu to remove the bandage. He winced and simulated pain, although I could find no trace of any injury. But as accusing him of being a liar was not going to help Pippa, we went next day as usual to search for her.

All we found was her spoor leading to the river, but no pugmarks of the cubs. Where did they get water?

It was now four days since I had given them food, and I was very worried. The following morning we hunted again without result, and it was only on the sixth day that we found the spoor of two cheetahs leading toward camp. Our arrival there coincided with that of Pippa, who, desperately hungry, gorged herself with zebra meat and then led us in a straight line for some three miles to a large tree under which the cubs now rose like jack-in-the-boxes. I was happy to find them fit and to see that they had grown a lot in the last few days. They were seven and a half weeks old and their ruffs now covered only their shoulders. Judging by their black droppings, which obviously contained digested blood, Pippa must have killed. Or had the father, perhaps, at last fed his family?

Whity was the most timid of the cubs, and she was always the last to arrive at the meat over which the other cubs were already fighting. Young as they were, they defended their food even from Pippa and hung on to it if she tried to drag it away.

I usually kept some distance away from them while they ate, and then came nearer only gradually. When they became drowsy they did not mind my sitting among them and even allowed me to pick a tick or two off them, providing Pippa were close.

For the next six days the family remained near this large tree, which was easy to find and so popular with them that the boys called it the Hoteli. Little Dume was the guardian of the pride and the most lively of the cubs. When the others were tired out from playing he would still race around, pulling his sisters' tails or leaping high into the air just for the fun of it. He was always on the alert to prevent me from stroking his mother, and if I did so he pounced at me, striking quickly and repeatedly with both his front legs simultaneously: a most effective defense, in view of his sharp claws. Gradually he turned this into a game in which he struck with one leg, not using his claws, and spanked my hand until finally he kept his paw inside my palm and allowed me to stroke it. Whity was the most curious of the quartet. She was always patroling around, showing great pluck and investigating everything. She snarled at me but also came close, waiting to be touched as though to find out what I did to Pippa. She ate the least but was nevertheless very fit. Recently Pippa's teats had been reduced to almost normal

Cubs at the Hoteli tree at 7½ and 8 weeks

size and seemed to be drying up. Although the cubs were now eight weeks old, and rather large for suckling, they still fought for the best teat and they must often have hurt their mother.

One morning we found the spoor of the male leading toward Pippa. On our arrival next day we noticed a lot of vultures dispersing about half a mile from the Hoteli tree. After having fed the family we investigated the spot and found the almost complete skeleton of a Grant's gazelle. That it had been killed by a cheetah was evident from the surrounding spoor; had lions been responsible, there would have been no bones left. I had no doubt that this cheetah was the cubs' father, but judging by the family's appetite, he had not invited them to share the buck.

CHAPTER

12

Bush Fire

THE COUNTRY was now very dry and the grass had become mere straw. It is customary to burn it systematically before the rains begin and thus not only kill all parasites but encourage new grazing; if this were not done the animals might move away because the vegetation would have become too woody. Most of the Meru Park had already been burned except for the plains close to my camp and the area where Pippa was living. As time was short and the Park Warden was away, I saw no harm in helping to burn the plain across the stream, taking on from where a previous fire had stopped about a mile upstream. First we cut firebreaks twelve feet wide on three sides around the camp; we expected the stream to act as a protection on the fourth side. Then, after carefully observing the wind, we set the plain alight. Soon the flames began crackling, and I took pictures of the racing fire across the stream with the camp in the foreground. When it had passed and left the grass a smoldering ash we had lunch.

It was Sunday; Guitu and Stanley went to the Rojoweru to fish, and I wrote letters. Suddenly the cook yelled that the fire was coming near to my Land-Rover, which was parked under a tree about a hundred yards away. The wind had changed and blown a few sparks across the stream which had ignited the grass. Running as fast as I could, I drove the car onto the road in the nick of time. Meanwhile the flames jumped the firebreaks and blazed with terrifying speed toward the camp. Frantically we carried buckets of water to put them out, and we also cut branches with which to beat down the fire.

Nearly suffocated by smoke, working to the point of sheer exhaustion, we managed to save the tents but lost a partly dismantled jeep which George had left with us. Unable to remove it, we had to watch it burn and were extremely lucky that the petrol tank was empty. By then the two fishermen had returned, and for the next five hours we worked, gasping for air in the stifling smoke, burning our skin and singeing our hair. Footsore, and with blistered hands, we got the fire under control by sunset, but long after dark we went on drenching the simmering logs and smoldering elephant dung.

When I dropped down, utterly spent, the sky was deep red and the air thick with smoke. I saw many birds escaping from the fire, which had now spread across the road and onto the plains beyond. All I could do was to pray that it would not move in the direction of Pippa's family. Already marabou storks were picking sizzling insects out of the smoldering ash, and it made me feel wretched to think of all the tortoises and snails which could not, like smaller rodents and lizards and snakes, dash underground for safety. Suddenly I heard the piercing trumpeting of elephants which appeared out of the burning bush and ran, in single file, toward the stream. They were silhouetted against the fire and screaming loudly. I prayed again for all the animals—that they might escape from this furnace. Tired though I was, I spent all that night watching the smoldering trees which we had not been able to extinguish and listening for the slightest suspicious crackling.

At first light we went to Pippa. Thank God, the plains in her direction were unburned. For two and a half hours we could not find the family, then Guitu announced that his heart was telling him they were in a certain direction! He led us confidently and we did indeed find the cheetahs where he said they would be, some five hundred yards nearer camp than when we had last seen them. The cubs were very shy, and I wondered if this were due to the presence of two elephants who remained close all the time we were there.

On our return, we found the Park Warden in camp. He told me that George had been injured by a buffalo. Taking medicines, we drove off and found poor George sitting on his bed, moaning and covered with blood. He could not lie down because of the pain in his ribs. After I had washed him and forced him to eat some food, he told us that he had been after a buffalo which had given trouble and which he wanted to shoot for the lions. He had hit the animal twice but lost him when he disappeared into the thicket. He was searching for the wounded beast when it suddenly came out of the bush, charged him from two yards, and knocked him down. Luckily, while trying to get at him with his horns, the buffalo fell dead. It was a very narrow escape, since wounded buffaloes are notoriously dangerous, and George was fortunate to get away with a few scratches on his head, some fractured ribs, and a minor fracture of one foot. I spent the night with him, then a Flying-Doctor plane took him to Nairobi. I did not fly with him since I could be of more help by looking after his lions during his absence, and we could keep in touch by radio. After a few days George returned; he was most anxious to know about Girl, who in his absence had produced two cubs, fathered by Boy.

Not long afterward, still walking with a stick, George chose a time when Girl was in camp to take me to her lair high up on Mugwongo Hill. From here we had a magnificent view across the vast plains stretching to the far Jombeni range while all around us were big boulders broken from a cliff at the base of which Girl had found an ideal nursery: it was under an overhanging rock which tapered to such a narrow cleft that her cubs were safe from any predator. George imitated Girl's mhm-mhm, and soon one of the little ones crawled to the opening and looked fearlessly at us with large, bluish eyes. It was twelve days old. Only once—in the case of Elsa— had I ever even seen so young a lion cub, and I was amused by his long nose. George called him Sam. Meanwhile, the other cub also appeared and pushed his brother more into the open. Sam stretched himself in the sun and, without any sign of nervousness, had another look at us. Obviously he found it odd to find us there instead of Mom after hearing the familiar mhm-mhm. It takes about six weeks before the vision of a lion clears, and so I was surprised at the great interest this tiny cub already took in his surroundings; he watched us and also a lizard and a beetle which crawled across his paws.

By the time he was four weeks old Sam was in command of all of George's seven lions. He loved playing with them as long as they were gentle, but should one dare to be rough with him he miaowed in protest and, clouting back, put the big lions in their place. Knowing he was the pet, he did exactly what he liked and feared no one. The placid self-assurance of this "infant king of all the animals," compared to the high-strung alertness of the cheetah cubs, was fascinating to observe.

Meanwhile, Pippa had moved her family steadily nearer to my camp. But our searches were now greatly handicapped by the rains, which washed all spoor away. Once for a week we could not find the family, then Pippa turned up at teatime, thin and hungry. How starved she was I could judge by the way in which she wolfed down some high meat which a cheetah would not ordinarily touch —they are not carrion eaters. After this she led us across the road for about a mile into the forest to a patch of big acacia trees. Their trunks were smoothly polished from the continued rubbing of elephants, and the ground around was carpeted with elephant droppings. On our way we passed within thirty yards of one of these giants, and I needed to behave as though I were much braver than I felt if I were not to lose Pippa, who walked along very fast ignoring this elephant. Finally she rushed away, stopped, listened, and then prr-prr, and I saw the cubs under a tree. They too were thin and rather shaky on their hind legs, and I was very sorry that I had only some high meat to give them. As soon as they had eaten, little Dume bit playfully at my fingers and then began his swiping game while his sisters reserved their affection for their mother.

She had moved the cubs at least two miles from the Hoteli tree to this elephant paradise. The area had not been burned and, being mostly black cotton soil, was covered with luscious grass in places, and in others was very muddy after the past few rainy days. For this reason most of the elephants were moving out to more sandy ground, but buffaloes seem to know how to avoid getting stuck, and, judging by their spoor, they loved the place. So did Pippa and she made her home here for the next month.

It did not take us long to get the family in good shape again. There were many broken trees around which the cubs loved to climb. They also enjoyed balancing on fallen logs. When they got into trouble, Pippa often demonstrated how to turn a precarious angle. They were more friendly now, and though they kept constantly on the alert for danger, they no longer minded Guitu and Stanley coming near.

One of the female cubs was particularly affectionate. She was the thinnest of the four and was often covered with many ticks and camel

Cubs learning to climb, 10 weeks; now more confident, 16 weeks

flies (hippoboscids), which she allowed me to pluck off. (I don't know whether these brownish flies derive their name from living mainly on the blood of camels or because they are as tough as these animals, but the fact is that they are impossible to kill by squashing, and even if I pulled them in half both sections moved back to their meal unless I tore their legs off.) Since Whity was the first of the three sisters to get a name, I called the thin cub Mbili, the Swahili for "two," and the third female I called Tatu, which means "three." Tatu always kept her distance and was extremely shy but very strong and self-willed, and she tucked in very well at meals. All the cubs had distinct characters. At this stage I found Mbili and Tatu easier to recognize by their characters than by their physical appearances. Whity had lately developed into a very handsome animal with most expressive eyes, sensitive features, and beautiful coloring. She was Guitu's favorite, while I liked Dume best.

One day our "hearts," to use Guitu's expression, co-operated extraordinarily well. We had looked all morning for the family without result when Guitu's heart told him that they had moved back toward the Hoteli tree. We searched in that direction but could not find a trace and, hot and exhausted, went home for lunch. I was very tired from the long walk and looked forward to a rest, but suddenly I had a strong feeling that Pippa was at the elephant forest, and I insisted on returning there. As soon as we arrived I called and Pippa appeared and led us halfway to the Hoteli tree where, prr-prr, the cubs showed up. How did Guitu's heart know that the family had moved there? How did I know that Pippa later had returned to the elephant forest, and how did she sense that we would look for her there again so that she could lead us halfway to the Hoteli tree and to her hungry cubs? Though our hearts had sent all three of us in different directions, they had co-ordinated to give a positive result.

I was interested to observe that while Elsa had always brought her cubs to our camp for meals, Pippa left her young in the bush and came along to guide us to her family when feeding help was needed. The last time I had seen the cubs suckling was when they were eight weeks old. Now, at ten weeks, the hair round Pippa's teats was again sticky and I wondered if they could still get milk from her dry teats or if they suckled merely for comfort.

That night it rained very heavily, the flooded stream rose fifteen feet, and the water was almost level with the studio. At dawn I listened to the glorious chorus of the awakening birds and the low calls of two lions mingling with it. Soon I watched them passing our camp; they moved slowly downstream and looked at us as though we were a natural feature of their lives.

On our way to Pippa we found the spoor of leopards, jackals, and hyenas and saw two reticulated giraffes entwining their necks in love play; their netlike markings made a complicated pattern as they twisted and turned before disappearing with their undulating gait. How enchanting these animals were! Thinking of the many people who have to live a city life, little as they may like it, I realized how lucky I was to be camping among these wild animals and to have Pippa's trust even if it did involve a life which had its bouts of loneliness.

After a four-hour search we detected Pippa high up in a tree in the elephant forest. The family looked very bedraggled and ate ravenously. This was the last meal I was able to give them for three days; during that time we plodded along through knee-high grass with heavy clods of mud on our shoes, and once we ran into a herd of some four hundred buffaloes which had churned the ground into such a morass that walking became still more difficult. Another time we watched a giraffe baby-sitting for four youngsters of different ages. These big creatures seemed to be the only animals that were still living in this high vegetation, which we could almost see growing. I was worried because I could not imagine how Pippa and the cubs would cope with the rising jungle, particularly as it rained every night. When at last we found them they were all surprisingly fit and very lively; nevertheless, they ate up a goat in no time. Indeed, the cubs were so absorbed in eating that they did not at first notice my taking ticks off them, but when they realized what I was doing they jumped away. Perhaps to show his disapproval of my interfering with their meal, little Dume stalked me from behind and bit me in the back.

Next morning I had still more reason to be proud of Pippa, for not only had she taken good care of her cubs during the rains but we found the family on a kill of a waterbuck fawn. All ribs, and the front and hind legs, were already eaten, as well as the stomach. This surprised me, but as the fawn had obviously still been suckling, the cheetahs probably liked the milk-containing stomach. Pippa had no scratch though, judging by the surrounding spoor, she had a tough fight with the fawn's mother.

During the following days we discovered that Guitu's "heart predictions" were not coincidences, for whenever he had an intuition we found the cheetahs where he said they were, whereas when he had no inspiration we drew a blank. On many occasions Pippa was waiting for us perched high up in a tree and we were able to see her from a long distance, which shortened our search. The cubs were now twelve weeks old, and the dark pigment of their eyes had cleared to three distinct shades going from dark brown to light amber. They had discovered a wonderful playground between a colony of termite hills and chased each other around the conical towers. They played hide-and-seek, peeped around the air funnels to ambush each other, scrambled up the pinnacles to plunge from their tops onto the back of a victim, and finally hopped away and onto Pippa, who also skipped and jumped around as though she were a cub. There were several small trees near the anthills, and once Whity got stuck between two forked branches. Struggling to free herself made her predicament still worse, so, fearing that she might injure herself, I pulled her out. Screaming blue murder at being handled by me, biting and wriggling, she slipped out of my hands and bolted; but, at least, she was unhurt. The family was so happy in this place that they stayed there for five days; by then the red earth of the ant-hills was smoothly polished from their games.

By now the grass was waist-high and a real trap for the cheetahs. Only browsers like elephants, giraffes, and gerenuks could cope with this profusion, and even they avoided the steadily widening swamps. We saw no smaller animals which Pippa might have hunted although we searched for days, not only in the elephant forest but also on the plains beyond. These had been burned and, with their new grass, they looked like a Garden of Eden. They were dotted with antelopes of all kinds grazing among blue pentanesias, white heliotropes, and bright red Gloriosa lilies. But where was Pippa? It rained and rained, and we heard reports of bridges' being washed away and of people being drowned. As for ourselves, we often got bogged down but plowed along five to six hours daily without finding a sign of the family. Could the cheetahs survive? So long as Pippa was all right I hoped that she would somehow manage to feed the cubs, for I had recently seen her catch a francolin at its take-off by jumping after it into the air and hooking it down. All the same, I had visions of her getting hurt while she was hunting, and if that happened the cubs must die.

One day we slithered along a muddy road in the car with the meat we had brought in case we found the cheetahs: it was very high but nevertheless seemed attractive to a lion whom we met close to the road. We stopped to look at him sniffing at the meat until he came too close for safety and we drove on. When later we returned, we found the trees close to the place at which we had met the lion loaded with vultures. My heart beat fast; were they watching a cheetah kill? To my great relief, the lion was on a dead giraffe.

Camping had become very trying, because during the rains not only did the snakes and scorpions increase but the rains stimulated the breeding of sugar ants, whose eggs we found in cardboard boxes and in books, and almost every wooden tent pole was covered by an earthy coating which concealed the destructive work of termites. Reading after dark was now impossible as my lamp attracted too many insects, and since the palm-thatched roofs were no longer rainproof I spent the greater part of each night shifting basins around to catch the dripping water.

For a week we had looked everywhere for the family except on the Gambo plain across the stream. Pippa had avoided this area during previous rains: perhaps she feared that she would be cut off from us by the floods. Now the plain was teaming with animals, and my last hope was to find her there. After a long search we traced a day-old spoor of a cheetah about two miles upriver and later saw two more tracks only half a mile from camp. If these belonged to our family, why did Pippa not come to camp? Calling her name, we went on looking for her until it got dark. When we were close to camp I suddenly felt Pippa rubbing against my knee. She looked very small and thin. Luckily, we had fresh zebra meat, of which I gave her a large chunk. She immediately carried it about four hundred yards, then she dropped it and anxiously called i-hn, i-hn i-hn i-hn, waiting for the cubs. I sent Guitu for more meat. As soon as he had gone the cubs appeared and, glancing cautiously at me, pounced on the food. All were in good condition and had grown a lot; their legs were very long and out of proportion to their bodies. Though they were hungry and fought for the meat, Pippa must have killed at least

View of the men's quarters

Guitu and Stanley

twice during these eight days to keep her family so fit. One of them trembled with excitement and ate so rapidly that it all came up again. Only when I offered this cub a piece of meat at a little distance from the others did it calm down and even allow me to hold the food while it gnawed away happily. I believed it to be Dume, because he was always the least able to defend his share, but it was too dark to be sure. After they had finished about twenty pounds of zebra, they disappeared. To celebrate the occasion, I presented the men with sugar and posho (maize flour) to thank them for their efforts to help Pippa and the cubs during this strenuous week.

The family remained within a mile of the camp upstream, for several days. Although I took great quantities of meat to them every day, Pippa had such an insatiable hunger that she often tore the meat out of the cubs' mouths. Finally, I got so angry at her selfishness that I hit her. It was the first time I had done this, and she was as surprised as I was upset at having to punish her in this way. Usually she never purred when her cubs were close, in order not to arouse their jealousy, so I was touched when she now came to me and, purring, rubbed herself against me, evidently wanting to make friends again. Nevertheless she understood the lesson, and for the next two days she sat aloof until the cubs had had their fill.

They were now fourteen weeks old, and I was certain that they were all weaned. Thinking that Pippa's greed might be due to tapeworm, I took cestarsol tablets along, and while the cubs were busy on a complete goat carcass I wormed Pippa. Within fifteen minutes she discharged an unbelievable quantity of worms; she took care to defecate at some distance from the feeding cubs. For the next two hours she was off-color. Dume snuggled close and licked her while his sisters gorged themselves on the goat. Attracted by the meat, the place was soon swarming with ants which attacked the carcass fiercely but did not molest the cubs, who ate unconcernedly. When Pippa had recovered she had her share and then "buried" the remains by scratching earth all over it. It was interesting that she did this only when the carcass had been complete (even though we had killed the animal); she never buried any cut-up meat. I always watched the feces of the cubs, and though so far I had found no worms, I wondered why Dume had recently grown thin and had so many ticks, since they always concentrate on sick animals. I could find no symptoms of illness, but I always kept a few titbits on the side which I hand-fed to him. He soon realized that this was a much safer way of getting his food than by fighting for it with his sisters, and from now on he often let me hold the meat while he ate. Otherwise he was active enough and the leader of the cubs, although he was the smallest.

Pippa's next headquarters was on a termite hill flat enough for all the family to rest on it while they kept a lookout over the plain. It was overshadowed by a small tree which provided endless games for the cubs. If I placed a piece of goatskin on its branches, all four competed to tear it off. Whity usually won. She then paraded the trophy provokingly around and got chased by the other cubs while Pippa reclined in a dignified manner on the hill. But her rest never lasted long, for the cubs would sneak up to her, pull her tail and nibble at her ears, and then roll over each other down the hill. I called this Anthill No. 1 because it soon became a favorite rendezvous for all of us whenever Pippa was in that area. Our presence had not escaped the notice of a honey guide who came one morning to the little tree and, chattering agitatedly, attracted our attention. This brownish bird is well known for its habit of guiding people to bees living in places that are inaccessible to the bird. The honey guide's hope is that the human beings will help him to get at the honey. Guitu now followed the twittering bird for about four hundred yards, then he saw bees swarming in the hollow of a tree. Chopping at the opening, he got stung, but he found the honey which he shared with the honey guide.

Most animals keep to their territories during the wet seasons, so I was surprised when I saw a strange lioness close to camp with three cubs about eight months old. My interest was first roused by the terrific din made by the baboons perched on a tree some three hundred yards away and across the stream; going to investigate, I saw a very thin lioness, with equally thin cubs, walking toward Pippa's anthill; they must have been extremely hungry to move at this hot hour. Fearing for the family, I called Guitu and between us we maneuvered the pride in the opposite direction. When later we went to Pippa, she walked away, which she had lately taken to doing if we visited her in the afternoon. She was prepared to put up with us once a day when we took her food, but for the rest of the time she wanted to be alone with her cubs.

When George called again I took him to see the cheetahs. We

approached them silently, but Pippa had spotted us and crouched low while the cubs bolted, except for Dume, who sat with his Mom. Leaving George twenty or so yards behind, I carried meat to Pippa, but it was an hour before she felt sufficiently reassured to eat. I then looked for the cubs, whom I found at a distance in a thicket, and I offered them meat. Instantly, Pippa placed herself between her young and me and never left this protective position while we were there. It was again little Dume who, as if to protect his mother, came and spanked my hand. When George approached cautiously within sixteen yards, the cubs spat and growled at him. We quickly withdrew.

After seeing with what suspicion Pippa reacted even to George, whom she knew well, I became more than ever determined to keep strangers away from the family. Next day the cheetahs were relaxed after having a good meal and licked each other's tongues affectionately. They did this frequently until eighteen giraffes appeared. Promptly brave little Dume set off to stalk them. After he had ventured a hundred yards, Whity joined him, but then Pippa called prr-prr and all the cheetahs walked away.

They found an ideal lair on the Gambo plain, and there they remained for a long time. It was a sheltered place between three large, thornless bushes which had previously been occupied by buffaloes. Concealed by the foliage, the family could overlook the plain in every direction and also eat their food unmolested by vultures, which could not see it from above. These scavengers had lately taken to following Pippa: knowing that sooner or later she must make a kill, they waited for their share. Although the family enjoyed peace so far as these birds were concerned, the cubs now took to fighting fiercely among themselves over their food. Nose to nose, two cubs would crouch with flattened ears, giving threatening squeals, each hanging on to the piece of meat. Sometimes they did this for so long that meanwhile the rest of the family had had time to finish all the remaining food. As the combatants were well aware of this risk, it must have seemed more important to them to test each other's strength than to eat. Little Dume had a tough time of it, for in spite of his courage he could not stand up to his stronger sisters. Luckily, he was now quite at ease with me and always rushed forward to get his hand-fed share. In spite of this he never put on weight, and one morning he had severe convulsions. I was alarmed and did not know how to improve his condition, except by increasing his intake of vitamins and milk. Dume was a bad eater and needed a lot of coaxing; for one thing, he was far too interested in everything that was going on to concentrate on his food. He was extremely quick in his reactions and was always the first to spot any danger. It was interesting that none of the cheetahs took any notice of three buffaloes who once came very near. A few days later the cubs also ignored two elephants who approached so close that we quickly retreated. Yet at the faintest lion call the family always cleared out, though they returned as soon as the lions had left.

The cubs played wonderful games on the branches of their new home; in fact, they spent more time up in the shrub than on the ground. I never tired of watching their antics; at times Pippa became jealous and, just to draw attention to herself, joined in the fun. The cubs jumped up and down on the branches like monkeys, often landing on top of their mother, or used each other as steps; Pippa, being much bigger, was at a disadvantage. They were all very happy, and their chorus of simultaneous purring was most impressive. Although I always took more meat than the family could eat, I often found that Pippa's teats had been suckled, presumably merely for pleasure.

It was about two months since we had seen traces of the cubs' father, then one day we found his spoor near Kenmare leading in the opposite direction to that of his family. Like the local lion, he moved around within his territory in circuits lasting two to three weeks. He had to move in order to find a prey, for naturally the hunted animals temporarily left the area while he was on the prowl. The fact that he had not been near his family lately was probably due not so much to our presence as to the habits of cheetah and lion mothers, who avoid mating during the period in which they are busy rearing their young. So far as lions are concerned, we knew this occupies them for up to two years; but no facts were available as to how long this "voluntary birth control" lasted with cheetahs.

After Pippa had "resided" for twelve days at the buffalo lair the ground became so infested with ants that the family moved away. This was the longest time that I had known the cheetahs to remain in one place, and it had obviously been made possible only by our bringing food. Little Dume was again not well, and for the

Pippa and the cubs at buffalo lair, 16 and 17 weeks

first time he showed signs of rickets by walking with his front legs
bent outward. On George's advice I added some Farex to his diet
of meat and Abidec. The cubs loved it, particularly Dume, who
could not get enough of the Ideal milk into which I mixed this baby
food.

One morning during a downpour I arrived in a green plastic raincoat. Promptly the cubs bolted and showed up only after I had taken
off this unfamiliar garment. I got drenched—not an unpleasant
experience in this warm climate; I was therefore alarmed when
I saw Dume shivering. Next day he limped badly on his right front
leg and reacted as if in pain when I touched his shoulder. He had
no temperature, and since he ate well I assumed that he had strained
a muscle when jumping off a tree. The following morning he was
worse and, knowing that he was vulnerable, kept in hiding. Fearing
that he might become an easy prey to predators I wanted to take
him to camp until he recovered, but Guitu advised against this,
believing that I would lose Pippa's trust if I took him away. After
watching Dume for two hours, I drove over to the Park Warden to
discuss the problem with him. He too suggested that it was best to
leave Dume with his mother unless she were to abandon him. Hoping to protect the family from possible danger, I returned in the
afternoon but could find no trace of them, though with Dume so
handicapped they could not have gone far.

By next morning they had moved a hundred yards or so. It was
drizzling, and the cubs, invigorated by the rain, chased each
other, splashing through little puddles and becoming marvelously
muddy. Little Dume wanted to join in, but after a few steps he collapsed. He was now very conscious of his condition and kept aside
most of the time, but eventually he came to me and licked my hand.
Pippa meanwhile had a tussle with Whity over meat. Trying to take
a piece away from her, she walked in circles around her daughter,
who, lying on her back, held on to it and, rolling parallel with her
mother so as not to lose sight of her, scratched and bit whenever
Pippa tried to snatch the meat. Finally, Whity won and Pippa
walked off. Watching this skirmish, I wondered if it might not be a
well-intended lesson given by Pippa to teach her children that they
must defend their food.

Worried about Dume, I drove to Leopard Rock and radio-called
Dr. Harthoorn. It was the twenty-second of December and he had al-

Whity inspects meat basket

ready left for a Christmas holiday, so I contacted another Vet who advised me to add steamed bonemeal to the cub's diet but to leave him with his mother. He assumed that Dume had strained a muscle and would recover within two or three weeks. Next day, to my relief, he seemed slightly better but nevertheless kept close to Pippa and followed her wherever she moved. The fact that she clouted him once during this time made me feel happier: I believed she would not do this if he were seriously ill.

On my return I found George in camp, deeply distressed because a wild lion had killed Sam. I knew what this meant to George. We had both loved this endearing cub, who was such an outstanding character. It was a shocking blow that he should die in this way and, like Taga, again at Christmastime. Happily, on the twenty-fourth of December Dume was better, and he even played quietly with his sisters: Whity especially never left his side. Hoping that he would soon be well again, I went home and prepared the Christmas Eve dinner, at which I expected George, his brother, and Ken Smith, whom readers of *Born Free* may remember as playing a vital part in Elsa's life on two occasions. They came, together with young Arun, and we had as pleasant an evening as was possible.

CHAPTER

13

Death of Little Dume

ON CHRISTMAS DAY Dume also lost the use of one of his hind legs. Greatly alarmed, I wanted to take him to camp, but unless I could get a Vet to sedate him the capture might upset him so much that it would do more harm than good. But, of course, all offices were closed for the holidays and communication even by radio was almost at a standstill. During the three days it took me to arrange for a Vet to fly out to us, Guitu spent all the daylight hours with the cheetah family, helping to protect them from predators and also watching their movements, which Pippa had reduced to a minimum. Dume got worse each day. Since he was now an easy prey for any lion, I did not dare leave him in the bush at night, so I asked George to help me catch him. Not to upset the cheetah as his presence had done during his first visit, he remained at some distance watching Dume through field glasses. I approached the cub with a piece of meat, but however casually I tried to behave, he must have sensed my intention and staggered off on his two good legs at such a speed that I felt cruel chasing him, and so I decided to risk another night in the bush. It would be the last, for the Vet was due to fly in next day.

In the morning we had quite a job finding the family; they had obviously become suspicious because of our attempt to catch Dume. Now I only offered him very little food so that the sedative I had placed in it should have a quick effect. But Dume was not to be fooled and stumbled off whenever I came near. This affected Pippa, and she took the family away. At lunchtime I collected the Vet at the

Kenmare airstrip and returned with him immediately. Long before we came near Dume bolted and, joined by Whity, disappeared. I was worried, because poor Dume had had no food that morning and very little the day before. But, as we did not wish to frighten him still more, we confined ourselves to making friends with Pippa. Approaching carefully, we sat down within two yards of her, and after we had talked quietly to her she allowed the Vet to pat her, and she even nibbled at his hand. That was more than we had hoped for and now, confident of her friendliness, we went home. Next morning George came over to help us, and after collecting a goat from Kenmare we drove with the Vet half the distance to the cheetahs' lair. I told both of them to stay there and wait for the news I would send back. Guitu and I then went ahead with the goat carcass and almost ran into a sleeping rhino, which until it moved looked exactly like a termite hill. Carrying the heavy carcass between us, it took us two hours to find our cheetah and get rid of the goat. All the family pounced on it except for little Dume, who kept hiding. Did he know that I had added a tranquilizer to his milk? More than ever I was convinced that animals can read our minds. Giving him time to settle down, I sent Guitu to guide the Vet to within five hundred yards of us to a place where he could not be seen by the cheetahs. He was obliged to sit there for two hours, since it took Dume all that time to decide to come near me. Though he must have been hungry after two days without food, he bolted every time I held the bowl of milk out to him. To win his trust, I had to give him a small piece of liver in which I had concealed his Abidec ration; it was only by exercising great patience that I was at last able to coax him to take the tranquilizer by dripping the mixture of Farex and milk carefully on his paws off which he licked it and so took the whole dose.

I then joined the Vet and we waited for another two hours to give Dume time to get drowsy. Since the cat species react unpredictably to any drug, the Vet had based the sedative on a minimum weight of ten pounds, intending to increase it if necessary. Obviously, this was too little, for when I returned after two hours, Dume was still wide awake; the fact that his nictitating membrane partly covered his eyes was the only evidence of his having taken largactil. The goat had been eaten, and after Pippa had buried the remains she had left with her cubs for a bush a hundred yards away. The Vet and I had a picnic lunch, and we let time go by for the tranquilizer to have its

Pippa with Dume, 17 weeks

Last photo of Dume, 17½ weeks

effect, but even after this interval little Dume was far from sleepy. Since he gave us no opportunity to increase the dose, we decided to catch him as best we could and then inject a fast-acting anesthetic. We approached, but, seeing the Vet, all the females bolted into a thicket some hundred yards away while I ran after Dume, who hobbled for his life at such a speed that I had a hard time catching up with him and could get close only when, in his final effort to escape, he struggled up a tree, from which I pulled him down. He must have reached the limit of his strength, for he was quite still except for his fast-beating heart. Pippa had raced parallel with us and now sat within three feet, watching me patting little Dume to calm him down. She did not interfere then or later, when the Vet caught up with us and injected the fast-acting anesthetic, after which he manipulated the cub's legs. Unfortunately, he could not diagnose the degree of the injuries and insisted on taking Dume to Nairobi for an X-ray. To take advantage of his semi-conscious state, he suggested driving straight to the Leopard Rock airstrip, from which the Warden could fly them both to Nairobi. So I sent Guitu to George, asking him to get us by car. While waiting for him I sat with little Dume in my lap. I dreaded this visit to Nairobi, where he would be deprived of every familiar thing he loved, but if I wanted to save him there was no choice. By now Pippa had joined her other cubs, and all watched us very alertly as we took Dume away. During the fifteen-minute drive to Leopard Rock poor Dume growled all the time in a very strange voice; probably he was objecting to the car, since driving was a new experience to him. At Leopard Rock we put him on a scale, and the Vet, seeing that he weighed eighteen pounds, gave him another injection of largactil for the flight. I could not fly with Dume to comfort him, because the plane was a two-seater, and also I had to help Pippa over her bewilderment and try to keep her trust. I arranged for the Vet to keep in daily contact with me by radio, and he assured me that I had no need to worry since he and his wife would nurse little Dume in their home and see that he did not fret too much. Although I knew that Dume was in good hands, I wondered if I would ever see him again, and it was with a heavy heart that I watched the plane take off.

I went straight to the cheetahs and found them at the same place from which they had watched us taking Dume away. They all dashed off at the mere sight of us, and it was half an hour before Pippa returned. She sniffed the ground where Dume had been and crept into the thicket where he had hidden, anxiously calling i-hn i-hn all the time. It was torture to me to watch her looking for her child. Finally she settled on the tree where I had grabbed Dume and surveyed the surroundings. I offered her water; she did not touch it. Stroking her, I whispered that I had only taken little Dume away to get him fit again, since in his present state he had little chance of survival and jeopardized the lives of the other cubs because, in case of an attack, she would be obliged to protect him. As though she understood the meaning of my words, she started to purr. By then the sun was setting and I could imagine little Dume landing at Nairobi, fast asleep and unconscious of his frightening mode of transport. Thinking about his illness, I now remembered that he had dragged his front leg for nine days, and that four days later he had injured his hind leg; owing to his handicap, he had kept away from the feeding competitions, which had no doubt been the cause of his getting out of condition so fast.

In the morning I put on the same clothes I had worn the day before, hoping that Dume's scent on them might give Pippa confidence in me. She was again at the tree where I had caught Dume; the cubs ran away instantly. Pippa sniffed for a long time at my shorts and then settled for her meal. Later on, the cubs reappeared; they were extremely shy and did not play, only sat on fallen trees and looked around; so did their mother, calling i-hn i-hn continuously.

That afternoon the Park Warden sent a message from the Vet saying that the X-ray revealed a fracture of the humerus (below the shoulder) of the front leg and a fracture of the tibia in the rear leg. There would be no need to immobilize Dume, no pins or plaster, since the fractures were not serious, though the hind leg would remain slightly shorter but not so short as to be a handicap. After ten days another X-ray would be taken, and if this showed good progress I could have Dume back but would need to confine him for three to four weeks in camp until he was again fit for wild life. Finally, the Vet asked me not to worry, as he had vaccinated Dume against feline distemper, which was common in Nairobi.

That was good news. All the same, I felt that I should like to fly to Nairobi as soon as possible to give moral support to Dume, but when I saw Pippa next day I had to give up the plan. She had not budged from the place of the cub's capture; she sniffed around sand

Pippa searching for Dume

patches where he had been and called for him continually, while the remaining cubs sat quietly in trees and looked out onto the plain.

On New Year's Eve I had borrowed a phonograph from the Park Warden and after it got dark played the record of *Born Free*. The music became more meaningful in the stillness of the African night, and I thought of a young author, John Heminway, who had visited us recently. He was writing a book about people living in the bush, and after interviewing George, myself, and several other people he summed up their motives in these words: "People of the bush have a need for unlimited freedom which only life close to nature can give." Conscious of how fortunate I was to live such a life, in spite of the sorrows and anxieties that relationship with animals sometimes entails, I toasted a happy life for all and especially for little Dume.

For six days the family remained put at the place of capture, searching and calling for Dume. The extent to which this little male had been the leader of them all I realized only now when I saw his family listless and subdued. It was heartbreaking to witness their distress. I could not communicate with the Vet over the New Year's holiday, and when at last we spoke together on the third of January I learned that Dume had been on a hunger strike for the first few days and had only now started to take food and settle down. In expectation of his return, we prepared an enclosure some twenty yards square around a small tree. It was close to my tent and had a sheltered sleeping place. On the sixth of January the Vet told me that Dume was improving fast and he hoped that after another X-ray, on the ninth, I could get him; meanwhile I should make a six-by-six-foot crate in which to confine him for three or four weeks before letting him run about in the larger compound.

The following morning, watching the cubs jumping off trees and striking forcefully at each other in their games, I was amazed that they could behave like this without injuring their delicate legs. Recently Pippa had treated roughly and even attacked her children with such deliberation that I was convinced she was teaching them to defend themselves.

During the night of the eighth to ninth of January, I woke up with a strong feeling that something had gone wrong with Dume. Next morning I got through on the radio to the Vet, who said: "Dume died last night. Until the sixth he did well and both fractures were almost healed. In the evening he vomited, but after I gave him some medicine he started eating again. This morning I found him dead. The post-mortem showed that he died of feline enteritis, although I had injected him with four cubic centimeters of Hoechst feline enteritis vaccine." Fighting my tears, I asked if this meant that Dume had died of distemper which he had caught in Nairobi. The answer was "Yes." Knowing how plucky little Dume had always been, I feared he had succumbed to the infection more easily because fretting had diminished his resistance and because he no longer had any wish to live. I dreaded going to his family. They were all still in the same area where Dume had been captured, and I found them waiting for their food. After they had eaten I sat with Pippa. From my despair she seemed to sense what had happened and neither purred nor licked my hands, as she had previously done when I had conveyed Dume's recovery to her; she only listened quietly, then called her cubs and took them away.

I was too upset to carry on with my daily routine and drove to Elsa's camp, hoping her spirit would ease my distress. I kept thinking that I should have gone to Nairobi so that little Dume would have had my familiar presence to keep up his morale.

Suddenly I was distracted from these thoughts by eight elephants who appeared on the opposite riverbank. The adults took a long time filling their bellies and blowing water over themselves and then over three small calves. Later they all leaned side by side against the muddy riverbank, which was eroded at that place, and, keeping the youngsters in the middle, rubbed against it with such rhythmical movements that they looked like a frieze which had suddenly come to life. I believe that elephants have an abstract concept of death nearly akin to our own. They bury other elephants and even people they have killed under large piles of brushwood, and to our knowledge they have returned repeatedly to a place where they have killed someone. On one occasion, elephants tried for ten days to dig up one of their victims who had been buried six feet deep. Indeed, we had witnessed two cases which appeared to indicate that elephants even set up memorials to their dead. In one instance they carried the shoulder blade of a dead elephant over a mile to drop it at exactly the spot at which he had been shot, and in another they carried the two tusks of the dead animal a long distance to place them side by side. There was also an extraordinary case which appeared to be a

Pippa and cubs on cobra hill, 21 and 22 weeks

mercy killing; it took place in South Africa when the leading bull of a herd actually stabbed an old cow, who was fatally ill, through her brain with his tusk and so put her out of her misery. Many people deny that animals have any feeling for their dead except that of sometimes missing them. Having witnessed the reaction of Elsa's cubs to her death, as well as Pippa's and her daughters' search for Dume, I am now convinced that their emotions go far deeper than that.

This belief was strengthened the next morning when we had to search for several hours before discovering the cheetah family. They were far outside the area which had been within Dume's orbit and where they had remained since he had become ill twenty-four days ago. Was it a mere coincidence that they had moved away as soon as Pippa sensed from my behavior that Dume would never return?

We found them resting on a termite hill. Three buffaloes appeared and came uncomfortably close. The cheetahs took no notice of these formidable beasts but were far more interested in a black cobra wriggling along the base of the termite hill and craned their necks toward the deadly snake. It was the longest cobra I had ever seen and as thick as my arm. My yelling to prevent the cubs from going near it had no effect on them, but luckily the snake quickly disappeared into a hole. The ground around this cobra hill was riddled with big ant-bear holes and was obviously often occupied by snakes, which made me worry about the safety of the cheetahs. But they liked this place and later often chose it as a playground. Today the cubs were full of beans, chasing around and up and down the hill, leaping from its top onto each other or rolling all together down its slope. When, tired out, they rested on the hill, Whity for the first time took my hand into her mouth, and Mbili actually allowed me to pat her. Only Tatu remained as shy as ever and even sneaked off if I looked at her for too long.

14

The Harthoorns to the Rescue

THAT EVENING a party from Switzerland called at my camp, among whom was Dr. De Watteville, a leading international gynecologist as well as a great animal lover. When we were discussing the breeding difficulties of cheetahs in captivity, he suggested that one reason might be that the sex activities of females are controlled by their mental reactions to their environment. Since a cheetah's well-being depends on vast space to satisfy its need for exercise, and it also has a strong instinct to conceal itself, the female might be severely affected by living in unnatural surroundings.

The longer I lived near Pippa's family, the more I marveled at their sensitive reactions to each other and everything around them. Therefore I was surprised to see to what an extent their visual reactions depended on color rather than on physical characteristics. Again and again the cubs bolted at the sight of my green raincoat, or green khaki, instead of the familiar cream-colored cloth coat. Though we human beings also respond emotionally to color, we depend more on features and movements when it comes to recognizing people. Of course my experience is limited to lions and cheetahs, but certainly they never recognized us when we wore unfamiliar clothes. Having recently read some controversial articles about the purpose of stripes, spots, and other patterns on animal hides in which it was suggested that the slightly different marking of each animal helps the herd to recognize the individual, I drew black stripes with charcoal over my cream-colored cloth coat. My staff was impressed by my fancy dress, but the cheetah family paid no attention to the stripes and seemed not to notice the new pattern.

Bolting from strangers, on the other hand, depends entirely on the animal's tameness. This became very obvious when a film unit arrived to shoot a documentary of our rehabilitation work. Since George had recently encouraged visitors to see his lions, and even allowed them to walk among the animals, his pride accepted the crew. But I had kept strangers away from the cheetahs, and I now agreed to co-operate if the filming was done by only one person and then only if it was proved that he did not upset the family. Although we used great tact and patience, Pippa and her cubs bolted on the second day and kept away for a whole week. When late one afternoon we eventually found them, Pippa alone followed us to within half a mile of camp, and there she sat firmly. By the time I had collected food it was too dark to see, but judging from the barkings of baboons the cubs must have been near. They had had no meat from me for a week, yet they did not show up, and after a wait of two hours I went home. All the following day we looked for them. After dark Pippa again appeared alone and kept the cubs in hiding. Much later she released them with her prr-prr and all had a good meal.

On our way home we met five Grévy's zebra with a foal hobbling on three legs, a front one dangling limp. We had frequently seen this group during the last three weeks since they kept within a very small area and obviously restricted their movements to help the foal recover from its injury. Thinking again of the Grévy's mare successfully protecting her suckling foal, which had a much worse injury than Dume's, I realized that I should never have separated him from Pippa and questioned whether we had the right to interfere with the lives of other species. Was not each species destined to live by its own instincts and share the responsibility for survival with its own kind only? Had we not by now enough evidence to recognize the disastrous results our interference had had on the balance of nature? Why had we evolved a conscience that took us outside our own realm? Yet was I quite sure that I would not again interfere if anything should happen to one of the cheetahs? I did not know the answer.

Next day we found the family had moved still farther off in the direction of a densely wooded section of the plain which we called the Buffalo Forest because the ground there was patterned with their spoor. It was about an hour's walk from camp and halfway between the stream and the Rojoweru. The cubs were busy jumping on and off a fallen tree. Suddenly I noticed that one of Mbili's front legs was now turning slightly outward. A little later she sat apart, shaken by convulsions which were like those Dume had had at the beginning of his illness. I was horrified. Why, after the cubs had developed so splendidly for four months, was she now showing symptoms of rickets? All I could do was to feed her a double ration of Farex, which she liked, but I had to use all kinds of tricks to coax her to take the Abidec and the bonemeal. Only too late did I learn that felines need large quantities of minerals during the period when they grow fast and try to get these by eating mud and licking sand off each other. During the following days the cheetahs remained at this place, disregarding the buffaloes which were around. Mbili kept rather quiet, and I was glad to see that her leg improved. Luckily, she was so fond of the Farex and Ideal milk that she always rushed to me to get her fill before her sisters could fight for the rest, pushing their heads into the small bowl and spilling its contents over each other.

Our peaceful time came to an end when lions invaded the area on one of their periodic hunts. On our way to Pippa we met five lionesses, and when later we almost collided with two elephants at the Buffalo Forest I was not surprised to find that the cheetahs had cleared out. During one of our searches we disturbed a lion from his slumber; suddenly his dark-maned head rose above the grass no more than twenty yards away from us. He took a long look at us and then trotted off. On another occasion we found two lionesses occupying one of Pippa's favorite drinking places on the Rojoweru, and soon afterward we put up a cheetah bounding from a thicket straight toward the lionesses. He may have been Pippa's mate, for he was dark-colored and later we found her spoor and that of the cubs within about four hundred yards. During the night the lions passed our camp and walked along the road to Kenmare. This was in the opposite direction to the one in which we found the cheetah family after an absence of nine days. We were on our way home after a tiring search when we spotted circling vultures far way. Guided by them, we met Pippa furiously defending the last remains of a young waterbuck. The cubs were resting with bursting bellies and licking the blood off each other. Very thirsty, they rushed to the familiar water can and lapped and lapped. I watched them attentively to see

Whity helps herself to titbits of liver

that they did not spill the precious water which we had carried all the afternoon, and I was so absorbed that I did not notice three elephants emerge from the bush. When I saw them they were already almost on top of us. Dropping everything, we ran.

When we returned next morning to recover the water bowl, there was no sign of the family except a few remains of guinea fowl probably killed by Pippa. During the following week she made her headquarters under an isolated acacia growing at a bend of the Buffalo Forest; we called it the Corner Acacia. This tree was a typical umbrella acacia; its trunk grew straight, without supporting branches, to a flat crown. It was, of course, an irresistible challenge to the cubs to climb up the twenty-foot-high trunk which they could now do almost as well as Pippa. Hooking their claws into the bark and heaving their bodies inch by inch up the tree, going up was not too difficult, but coming down was quite another matter. This they did by clinging to the bark, then jumping, and landing with outstretched legs on the ground. One has to be familiar with the structure of a cheetah's legs to appreciate these acrobatics; I was amazed that their thin bones could stand the impact of such jumps without breaking.

Within ten minutes' walk there was an even better lair under a large tamarind which overshadowed a termite hill, ideal to rest on and also for looking around. The tree grew at the point where the Gambo plain drops in a gentle slope down to the Rojoweru, half a mile away. As the hide-out was concealed by its low branches, the cheetahs could survey not only the river bush but also the plain in the direction of the camp, which was not more than a twenty-minute walk away. Though several times we found the pugmarks of the family going from the tamarind along a narrow game path leading to the camp, Pippa never brought the cubs nearer than four hundred yards. They were by now five and a half months old, and it was interesting to study the area they had covered since their birth, for this showed that Pippa had taken them in a circle of about five miles' diameter around the camp.

Since the rains had ended the elephants had returned and were again crossing the plain in several small herds. They moved quite noiselessly, and we had a narrow escape when we came face to face with one hidden by a bush. I could now watch their nightly visits to "the tree" across the stream in comfort from my bed as I had moved it into a position which enabled me to shine my flashlight on

At the tamarind tree

them without having to raise my hand. Even so, I was obliged to keep awake and to watch out; how I envied the cheetahs their nonchalance in regard to elephants (and to pachyderms in general).

On the sixteenth of February we spotted the family under a small bush near the Corner Acacia. I dropped the meat and all rushed up to it except Whity. When she finally appeared, I was horrified, for she came hobbling slowly, dangling her left front leg, which was limp from the wrist. Watching me with suspicion, she moved near Pippa, whom she kept from now on between herself and me. Whity had always been very friendly, but now she spat with fury if I even looked at her and raged when I tried to come near. What was I to do? She could not put any weight on her leg, which appeared to be broken. I decided to leave her with Pippa. Later I radio-called Dr. Harthoorn, who agreed that this was the best plan, but he offered to send a tranquilizer in case Whity should get worse and I should have to bring her into camp.

From this expedition I returned home just in time to help chase an elephant who was walking into the kitchen: he crashed into a tree not more than twenty yards from the men's tent before he lumbered off. Soon after dark there was much lion growling and the agonized barking of a zebra very close. For most of the night I listened to the howling of hyenas and the yelping of jackals joining the kill. Next morning we cautiously approached the place, about two hundred yards upstream; it was not difficult to locate because the nearby trees were loaded with vultures. We could not investigate the kill itself since the lions were still on it, but we found, at the spot where the fight had taken place and from which the carcass had been dragged into a thicket, the front leg of an immature Grévy's zebra severed at an old break. This left no doubt that it was the poor foal we had been watching for seven weeks and which had at last fallen victim to its injury. It was evidence that even the bravest mother could not protect her young if it were handicapped. Was this to be a warning to me in regard to Whity? We went on to the Corner Acacia. Whity was no worse and could run quite fast on her three legs and even strike back if the sisters played too roughly with her, but she could not defend her food from them. Expecting this, and in the hope that I could hand-feed her, I had brought with me the khaki gloves which I had used in handling Taga. It needed inexhaustible patience to convince Whity of my friendly intention, but I was determined that she should not get out of condition, so the sooner she accepted food from me the better. Gradually, while taking good care never to become isolated from the family, she made friends with me. Meanwhile Pippa scrambled up the tree and, balancing on the thin top branches, called provokingly, prr-prr, as if saying: "Look, see what I can do!"

I could not imagine why she encouraged the cubs to indulge in such a dangerous exercise, except that perhaps after Whity's accident she didn't want them to become afraid of climbing, a skill they might need for survival. Perhaps cheetahs have developed their tree climbing habits only since man has forced them away from their natural habitat on the open plains and into a more wooded country. But even though they have mastered the technique of climbing, they are not equipped by nature with retractable claws, adhesive pads, or the low build characteristic of tree-climbing animals.

Perhaps the main reason for the high mortality among young cheetahs is the leg injuries they sustain in trying to learn a skill for which they are not built?

By next morning we found that Pippa had moved the cubs half a mile away, obviously to evade the vultures which had kept a macabre watch, for the last two days, on the Corner Acacia. This long walk had done Whity no good, and she moved very cautiously but she was also extremely shy, which made it very difficult for me to hand-feed her and ensure her getting all her supplementary rations. She was a strikingly handsome animal and by far the strongest of the cubs, so it seemed doubly cruel to see her suffering from such a severe injury. That evening, while I was having my bath, I heard a lion roar so forcefully that for the first time I was frightened by a sound which I love. Jumping out, I saw the lion walking to the Grévy kill. His shattering roar continued until he reached it; then he stopped. I thought of Whity with anxiety.

The following morning we discovered that Pippa had taken the cubs still farther off to a burned tree which had fallen on some charred ground. The cubs loved rolling in the ash and looked like spotted chimney sweeps. It must have been very frustrating for Whity not to be able to join in the fun. She spent most of the morning suckling Pippa. The cubs were six months old today. Pippa was very gentle and remained still whenever Whity came to be comforted. Torn between the various possible alternatives for helping

Pippa gives tree-climbing lesson

the cub, we went home, only to run into another lioness and hear still more calling in the distance.

This made me decide to take Whity into camp, so I drove to Leopard Rock and asked the Park Warden to fly to Nairobi and get the tranquilizer, which he agreed to do. The following morning we searched for the family without success. Meanwhile the largactil had arrived with instructions to give one milligram per pound of body weight. My guess was that Whity weighed about twenty-five pounds, and I prepared the dose accordingly. We had a very hot search until we finally discovered the family in a belt of thornbush about one and a half miles farther away than they had ever been before. Whity was very hungry and greedily ate the small piece of meat which concealed the sedative. It was supposed to take effect within thirty minutes. After two hours she was still wide awake and came for a drink. By then the sun was getting low and, fearing to lose her in the dark, I waited until her head was in the water bowl, then I grabbed her. Instantly she bit me in the arm, thigh, and leg, and as the blood was running all over me I had to let her go. This put an end to any attempt to catch her. Since I could not leave her alone in her sedated state, I persuaded Guitu and Stanley to wait into the night with me for the largactil to have its effect. Luckily, there was enough moonlight for us to watch the family for another three hours. By then Whity seemed drowsy and I inched myself carefully near her, but whenever I got within touching distance she bolted. Listening to hyena howls and lion whuffing, we waited for her to become more sleepy; but Mbili and Tatu kept protectively between us and gave the alarm the moment I moved. Pippa was the only one who still trusted me, so I waited until Whity snuggled up to her, then, pretending to play with Pippa, I got near enough to throw a towel over Whity's head and grabbed her. Before I knew what was happening, she rushed to the nearest tree and struggled up it. Seeing me following her, she then jumped eight feet down and disappeared in the dark. It was five and a half hours since she had taken the tranquilizer, and the effect, however slight, seemed to have worn off. The situation was hopeless, for now that she was fully conscious and able to escape we risked separating and losing the family in the dark if we continued chasing her.

Meanwhile my arm was hurting badly and two fingers were getting numb, so I returned to camp; there I got the car and went to

Leopard Rock for an injection of penicillin. My mind concentrated on Whity, I drove straight through a dust whirl and barely missed hitting six elephants. I noticed them only after I had passed them and heard their protesting trumpetings. We arrived at Leopard Rock long after midnight and everyone was asleep. I was sorry to have to rouse the Warden. He kindly arranged for me to have a bath and supper while the African dresser was called to do the injection and patch me up. Finally, I was to be escorted by a driver on my way home in case we should meet more elephants.

After a sleepless night we started at crack of dawn, and I was much relieved to find the cheetahs all fit not far from where we had left them. Whity was still slightly dopy and so thirsty that I had to let her drink before giving her a double dose of largactil. This soon had an effect, and growling frequently she followed Pippa five hundred yards to a lone balanitis tree right in the open plain. Pippa always preferred these trees as they have less vicious thorns than acacias, which often stick painfully into animals' paws. But today I was not sure if this was the only reason for the move or whether she had chosen the place because of the presence of an elephant who was browsing in a bush not more than a hundred yards away. Even though his back was turned toward us, we had to watch him constantly while we were trying to catch Whity. Her nictitating membrane was by now exposed and her head drooping, but she was alert enough to move away as soon as I came near. We played this game for more than two hours, then I remembered the Harthoorns' advice to give up after such a lapse of time because the effect of the drug would be wearing off. I did not dare to give Whity more than fifty milligrams of largactil, so, calling it a day, we offered her some food, the first she had had for forty-eight hours. Ravenously she tucked in. I decided to make a last attempt to catch her and, pulling a towel over her, picked her up. Outraged, she struggled, biting and scratching, and was joined by Pippa, who attacked me so fiercely that I dropped Whity like a hot brick. All the cheetahs ran off straight toward the elephant. Far too close to the elephant for us to follow them, they then settled under a tree, and from this safe position Pippa watched our movements while Mbili and Tatu played. After we had watched them for an hour, Whity showed no sign of falling asleep, so I left Guitu on guard and drove to Leopard Rock to radio-call the Harthoorns.

Because it had proved impossible to catch Whity by tranquilizing her, they agreed to come in three days' time to immobilize her. Though Toni was a world authority on this new method of putting animals "out" temporarily, I was terrified of overdosing Whity since we could only estimate her weight. But Toni assured me that she would not be overdosed and would come to no harm. Because Pippa moved the cubs daily over long distances, I thought that Whity had no chance of recovery unless I could confine her at my camp. But so far all my attempts to help had resulted in failure, and worse, I felt that the glorious relationship between the family and me had come today to an abrupt end. How was I to introduce the Harthoorns to the cheetahs if even Pippa now distrusted me?

Next morning, to my surprise, the cheetahs were very friendly, and even Whity came to get her meat from me. On the second day we found that Pippa had moved about seven hundred yards and saw that Whity's foot was swollen. She kept aside all the time and only got very little food. On the third day we found Pippa, Mbili, and Tatu back at the burned bush, but no sign of Whity. I searched and searched until at last I found her hiding under a bush which she left reluctantly at my approach, limping off to her family, who pushed her away. However cunningly I tried to offer her meat, they tore it from her. Intimidated, poor Whity then retired inside a deep thicket where I could not follow her. If I left meat outside her lair I knew that the others would steal it, so I pushed a lump with a stick through the thorns, but very soon it was so covered with ants that Whity could not eat it. She never left the thicket, and all my efforts to give her food were unsuccessful although we spent most of the day trying to feed her. I was very sorry for the cub but I knew that her empty stomach meant that she would absorb the drug more quickly when the Harthoorns arrived with it.

Early next morning they flew in at Leopard Rock, where I collected them and took them to my camp. George also came to help. During a quick breakfast we devised a way of catching Whity. Since it was essential not to frighten the cheetahs, we decided that we would all walk half the distance to the place where I had left the family on the previous afternoon. There Toni would prepare the sernilan and inject it into a small piece of meat which Guitu and I would take along with other food. If I was successful in doping Whity, Guitu would collect Toni and guide him to us while his wife and George would wait on the spot in case we needed help. The drug needed thirty minutes to take effect, so Toni would have time enough to catch up with us and treat Whity instantly if she was over-dosed. We set off.

It was an hour and a half before we found the family in a dense commiphora forest; certainly Whity was safer here than in the open. When we arrived she was hiding, but seeing me drop the food she could not resist coming along and quickly took the doped meat. Having starved for two days, she naturally wanted more and I felt a brute to prevent her from getting at the meat and then seeing her hobble off, watching the others eat. After the family had had their fill, they moved fifty yards away and were soon joined by Whity, who showed no sign of drowsiness although it was an hour since she had taken the drug. Pippa licked her affectionately for a long time, then walked with Mbili and Tatu out of the thorny forest far into the plains, without stopping once to see if Whity were following. Meanwhile I had sent for Toni. When he arrived I asked him to look out for Pippa, but there was no necessity for she appeared to have abandoned Whity.

Toni and I sat within twenty yards of the cub watching through our binoculars: gradually her head started swaying, dropping lower and lower, until she fell onto her side. We had estimated her weight at forty pounds, but it had taken much longer for the drug to take effect than Toni had calculated; at least the result now seemed posi-tive. Prepared for a struggle, we walked carefully up to Whity, but she was completely immobilized and, though her eyes were wide open, never stirred while we placed her in an air traveling bag. It was a hard job carrying her the long way back in the heat of the day, two of us sharing the weight and one supporting her head so that she did not suffocate. We were all glad when we reached camp at teatime.

Toni then gave her some largactil to make sure she would not become active before he had examined her. I held my breath while he carefully manipulated the injured leg until he diagnosed radial paralysis. This meant that Whity did not have to go to Nairobi for treatment and I could keep her here in confinement until the tem-porarily paralyzed main nerve and consequently inactive muscles recovered. Though this injury was, in itself, minor, it could become dangerous if the insensitive part of the leg were bent inward, for then it might break if any weight were put on it. The Harthoorns bandaged the leg with plaster of Paris and, profiting from her immobilization, examined Whity's teeth. She was six months and one week old that day, and it was interesting to see two of the permanent molars already breaking through. Cheetah cubs are believed to depend on the kills of the mother until they are two years old, like lion cubs, who develop their permanent teeth only after twelve months. But since Whity had already changed her teeth, it looked as though she would be capable of killing much earlier. Now, if I could keep in contact with the family, I might well be able to find out the truth about when a cheetah cub starts killing and becomes independent of its mother.

Giving Whity a vitamin B complex injection, we placed her in Taga's sleeping crate inside my tent so that during the night I could watch her coming around. The Harthoorns told me to keep her sedated for the next ten days with half a tablet of largactil per day but said I could decrease the dose if she got used to her confinement. Then they left. I hoped that Sue and Toni knew how grateful I was for their help.

After they had gone I felt dizzy and sick and went to bed to recover from the strain of the last hours. It had been a great help to us, in catching Whity, that Pippa had not returned, but I was alarmed that during the last few days she had interfered with Whity's feeding and now seemed to have abandoned her. Even if we had rescued Whity in the nick of time, what was to become of her? Would I be able to return her to the family, or would she end up as a pet?

She came around at 5 A.M., and to prevent her from struggling I gave her half a tablet of largactil and some glucose. After she had calmed down I moved her into the six-by-six-foot enclosure we had made for Dume. To this we had now attached a slightly larger annex connected by a door which I could open as soon as she was fit enough to have more space. Both were completely wired in, overshadowed by a small tree, and stood inside the large compound.

At 10 A.M. I heard the sound of a struggle, and before I could prevent her, Whity tore off the plaster of Paris. As it turned out, this was just as well, for later I would have found it impossible to remove it without giving her an anesthetic. Now at last I was able to give

The Harthoorns examine Whity

Whity convalescent in compound

her a good meal, the first she had had for three days. I hid another half largactil in it.

Soon after this young Arun arrived. He had agreed to baby-sit for the next few days during the time I would have to spend with the rest of the cheetah family.

On our way to them we passed the bush where, twelve days ago, we had first noticed that Whity was ill. There were fresh cheetah spoor there as well as at some of the other places where the family had lately been. Finally we found Pippa sniffing around the spot where we had caught Whity. Ignoring us, she went on calling and looking for her while Mbili and Tatu ate the meat we had brought. Only after a long time did she join us, lick my hand, and settle down; she was exceptionally quiet. Later, she and the cubs followed us on our way home as far as the Corner Acacia, where they remained.

When we arrived in camp Whity was still sleepy, but toward sunset she became more active. Walking along the wire, she looked around drowsily, then suddenly started making heart-rending calls, her body jerking with every sharp chirp. After some time I succeeded in quieting her and we sat together, but soon an elephant appeared on the far bank of the stream to start his nocturnal browsing. Poor Whity trembled with excitement; evidently, she felt trapped in the enclosure. She shook even more when a lion whuffed at a distance, so I placed a camp bed close by and spent the night near her. For the next ten days she had to be kept sedated, which had the disadvantage of making her constipated as well as raising her temperature. The Harthoorns had warned me about this and advised me to counteract it by sprinkling water over her during the hot hours: this she liked. She ate well and showed her contentment while chewing the meat, by a new, charming sound, nyam-nyam-nyam, but I never heard her purr.

Unfortunately, Whity took a dislike to Arun and rushed furiously against the wire at the sight of him. But there was no one else I could rely on to chase the baboons away. They terrified the cub to such an extent that she defecated the moment she heard their barkings. Arun kept well out of sight during his baby-sittings. Chiefly, Whity was utterly bored, and the more frustrated she felt the fiercer she became. Soon she even spat and growled when I approached and I could calm her only by offering her milk and Farex. She liked this mixture so much that she developed a ritual licking of the bowl till it was spotlessly clean. While this was going on I was able to stroke her and make friends with her. Unlike semi-nocturnal animals, Whity usually settled down at sunset, and then I could sit close to her and even listen to the news on the radio. It puzzled me that so long as I kept the transistor turned low she did not object to this artificial sound, whereas thunder and lightning made her panic.

Her teething pains added to her discomfort, and I could not quickly enough replace the bits of wood which she chewed into pulp. Eventually she became so unmanageable, even striking at the milk bowl and splashing the contents over me, that I stopped the largactil, for I had been told that human beings sometimes become aggressive under the prolonged influence of sedatives. It helped a little when I opened the door to the annex and she had more space to move in, but even so she grew fiercer with every day. In one way I was glad of this, since I did not wish to spoil her wild instincts, but how was I to handle her during the time she had to be confined when she struck at me or retreated to the farthest corner when I brought her her food? Whity had always had the most beautiful, soft eyes; now they were murderously hard and her expression was full of hate. But why indeed should she like me now? In the past, she had only tolerated me as Pippa's friend and as her food provider. True, I still continued to feed her, but I had deprived her of her family and her freedom.

After a few days her leg was well enough for me to let her into the large compound. When I opened the door she made no attempt to leave the inner enclosure, and it was only after several hours that she dared to take a quick look at her new run, then she hurriedly returned to the familiar enclosure where she remained until the next day although the doors were open. Whity was reacting in a way that is typical of all wild animals who, after capture, cling to their catching crates as the only place they know rather than rushing into the bigger but strange enclosures of a zoo. This reaction is understandable but is often misinterpreted, especially by animal dealers who, to justify their trade, say that animals like small cages.

Poor Whity, could I expect her attitude toward me to improve in this larger compound so long as wire separated her from her family and her free life? All she now had was a better opportunity to run away from me, whom naturally she blamed for all these strange happenings.

Meanwhile, Pippa had brought the cubs gradually nearer to camp and now again lived at the tamarind anthill, where Mbili and Tatu had marvelous games on its low branches. Pippa herself never joined in their fun and was always subdued.

On the day I released Whity into the large compound, Pippa came within a mile of camp, which was nearer than she had been for a long time. This seemed a good opportunity to try to coax her to Whity so that they might comfort each other until I could unite them all again. All started well: the family was very hungry and eagerly followed the meat basket, but after a while they became suspicious and, sitting down every few yards, took two exasperating hours to reach a spot about 150 yards from camp, where they stayed put. Nothing would make them budge. I let Pippa sniff my shorts with Whity's scent on them, hoping this would entice her to come nearer. I called Whity's name and pointed toward her; I went to her enclosure, hoping that Whity would join me in calling for Pippa, but all I achieved was to make Pippa jump onto a tree and gaze toward the compound without coming a step nearer. In a last effort to keep her close to camp, I dropped the meat; they all pounced on it and, after quickly gulping it down, walked back to where they had come from. Desperate, I returned to Whity. She sat glued to the wire, staring at the plain. Hoping to divert her mind, I brought her milk, only to have it thrown into my face. I refilled the bowl and waited for her to come for her favorite drink. After an hour I lost patience and left; instantly she lapped it up.

I saw no other way of making the situation bearable for Whity than giving her a quarter of a tablet of largactil every day. She soon responded to this and allowed me to hand-feed her. Since I had failed to induce Pippa to come near Whity with a bait of meat, I had to find another device if I hoped to reunite the family again. It was impracticable to immobilize Whity because we were not sure whether Pippa would remain with her until she came around. She might even abandon her in her sedated state, believing that she was dead. I ordered a sound recorder and hoped, by putting Whity's call on the tape and playing it back to Pippa, that she would come to collect her daughter. Should this also fail I would have to tame poor Whity. To prepare for this alternative I ordered a harness so that I could train her to walk on a leash, also a football and some balloons for her to play with. In the meantime I made a paper ball and hung it from a string so that she could punch at it. I also wriggled a rag at her and rolled a small tire in front of her for her to catch. She made a few attempts to play but soon got bored with these lifeless toys. Cardboard boxes and egg cartons were more successful, and she spent a long time tearing them to shreds, but they, too, soon lost their novelty. She sat for hours staring out onto the plains, calling for Pippa or running up and down along the wire; she was especially active when she saw us going to her family. They had moved back to the place where Whity had been caught, but after we heard a lion whuffing during the night in that direction, they disappeared and we could not find them for three days.

For Whity's safety, I had to lock her up during the night in the small enclosure; this she resented bitterly. It was a cruel irony to have to tame this wild animal in the hope of giving her back to the wild. The most important thing for her was not to lose touch with the family, and we trusted that one day they would accept her. Our recent searches had given no clue as to the cheetahs' whereabouts.

On the evening of the fourteenth of March I could not induce Whity to go into her sleeping quarters, and she even allowed me to stroke her rather than leave the roof of the enclosure. She remained there until I went to bed. Later, when two lions roared, she made no sound but early in the morning I woke to hear her racing around, working off her pent-up energy. I asked Guitu to go and see if Pippa were back at the tamarind anthill; while he searched I fed Whity and tidied up her compound. She was surprisingly friendly and playfully interfered with my cleaning. Suddenly I heard Guitu coming back singing the little tune I had made up long ago when calling the family: "Pippa, Pippa, Pippalunka, Pippa Pippa Pippala, come-on—come-on—come-on, come-on, come-on," and sure enough, there came Pippa, Mbili, and Tatu, cantering to the rhythm of her song, and before I knew what was happening, Pippa rushed across the tree bridge and straight up to Whity's compound.

For a moment both stood puzzled, then they licked each other through the wire, purring. When the sisters appeared across the stream they craned their necks calling to Whity, and she answered them with a chirp. I opened the door, but at first Whity was too excited to notice it and, with arched neck, watched Pippa struggling against the wire. She passed the door several times until I managed at last to maneuver her to it, then out she shot. If ever there was a happy cheetah cub, it was Whity. With laughing eyes, she jumped

Cheetah family on termite hill

up at Pippa, licking and hugging her, overwhelmed with emotion, then, clinging to her mother, she followed her to the refrigerator. I had only some very smelly remains of goat, so I was not surprised that Pippa refused it. By now the other cubs had also come into camp and, overjoyed at seeing Whity again, rolled over and over her and tumbled around until they were exhausted. I was alarmed to see how thin Mbili and Tatu were compared to Whity, and when I took the smelly meat to them they gobbled it up to the last scrap. While they ate, I went to prepare the milk and Farex mixture, but on my return I found that Pippa was already moving off. Anxious not to lose her, the cubs had but a quick lap and followed.

During the next hours we could only trace spoor criss-crossing in opposite directions, then the day became too hot to follow the spoor. It seemed almost a miracle that we had been able to cure Whity without having tamed her and that Pippa had collected her in such a natural way before a long separation or Shifta activities might have made a reunion impossible.

These guerrillas had been active recently, and for some time I had been afraid that I might be asked to evacuate my camp. At tea-time we continued our search and at dusk found the family about a mile away. Whity was limping on one of her hind legs and often resting. As a result she was behind the others when they pounced on the goat carcass. When, after a while, she came to get her share, I was horrified to see her mother chase her away, cuff her, and snatch the meat out of her mouth, although Pippa had already had plenty to eat.

What could have happened? In the morning Whity had been absolutely fit and all the cheetahs had seemed so happy; why, then, should Pippa now behave so strangely? I took some meat to Whity but she only ate a little liver. I examined her legs and found no injury except that one hind leg seemed a little weak. Had I released her too soon, and had the long walk been too much for her? I guarded the family with a flashlight until they had eaten all they could and was relieved to see Mbili snuggling up to poor Whity and comforting her. Hoping that the limp was only a reaction to fatigue, we went home at 9 P.M.

During the following three days we searched for the family from morning until dusk without finding a trace of them. After sunset, tired from the fourth day's exhausting hunt, I had just asked Guitu to empty the water can when I spotted four cheetahs' heads above the grass near the road halfway to Kenmare. As far as I could see in the fading light, Whity was all right and all were now friendly but plainly very hungry. Leaving Guitu in charge, I returned to camp and got some meat and water, which I took back by car. By now it was pitch-dark but Guitu had maneuvered the cheetahs onto the road and they had walked part of the way back to camp. Since I did not want to risk a car's interfering with their meal, I got them off the road, and only just in time, for soon several General Service Unit trucks came along, returning from patrol. The cheetahs were very nervous eating in the dark and kept looking around even though I constantly scanned the surrounding area with my flashlight for predators. They ate hurriedly and soon moved away. At dawn they all reappeared in camp but, as we had no meat, went off along the road in the direction of Leopard Rock. Knowing how fast the General Service Unit always drive, I was anxious to get the cheetahs off the road, but, gamboling alongside it and lurking in the grass, they kept on returning to it. For about a mile we tried to outwit each other. Finally I got a goat from Kenmare, and this induced the family to follow us across the stream to their old haunts, where they were safe from traffic accidents.

On my return to camp I found a note from the General Service Unit Inspector informing me that no one was allowed to walk beyond Kenmare after 6 P.M. because the Shifta were very close; he also told me that additional troops had been summoned and were stationed at Leopard Rock in readiness to fight them. Luckily, this was the last big operation which the General Service Unit carried out around the Park. Not long afterward, when successful negotiations between Kenya and Somalia settled the Shifta problem and made peaceful co-operation between the two Governments possible, the platoon was withdrawn from Kenmare.

Pippa remained on the other side of the stream and moved gradually up to a beautiful parkland of large acacias where there were plenty of anthills for the cubs to play on. Whity was now fairly friendly with me, though she always took great care to keep Pippa between us. It was interesting that she now purred; she had never done this while she was in camp but had called nyam-nyam-nyam to express pleasure—a call we never heard again. Her eyes had regained their soft, warm look and she was absolutely fit. It was Mbili

The three cubs

Cub on "Kill Acacia"

whose condition now worried me. She had always been on the slender side, but since she was by far the longest in body and always ate well, I thought she simply needed more time to fatten up. Now her pelvic bones stuck out alarmingly; thinking that she might have hookworm, I succeeded in taking samples of her feces and sent them to the Vet to analyze. The result of the test was negative, and no other parasites had been discovered which could have been responsible for Mbili's skinny condition. Since it was impossible for me to take a blood smear from her ear, I could only feed her well and hope she would improve. She quickly realized that, from now on, she was priority number one and got into the habit of rushing up to me well ahead of her sisters so that I could give her titbits before they interfered. She also was extremely cunning at judging the best time to get food: when all the others were occupied in some other way, so that she would not have to fight for her meat. It seemed odd that she did not object to my taking ticks off her, or even rubbing my hand against her as she ate, yet if I dared to touch her any other time she spat and ran away. Whity only cuddled up to Pippa, but Mbili made friends with all of us and sometimes even provoked her mother's jealousy. Tatu remained as shy as ever but was rather a bully when it came to food.

Suddenly I developed pain around my waist which became so unbearable that I had to see the doctor at Nairobi. He diagnosed shingles, which needed a lengthy treatment. I did not like to leave the cheetahs alone for too long, so I stayed for only three days in the hospital, then I went back to camp where for several weeks I went on with the codeine.

CHAPTER

15

The Flood

ON MY RETURN I found the family had moved farther upstream and near a ridge which led in a curve several miles long toward Leopard Rock. Gradually it broadened to a plateau, and though it rose to not more than two hundred feet above the surrounding country, it offered a superb outlook across the plains which were flanked to the left by our stream and to the right by the Mulika, both running parallel to each other within a mile of the ridge. This was ideal cheetah country, though five miles from camp was quite a way for us to carry our heavy loads. Near the beginning of the ridge were several dry water pools covered with a thin, saline crust which, judging by the spoor around it, attracted many animals. These salt licks were overshadowed by a grove of doum palms which seemed to be the temporary home of a large troop of baboons. Up to now Pippa had succeeded in keeping her cubs safe from these dangerous creatures, and I was therefore alarmed when one morning we met only Pippa and Mbili near the place, but saw no sign of the other cubs. Pippa seemed unconcerned and tucked into the meat we had brought, but little Mbili wandered around restlessly, calling for her sisters and looking in the direction from which we heard the barkings of baboons. Following their cries, we saw these woolly clowns clustering on the palm trees around the salt licks; at our approach they dropped to the ground like ripe apples and raced to some distant trees, from which they watched us searching for the cubs. It took us two hours to discover Whity and Tatu tense with fear hiding in a palm thicket. I tried to calm them down while Guitu collected meat, but though they were hungry they took a long time to come into the open and eat. I hoped to coax Pippa back to her daughters; so I walked after her and found her stalking a small herd of Grant's gazelles which took her in the opposite direction to her cubs. To make things still worse, a downpour started and drenched us to the skin. But I was quite determined to reunite the family, so I sloshed through the morass until I finally succeeded in maneuvering all three cubs back to their mother. To keep the family together, I gave them the remaining meat, which Pippa seized so greedily that she mistook my arm for part of it and gave me a hearty bite.

We were about two hours' walk from camp, and by the time I had got the car and driven to Leopard Rock for a pencillin injection my glands were rather painful. For three days I had to continue treating them, as well as taking codeine to cure my shingles, and I did not feel too happy as I walked daily for six or seven hours trying to locate the cheetahs.

One morning, after a long search, we were guided by the agitated gaggling of guinea fowl to the top of the ridge where we found the family surrounded by a large flock. It was a comic sight to watch the cheeky guinea fowl stepping up to within a few inches of the cheetahs, chuckling and clucking to provoke them. At last Whity made a halfhearted rush into the feathery crowd, but she soon sat down and yawned. This puzzled me, as the family appeared to be hungry and quickly got into action when they saw the meat basket, but it seemed that a meal of guinea fowl did not attract them.

It was April and the short but heavy rains again flooded us. After one night's downpour we almost ran into a sleeping buffalo on our way to the cheetahs; we only noticed the tips of its horns when we were almost on top of the beast. Before we could retreat, he staggered to his feet, dripping with mud. He was a funny sight as he looked at us while lumps of wet earth fell off him. Since neither of us could run on the slippery ground, the situation was awkward until the mighty animal lumbered off, slithering and skidding comically as he made his way over the bog. Both of us landed on our bottoms many times in a most undignified fashion before we located the family two miles farther on. The cheetahs had found a large sand patch which connected the ridge with the Mulika stream and was the only dry ground in this soggy area. When we met them they were

A morning at the sand patch

stalking a ratel. As soon as Pippa saw the meat basket she gave up the hunt, but the cubs pursued the fierce beast until it slipped into a thicket where they could not follow. Recently I had noticed tapeworms in the feces of the cubs, and I therefore dosed the whole family with yomesam, two and a half tablets for each cub and three for Pippa. They took them easily as I had concealed them in meat. Later they had a great game snatching bits of goatskin from each other and swiping at each other's legs.

That night it rained without stopping. I was anxious to know how the cheetahs had reacted to their worming, but we had to wait till after lunch to investigate for only then did the ground dry a bit. We found the family waiting on their sand patch, hungry but otherwise fit. Only Mbili looked alarmingly thin. This was probably because she was by far the most nervous of the cubs and too high-strung to put on flesh as easily as her more relaxed sisters. I could only hope the worming would improve her general condition. All that day the sky was overcast and it was late by the time the sun broke through and warmed us up. It was lovely to see the cheetahs in the golden glow of the sinking sun, gobbling their meat until they could hold no more. We left them, knowing that they would not starve, even if the rains interfered with our feeding visits for some days.

During the next forty-eight hours it poured almost constantly, which made it impossible for us to walk across the swampy ground. When at last we succeeded in reaching the ridge and walked along its top, we found ourselves surrounded by jumping fish about six to eight inches long. They leapt from a shallow trickle caused by the rain, which ran across a swampy patch and petered out after twenty yards. Guitu splashed after them and, assuring me that they were excellent eating, picked up fifteen fish within a few minutes. I was puzzled to know how these fish had arrived at the top of the ridge. To my knowledge there was no stream anywhere near from which a flood could have carried them. Neither could they have been dropped by birds or poachers since there were far too many of them.

While Guitu went on fishing I scanned the country through my field glasses until I detected the cheetahs far away in the plain below. Carefully avoiding puddles and shaking their legs frequently to free them from mud, they came along as quickly as they could and were plainly very hungry. I was sorry that we had little food to offer them: to make the best of it I smashed the bones into pulp which the cubs tore out of my hand. When Pippa realized that she had lost her share, she walked away in a dignified manner. I tried to make her return for a few titbits, but it was a long time before she allowed me to stroke her.

Luckily, it did not rain that night so we were able to take a fresh goat carcass to them next morning. While they ate ravenously we went off to photograph the fish. But it had not rained, the trickle had dried up, and all were dead and lying in heaps of six to ten together in the mud. I was surprised that not a single one had been touched by birds or carnivores although they were easy to see. I took some pictures of Guitu holding the dead fish, then I collected a few specimens which, after preserving them with salt, I later sent to Nairobi for the Fishery Department. They were identified as *Labeo gregorii* which occur in the Tana River and its tributaries. As they cannot live out of water, no one could explain how they had traveled to the top of the ridge, the nearest tributary being more than a mile away and 150 feet below the place where we had found them.

The cubs were now eight months old and losing the last of their deciduous teeth. On the twentieth of April their canines fell out; this handicapped them when they were eating because they could neither hold the meat nor tear off a big lump. The molars were the only teeth they had left for chewing; these must have been well developed since we had seen them breaking through two months earlier. The cubs were most endearing as they slowly munched the small pieces of meat I prepared for them and made smacking noises as they sucked them through their gaps. Pippa took advantage of their handicap, and if I had not protected the cubs' share they would have starved. However cleverly I tried to hide the meat, Pippa often got jealous and, misusing her authority over her children, walked off, calling the cubs to follow her. Reluctantly they obeyed, stopping frequently and watching me with hungry eyes as I carried their meat after them. When they could, they gobbled it up quickly before Pippa could interfere. Mbili in particular needed my help, and my plots to give her extra rations brought us daily closer together. I found it very difficult not to spoil her, for she was a charmer, though still very skinny in spite of her glossy coat. On the twenty-fifth I noticed that Mbili and Whity's lower incisors had come through, and from then onward their eating improved.

Meanwhile the increasingly heavy rains made the ground so impossibly soggy that it took us up to three and four hours to reach the family, by now marooned on their sand patch. Though it was easy enough for us to find them on the open ground, the kites could also spot them and, knowing about our daily food convoy, they hovered persistently near the cheetahs and even dived at us as we carried the meat basket. One morning we found the place churned up into a morass by a herd of buffalo. The family had cleared out. It took us three days to find them. They were under the overhanging branches of an acacia near the ridge from where they overlooked the sand patch without being themselves so easily seen. While I fed them, Guitu and Stanley settled at some distance, to guard us against any danger. Suddenly Whity craned her neck and, following her gaze, I saw a buffalo approaching steadily. All the cheetahs sat up erect as ninepins watching the huge bull grazing along, until he came uncomfortably close to the two men. Since they were obviously unaware of his presence, I yelled. Never have I seen a man react as fast as Guitu did. He picked up a stone, hurled it at the head of the buffalo, and continued his bombardment of the swerving beast, until it trotted up the ridge as fast as it could and disappeared. I was weak with laughter and only sorry that I had not had time to film the four cheetahs peering at the buffalo.

During the following days it went on raining, and we found it increasingly difficult to carry our cumbersome loads over the long distance. I appreciated the way in which Guitu and Stanley put up with all the drudgeries and was all the more grateful because they got little thanks for their efforts from the cheetah family, who barely allowed them to drop the meat, and if either of them dared to move, even at some distance, the cubs growled, spat, and even charged them.

One night at this time seemed darker than any I had yet experienced in Africa, and frequent lightning gave warning of a storm. Suddenly it started to pour as if a tap had been opened, and the downpour continued with such violence that I became alarmed. For hours there was no remission; the thunder and lightning increased and the rapidly rising stream roared. Normally it runs sixteen feet below the camp, but now it had risen to the level of our site and was a raging torrent, carrying debris and flooding the huts two feet deep. Wading in the icy water and drenched by the rain, we hurriedly carried heavy boxes containing valuable gear into the store hut, which stood on higher ground, while our tents collapsed over us and everything mobile was floated away. Our efforts to rescue our belongings were all the more exhausting because all of us had lost our shoes in the sucking mud and were staggering knee-deep in water without light. We were hit by logs and wreckage while trying to balance our loads above the flood. At last we could no longer move and collapsed onto a heap of soaking possessions and waited for daylight.

But it was impossible just to shiver in the dark sitting on a table with legs crossed to keep them above water, so I lit a kerosene lamp and started to read a book which had been sent me so that I might supply a quotation to help its promotion. Fascinated, I followed the experiences of Evelyn Ames on her safari through some of the East African Game Parks which she recorded appropriately as *A Glimpse of Eden*. Her delightful descriptions were a great contrast to my present surroundings, for she only knew the sunny side of Africa; all the same, her book kept me pleasantly diverted from my present misery. By dawn the flood had receded and we were able to spread out our things to dry and to repair our camp. Stiff with cold, I had never enjoyed hot tea as much as I did the cup which the cook now offered me. How he had been able to kindle a fire in this quagmire was beyond my imagination. But however uncomfortable we were, I feared the cheetahs might be in a still worse plight, so as soon as it was dry enough to move, we plodded along to help them.

How hungry they were I could judge by the sticky hair I saw around Pippa's teats, showing that they had again been suckled by her starving cubs. On our way we did not see one animal of the smaller species which they could have killed, and I wondered how wild predators who had no feeding help survived in these swampy conditions. As soon as we returned to camp, Guitu asked for leave. I could sympathize with him for being fed up with the weather but was surprised that he should insist on leaving us now, knowing that I was more than ever dependent on his help. Luckily, all turned out for the best since our friend, Local, was available and joined us on the following day. The sporting old rascal came just in time to share one of our grimmest periods. Although we had fires burning day and night, it was forty-eight hours before the ground inside the huts was dry, and then it was soon soaked again by another flood. Once more we had to move all valuables. We soon became adept at this exercise, for during the next week we had two more moves. Meru had never suffered such heavy rains for thirty years.

George was in Nairobi, and during his absence young Arun drove the Land-Rover into a ditch and broke the axle, so he was without transport. When George returned in the late afternoon he stopped for a short time at my camp, but he was in a hurry to reach home before another downpour messed up the road. Soon after he left it began to rain unceasingly. After dark I sat in the soggy studio and listened to the radio while the drumming of the rain drowned out everything else except the noise of the thunder. It was a night on which you would not wish your worst enemy to have to move about. Suddenly the door opened and George appeared; drenched to the skin, his face strained with exhaustion, he collapsed into a chair. On his way home he had to drive over the one and only bridge inside the Park which crossed the Rojoweru. It was a wooden bridge and had lately become very dilapidated; indeed, when driving over its rattling planks I always felt as if I were playing some huge xylophone. Now it had collapsed and George had crashed through. By a miracle his Land-Rover had stuck in the angle of the broken bridge, just out of reach of the raging torrent. He had managed to climb out through the window and scramble onto the bank and, grateful to be alive, had temporarily abandoned the car. Then he had walked the twelve miles to my camp without light or rifle, in the howling storm, with only lightning to guide him, while thunder mingled with lion whuffings. By now it was 10 P.M. and raining harder than ever. If we meant to rescue the car before the flooded river carried it away we had not one minute to lose. George changed quickly into some dry clothes of mine and ate a hot supper, then we drove off to Leopard Rock for help.

Slithering for ten miles from ruts into ditches, it took us two hours to reach our destination. There, with the help of the Park Warden we were able to organize a convoy of two trucks, two Land-Rovers, and a tractor, manned by every available person. Taking winches, jacks, cables, ropes, and shovels, we started to churn along the soggy road. Five miles from my camp I left the convoy in case we should have to make another move. I was lucky to reach home without getting stuck. Less lucky were the rest of the party, who spent most of the night digging each other out and finally had to walk the last few miles loaded with axes, cables, and winches, to haul the car from its precarious position. This operation took the whole of the next day and was completed just before the next flood carried the remains of the bridge away. George's camp was now completely cut off from Leopard Rock and from my camp, as the only cement fording across the Rojoweru was under deep water and no plane could land on the black cotton soil near his camp. My constant worry as to how he would be able to communicate if an emergency arose did not ease my own anxieties.

Kenmare Lodge was on the bank of the Rojoweru and as liable to be flooded as my camp. One night the boma where our goats were kept after dark and which was partly under water was attacked by five hyenas. It must have been easy for them to pull the rotting fence out of the soggy ground; they killed thirteen goats. That meant not only a financial loss of forty pounds but also the end of our meat supply for the cheetahs, since George could not get to us with a kill. Hoping to give the family a last good meal, we took one of the least mauled carcasses along while it was still fresh. After walking a few miles, I noticed four round ears above the grass within some fifty yards—lions. I motioned to the men to go in the opposite direction and, watching the lions through my field glasses, I stayed in the rear with Local and his rifle, thus protecting Stanley with the meat basket, who was walking in front of us. Attracted by the scent of the carcass, the lions followed, their bellies close to the ground. They were soon joined by a third. Luckily, this disagreeable situation came to an abrupt end when a large herd of buffaloes suddenly broke cover ahead of us and rushed off with the lions after them. We continued unmolested until we reached the cheetahs near the sand patch. They must have had far more rain than we had had in camp and looked pathetically bedraggled as they came hungrily toward us, but Pippa and Tatu sniffed disgustedly at the carcass and did not touch it: only Whity and Mbili gorged themselves. Meanwhile Local kept a lookout for the lions. And, sure enough, there they were again—all six ears. We threw stones in their direction until the cubs had finished their meal; when we saw the lions disappear up the ridge, we collected the remains of the meat and went home. Since the lions had chosen our usual route along the ridge for their retreat we had to go another way, which involved crossing the Mulika. As we groped carefully for a foothold, a small crocodile shot away from under our feet.

This gave poor Local such a fright that he fell into the water and hurt his ribs. Wet and limping, he remarked good-naturedly that he had had quite enough excitement today, to which we all agreed.

Our trials were not over yet. That night, utterly worn out, I watched the stream rising until we had no choice but to move everything to higher ground—for the fifth time. Exasperated by these moves, the cook went on strike and, saying he was ill, remained in bed while we got drenched and exhausted moving things between the huts, which stood like islands in a lake. By now I was not sure which of the two was the worse—bush fire or floods. Both were terrifying. All morning we worked hard to get our things dry again before we started out to find the cheetahs. Since I did not want to waste our last meat, we carried the carcass to the sand patch but could not find a trace of the family. After some time we understood the reason for their absence, for we saw a growling lion on the ridge who, without doubt, was one of the three we had met yesterday. Disheartened, we turned home with our smelly load until we came within two miles of the camp, where we saw fresh cheetah spoor along the road. Before I knew what was happening I was almost knocked over by Pippa, and all the cubs came bounding to the food basket. The cubs were hungry enough to gulp down the high meat, but Pippa stood aloof, although she had not eaten for three days. All my efforts to make her eat only resulted in her turning away whenever I came near, until she walked off into the dark with her young.

That evening was a very happy one for the men and for me, because it looked as though our long, exhausting walks had come to an end. However clever Pippa had been to find a refuge on the sand patch during these terrible rains, it had become almost impossible for us to walk the twelve miles, and we all blessed the three lions for having helped to move the family closer to the camp after their forty days' residence near the ridge. The most important thing now was to get more goats, since only one had survived the hyena massacre. So I hired a car from Leopard Rock and sent the cook with enough money to buy ten more. I expected him to be back in two days' time. Meanwhile, we killed the last of our goats, hoping it would keep the family close to camp. But by next morning the cheetahs had vanished. The following four days forced us to make the most exhausting searches we had undertaken since the rains began. Pippa had by now staked out a territory of some twenty square miles which it was possible for us to cover in good weather but very trying to investigate under the present conditions, with our muddy feet covered with red patches and sores like trench feet.

To top it all, one afternoon we got stuck in a bog, and I remember few occasions when I have been in such a panic. Five miles from camp we suddenly found ourselves sinking deeper with every step. Holding hands, Local and I supported each other while heaving our feet out from the knee-deep mud and grasping for any bush in reach to lift us a step forward. We lost our canvas shoes in the sucking mud, thorns pierced our feet, and we were unable to extract them because of the layer of sludge that covered them. It was dark by the time we got clear of this wet hell, and it was lucky that we knew the area well and did not lose our bearings on our way home in the pitch-darkness.

Next day Pippa crossed the tree bridge, leaving her cubs on the far bank. When I caught up with them I found them in excellent condition and not hungry, owing no doubt to having killed a Grant's gazelle whose remains we found under a large acacia. This "Kill Acacia" soon became their favorite feeding place: its low branches were ideal to climb and from them they could look across the plain unseen by vultures, which could not spot the meat below. I was glad to have the family so near to camp but was maddened by the thought that they must have been there all these days, while we had exhausted ourselves looking for them everywhere except here, and this because we had not been able to cross the stream until today. How they had got onto the far side I found out much later when I discovered a natural bridge some two miles upriver where the rains had sent a tree crashing across the water. Pippa seemed glad to be home again and responded most affectionately to my petting. Yet later in the afternoon I was not able to find the family although I called and looked for them until it got dark. Then Pippa appeared and rubbed her head against me, purred, and guided Local and me a long way to a small forest patch where her cubs were hiding.

For a week they remained around this area, even though one night we heard some lions very close. We usually fed the cheetahs at the Kill Acacia, which was in view from camp. We could see them sitting in the branches, waiting for their meal. They took less than two hours to finish a whole carcass, and Whity was an expert at opening it below the tail. All the cubs had by now learned to eat the tripe and intestines, which they sucked in spaghetti fashion, thus squeezing out the droppings. Pippa was by far the greediest and often tried to tear the meat out of her children's mouths, but they stood their ground, and, though the stalemates were often exasperatingly long, they never surrendered their share nor showed a submissive attitude toward their mother. Only Mbili sometimes walked away when the clouting became too fierce and thus failed to get her food. I therefore increased her extra ration, hoping she would soon be strong enough to stand up to the challenge of a rival. She was physically the weakest, yet she outwitted her sisters when it came to recovering a goatskin from a tricky place high up in a tree. I loved her funny ways of showing off and our bond grew stronger, for of course she realized her privileged position, and though she did not like me to touch her she often lay close to me and looked at me. One day I took my sketchbook along, but all the cheetahs reacted even more unfavorably to being drawn than Elsa had done. They seemed to know the difference between being looked at as a model and being watched with personal interest. All I was able to put on paper were a few sleeping cheetahs with their backs turned toward me.

At last the rains eased off and, with the exception of a few showers, did not interfere with our routine. Compared to the last weeks, we led a life of leisure until the family disappeared again and kept us well exercised for three days. On one of our searches we came at sunset to the Rojoweru. I loved this beautiful river, especially at the time of day when animals came for a drink and the river bush was tinted with a golden glow. I was listening to the peaceful bubbling of the water when I heard a strange rattling noise and soon discovered the quills of two porcupines sticking out of the undergrowth. Instantly Local and I froze. We watched the animals feeding on their way to the river, munching noisily and nosing leaves and grasses. They came within six feet when one of them noticed us. Terrified, it turned around, all its quills rattling in alarm, and passed so close between Local and me that we could easily have touched it. Puzzled by the behavior of its friend, the other porcupine came to within three feet, but as we stood still it did not detect us. It looked and looked, with its minute eyes, then circled undecidedly three times before it hurriedly joined the other. I knew very little about porcupines except that, even to lions, their quills can prove fatal. These otherwise harmless animals are nocturnal, and so I was amazed at their poor sense of smell.

On "Kill Acacia"

Siesta

My only other experience with the amusing creatures happened a few years ago while we were living at Isiolo. Close to our house was a burrow inhabited by porcupines. Some had the normal black-white quills, others black and terra-cotta red. It was the first time that porcupines with this unusual pigmentation had been observed, and they aroused great interest among zoologists. After some trouble we were able to send a pair of them to the London Zoo, where they received a lot of publicity, but after a short while their reddish pigmentation changed to the normal white. So quickly and surprisingly did this happen that several authorities were consulted, and the porcupines were then fed on plants that contained keratin until they recovered their sensational coloring. Though it was apparently possible to influence the pigmentation of quills by dieting, the problem of our Isiolo porcupines was not thereby solved, for they shared the same burrow and were eating the same food as the others, yet they had developed different coloring. For the last few days we had found no trace of our family.

When, after five days, the family turned up at the Kill Acacia, we were amazed when we tracked their spoor back to the Kenmare plains; we could not understand why they had hunted in this jungle, since their bellies were full. Stranger still, next morning they headed there again. We caught up with them crossing the rivulet two miles downstream. Hoping to entice them to the dry plain near camp, I waved the meat at them. Pippa promptly jumped in one long leap back to our side of the stream. The cubs watched her anxiously, but they could not make the distance and splashed into the water, except for Mbili, who searched for a narrower place from which she jumped across without wetting herself. This was the first time I had watched a cub jumping across; up to now, rather than risk falling in, they had waded through, as the water here was shallow enough to watch out for crocodiles. I never saw the family playing in the water—a contrast to Elsa and her cubs, who had enjoyed splashing about and swimming in much deeper water and often spent hours cooling themselves in the shallows. The only time Pippa swam was in the ocean when we were filming *Born Free,* and then she ventured into the sea only to follow me, never on her own initiative.

If cheetahs differ from lions in this respect they are like them in their affection for each other, at least as long as the cubs remain with their mother. Pippa's children made a well-balanced and happy team: Whity the most intelligent, Tatu the wildest and most independent, and Mbili the most friendly, the greatest explorer and most comic clown. They kept us constantly on the alert, especially Mbili, for whom any camera case, milk can, meat basket, hat, or binoculars hanging on a tree were, in her opinion, put there only for her to play with. Cunningly, she waited until we were off guard, then seized the object and shook it provokingly at her sisters, with the result that all raced off into the plain, scattering our possessions in the high grass. We chased after them trying to recover our things before they were chewed up. Hunting was still a problem for them, because almost everywhere the grass was now too high for the cheetahs to spot a prey and only the heads of waterbucks or ostriches were visible gliding above the grass, and these were far too large for a cheetah to cope with. If we did not provide meat, Mbili soon became very thin. The hungry vultures now followed the cheetahs everywhere, thus warning any prey of the predators' presence, and this added to their difficulties. Even the lions seemed to find it hard to get a kill and rarely came around, so I was surprised when I was wakened one night by a low growl and put the flashlight on just in time to stop a lion from crossing the tree bridge and walking into my tent. Promptly the family had cleared out. We found their pugmarks two days later along the road which passed the camp. When we caught up with them they were extremely hungry, and I could judge by their appetite how determined Pippa was to keep her young away from camp, even though she knew that I usually had meat there. A week later she led her hungry cubs in a close circle around the camp without calling in for meat. We saw them again late in the afternoon and they followed us home to collect food but remained five hundred yards from camp. It was dark by then, but we were obliged to carry the meat to Pippa as she made it plain that she would not bring the cubs a step nearer. The only time she had taken them into camp was when Whity was confined there, and even then they had stayed for only a moment. The fact that, as far as her cubs were concerned, she allowed only Stanley, Local, and myself to come near was satisfactory since it showed that the previous nine months and our long, exhausting walks into the bush to find the family on their self-chosen territory were now showing results and that the cubs were going wild, as I had hoped.

Family on termite hill

The three sisters

On the nineteenth of June they celebrated their ten months' birthday by chasing a one-horned oryx. I watched, fascinated, since these large antelopes are feared by most predators because of their long, straight, pointed horns, which can be fatal to their enemies. This oryx, which had one horn broken off and looked like the legendary unicorn, seemed to know that the cubs were only out to play and did not take them seriously when they dashed toward it. Later, Pippa became interested in a few ostriches which appeared on the far side of the stream. While she sat on an anthill, watching the birds intently, Mbili was busy trying to get at the full water can which I had hung high up on a tree. Twisting and jerking her slender body and jumping repeatedly, she managed to hit it down and promptly got a shower. Surprised, she looked at us, but when she saw us laughing she went on hitting the can as it lay on the ground and danced around it. Watching the family enjoying themselves, I remembered Pippa's ten months' birthday on the coast when she was living the life of a spoiled pet, and when her only fun had been a run along the beach on a long rope. How glad I was to see her enjoying her freedom with her cubs, all doing exactly what they liked.

Late in the afternoon I took a stroll along the road and came within three hundred yards of the ostrich which Pippa had spotted in the morning. I had seen this family of eight half-grown chicks and their parents many times. Although the young were still of a uniformly brownish color, they were easy to recognize because one chick was smaller than the rest. After I had watched them for a while through my field glasses they suddenly cocked their tails erect and, ruffling the fluffy feathers at the bases of their necks, stared in my direction. Looking around, I found Pippa and her cubs crouching in the grass behind me, their bellies to the ground, as they crossed the road, stalking the ostriches. After a few yards the cubs all stayed in one place and craned their necks while Pippa wriggled cautiously toward the birds. Trembling with excitement, the cubs remained absolutely still for what seemed an endless time, until I saw the ostriches break up into two groups, one running right, the other left, except for the small chick, which circled around and around until it flopped into the grass. Assuming that Pippa was killing it, I waited for ten minutes and then walked slowly to the place, while the cubs remained still immobile. I should have taken this as

Mbili and the water can

Cubs playing the skin game

a hint that Pippa had not yet completed the kill or she would have called prr-prr to the cubs, or released them by some invisible signal. When I came close to where the chick had dropped, it suddenly got up and, stiffly spraying out the wing feathers like fans, walked slowly away, exposing a terrible bleeding wound in its right hindquarter. There was no sign of Pippa. The badly mauled chick moved on into a grove of acacia trees where some of the scattered ostriches reappeared, then all went off into the bush. The light was failing rapidly and even with my field glasses I could no longer see what was happening, so I ran after the birds but had to give up when it became too dark. Usually, when Pippa missed a kill, she returned to her cubs, and they always remained behind as though obeying an order while she was stalking. But when I heard the cubs calling in high-pitched chirps, I guessed that she was still pursuing the ostrich.

Up to now I had never seen Pippa actually killing any prey and had only found her at a kill she had already made. But I knew that she suffocated her victims. This is the method predators prefer as it insures the quickest death without risking injury from the horns of the prey. If they cannot get at the throat they envelop the muzzle of the victim or, should this be impossible, attack at some vulnerable spot. To attack an ostrich by its throat would involve risking being stripped open by its powerful feet, so Pippa had obviously chased the chick in circles, swiping at its legs until it fell, then probably she had sat on it, holding it down and attacking its hindquarters, which the bird could not defend with its head. My arrival had interfered with the kill, and I could only hope that by now Pippa had succeeded in putting the ostrich out of its misery. As soon as it was light next morning we looked for traces of the kill but found nothing, so when, after two hours, Pippa and her cubs appeared from the acacia grove, with empty bellies, I assumed that the chick had got away.

CHAPTER

16

Impia

FOR THE NEXT FEW DAYS the family did not move far, being too full
of the meat of some zebra which George's lions had killed. On the
twenty-fifth of June I left them with bulging bellies, within half a
mile of camp. On my return I found the Park Warden, who had
brought with him a young cheetah cub which had been caught during a buffalo hunt at Nyeri. The Warden of that area had sent it to
me in the hope that Pippa might adopt it, as otherwise it would have
to go to the Animal Orphanage at Nairobi and ultimately to a zoo.
I peeped at the cub through the feeding hole of the wooden box in
which it had been placed four days earlier, at the time of its
capture. The cub growled and spat at me; as far as I could judge
by its teeth, it was not more than seven months old. We discussed
how to arrange a meeting between it and Pippa's family, who
fortunately were within reach of a car. Since neither of us knew if
Pippa would accept the newcomer, we could not let it go free until
we were sure that she would adopt it, for it was much too young
to look after itself. We must therefore move the cub from its
solid wooden box into Pippa's wired traveling crate and place
this near the family so that they could see each other and we could
watch their reactions. To do this, we had first to improvise a sliding
door to the wired crate, place both crates with their sliding doors
facing each other, then put some meat inside the wired box and,
after opening both doors, hope that the hungry cub would go to it,
for it had hardly eaten since its capture. While working on the box,

the Africans referred to the newcomer as "Impia," meaing in Swahili "New," and thus gave the young female cheetah her name.

When everything was ready, and both boxes stood door to door, we covered the wired box with blankets except for the side opposite the door, hoping that the view into the bush, as well as the meat, might induce Impia to enter it. Then we opened the doors and hid. Nothing happened except that Impia gave deep growls and retreated still farther from the door. After we had waited in silence for forty minutes, the cub inched herself cautiously toward the meat. Instantly we closed the door behind her and gave her time to calm down. Then we lifted her, silently, into a Land-Rover and drove within five hundred yards of the place where I left the family earlier in the morning. Walking on alone, I found them still sleepy after their heavy meal, so I sat next to Pippa, petting her for a while before I signaled to the Warden. He drove slowly to within a hundred yards of us and then for the rest of the distance he, Local, and Stanley carried the heavy crate near to the family.

The cheetahs watched all this most suspiciously and seemed extremely puzzled when they heard Impia's growls. As soon as the crate was on the ground and the blankets were removed, the men returned to the car. Now the responsibility rested with me. All would be well if Impia were instantly adopted by Pippa, but if she were resented I would have to keep her confined at my camp until she was tame enough to follow me around: I could then try to unite her with our cheetahs or, should this fail, train her to become wild again when she was old enough to look after herself. While I weighed the pros and cons of these alternatives, Pippa looked with interest at Impia, who chirped in a friendly manner, moved toward her, and sat down a short distance from the crate. Whity and Mbili were also intrigued: without any snarling or spitting, they approached Impia purring although she was stinking and covered with her excrement. Finally, Tatu too came along and, like her sisters, put her face close to the box, while Impia struggled against the wire in an endeavor to join the cubs. Since all the cheetahs were so friendly and seemed to like each other, I said a quick prayer—and opened the door.

After a few seconds Impia walked out quietly, went ten yards, stood still, looked around, and waited for the cubs to follow. Together they returned to Pippa and all played in a large circle around the car. Once Impia got left behind and chirped; to this Pippa responded with prr-prr, until the little cub caught up again. I joined the men inside the car and for half an hour watched the cheetahs making friends. As they chased each other around the bushes, little Impia got lost and called in distress. Mbili rushed to her rescue and brought her near to Pippa, who gradually led the cubs toward the road, where all of them soon disappeared in the high grass. The Warden and I looked at each other; it seemed too good to be true. We then got the crate and waited for two hours to give the cheetahs time to leave the road so that the Warden could drive home without frightening Impia. I could hardly wait until next morning to know if all was well, but we had to search from dawn to dusk before finding Pippa and her cubs about a mile from where we had left them.

Slowly they came across the plain, Whity and Mbili looking repeatedly back as if waiting for Impia, then they all settled on the road. Pippa moved about undecidedly, then she passed us without showing any interest and took her cubs back into the plain. I thought that it might take some time for Impia to get used to us and hoped that, meanwhile, hunger would bring her to the meat I intended to drop daily for her near the family. Early next morning Local went ahead spooring and found not only Impia's pugmarks but saw her walking on the road about a mile from where she had been released. Unfortunately, at this moment a truck appeared and the cub bounced off toward the Mulika plain where Local lost her among a patch of bushes. Soon afterward Stanley and I arrived by car with our heavy load. We searched the area without result and then searched for three hours only to find the family at the spot where Local had lost Impia. The cubs seemed far more interested in a bush nearby than in the meat and kept on looking in this direction, so I dropped some meat halfway to the bush. After making sure that our cheetahs had eaten to bursting point and were too full to bother about Impia's share, we left. Mbili was up a tree, apparently looking for Impia.

When we returned at teatime we saw no meat, no cheetahs, nor any spoor to lead us to them. By next morning Pippa and her cubs had moved across the road to the stream where they had found an ideal lay-up under a shady bush close to a salt lick. This place had been rather muddy during the rains, and now we always referred

Tatu and Whity

to it as "Mud Tree." It was about two miles from camp and soon became a favorite playground, made more attractive to them because, since the rains, a fallen tree provided a bridge across the stream to the Gambo plains. We found the cubs all looking with concentration in the same direction, so we dropped a lot of meat for them and left some for Impia a little farther off. Of course, by doing this we risked attracting other predators, but it was the only way to provide food for Impia till she was ready to accept our presence. Anxiously we went back at teatime, when we found only a bone left over from the cheetahs' feast. On our walk home we stopped a car whose driver told us he had just seen a cheetah cub crossing the road, going to the place where Impia had been released. As I knew of no other cheetah cub in the vicinity at that time, I assumed this to be Impia; if so, she must have walked two miles since morning.

Next day we found only the spoor of our family around the Mud Tree and lost it in the river bush, while Impia's pugmarks led from the Mud Tree half a mile along the road and then turned to the stream. Why were they splitting up? The following morning we traced her spoor along the road to within a short distance of the place of her release, and found Pippa and her cubs two miles in the opposite direction beyond the Mud Tree. Judging by the behavior of Pippa's cubs, little Impia had been close to the family for the first three days, but for the last three she had moved alone two miles between the place of her release, the Mud Tree, and the stream. I had no proof that she had eaten during these six days. Adding the four days from her capture to her arrival here, during which she had been on hunger strike inside the box, the poor cub might have had no food for ten days.

Tormented by the thought of Impia's starving to death, I drove to Leopard Rock and suggested to the Warden that we should trap her and look after her at my camp until she was old enough to be turned wild. He was more optimistic than I was, believing that she could survive on her own, but seeing how distressed I was, he ordered the Park's only trapping crate to be got from a farm where it was at present set up to catch a cattle-killing leopard. Hoping that Impia would still be alive when the crate arrived, we continued our search next morning. To my great relief, we saw her walking toward us along the road near the place of her release, but she turned off into the grass as soon as she spotted us. This was better than I had hoped for, the more so as a few moments later Pippa and her cubs appeared. Quickly I sent Local to collect meat and meanwhile guided the family off the road and in the direction in which Impia had bolted. When we reached a patch of trees we fed the cheetahs. As soon as their bellies were bulging, I dropped a generous meal for Impia a short distance away and left. However grateful I was to know that she was alive and still in contact with Pippa, I knew I was powerless to ensure that she would be the one to eat this meat, and this was most depressing.

That afternoon we left the cheetahs alone, because I feared our presence might interfere with their still delicate relationship, but I started off at dawn next day to look for them. Approaching the place where we had left the family, we saw some vultures dispersing, and at that moment Pippa and her cubs appeared. Knowing how quickly the birds would disappear into space, we left the family and went in their direction, trying to keep our bearings in the densely wooded bush. I searched every shrub for remains of a kill and became more and more anxious. Although there was no evidence that these vultures had any connection with Impia, I was harrowed by visions of poor, emaciated Impia getting weaker and weaker until death released her from a lingering agony, and this in spite of the fact that all the cheetahs had behaved in such a friendly way when we had introduced them to each other; I blamed myself for having been too rash, only now realizing that Pippa's friendly attitude to Impia might not have meant her willingness to share her food with her. I had acted as I did, hoping to save the wild cub the year-long ordeal of being tamed and then turned wild again, but I should never have risked her release while she was dependent on me for her food. She might have had to pay for my mistake by a slow death.

While I searched desperately for traces of the kill, the vultures soared higher and higher and went out of our view, taking with them the secret of whose earthly remains they were carrying toward heaven. Suppressing my forebodings, but with faith that Impia was still alive, we continued our search. Spooring in the high grass was often very difficult, and it was only on the road that we could reliably identify her pugmarks. Until now she had walked up and down it for about four miles and had remained within the adjoining plains which were bordered on one side by the Mulika, parallel to the road and within a mile of it, and on the other side by our stream; between the two there was a strip of open bush country four miles long and two miles wide. As long as Impia moved within this area she would at least have water. Next, we had to decide on a suitable spot to set the trap. We found a tree along the road halfway between the Mud Tree and the place of Impia's release, and attached a pulley to its overhanging branches. When, next day, the trap arrived, we placed it in a position which allowed us to open its door by pulley from inside the car. We did this in case we should catch a lion. Of course Pippa's family might also find the trap, and if two of the cubs entered it simultaneously the one behind might be killed by the released door crashing on its back. With this in mind we decided not to set the trap until we found Impia's spoor and, meanwhile, hoped to lead the family away from the area.

Although we camouflaged the box with greenery and made it almost inconspicuous, our cheetahs soon discovered it, and nothing we could do would make them budge from this suspicious-looking "bush." Meanwhile we searched for Impia from dawn to dusk. Each day I became more worried, even though Local tried to comfort me by saying that Impia might survive on squirrels, rats, small birds, or even frogs and dung-beetles. But when, after ten days, we had not found a trace of her, I resigned myself to believing that she was by now either independent of our help or beyond it. Although herbivorous animals, such as antelope, sometimes adopt orphans of their own kind, I had never known this to happen among predators in the wild state, and this should have been sufficient warning to me not to attempt such an experiment. No doubt one of the main reasons for the difference is the fact that predators have to work hard to feed themselves, and therefore resent an extra mouth to share their food with. To what extent their instinct to survive predominates over their maternal instinct I only now realized, and my misinterpretation of Pippa's friendly reaction to Impia may well have caused her to become the victim of a cruel death. On the ninth of July I returned the trap.

CHAPTER

17

Pippa Widens Her Territory

DURING THOSE WORRISOME DAYS, one morning when we were feeding Pippa and her cubs nine elephants with four small calves emerged from the bush close to us. Without breaking a stick or snapping a twig they moved so noiselessly that we were taken by surprise and had only just time to run away. Aroused by our movement and scent, the elephants seemed equally surprised and, huddling together, screaming, and raising their trunks, they tested for scent in all directions; then they crashed, trumpeting loudly, back into the bush. During all this pandemonium, the four cheetahs hardly stopped eating and seemed surprised that we should have run away. I envied their nonchalance during the next weeks when we often had to dodge small herds, or worse, single bull elephants who loitered during their migration in the same area as our cheetahs.

One morning we approached a place we had investigated half an hour earlier and saw the sky dotted with vultures arriving from every direction. Following them to the place of their descent, we found our cheetahs, panting, with bloated bellies and licking their bloodstained faces. The cubs were much too full to get up, and only Pippa dragged herself along and, with swaying belly, guided us about a hundred yards to what might have been a battlefield between herself and a half-grown ostrich, of which only the pelvic bones, the two feet, and a few vertebrae remained. I can only describe Pippa's expression as proud when she looked now at us, and then at her kill. She must have killed and eaten the ostrich during the half hour since we had passed the place, for the vultures, who are not slow to spot a kill, had just arrived. I shared Pippa's pride at having tackled such a formidable prey and was touched by her wish to show it to us; this seemed to be the only possible reason for her having walked the hundred yards, knowing that she would only find the bare bones which there was no need to guard against vultures.

The plain around here was perfect cheetah country with scattered thornbush and umbrella acacias, so I was not surprised that our cheetahs liked it so much and constantly returned to it. We called the place the "Ostrich Plain." The cubs had endless fun climbing up the trees and every day invented new tricks and games. They were well aware how much we enjoyed their antics and seemed to go on clowning just to make us laugh. Mbili was usually the leader, and after the family had finished eating she straddled bits of goat-skin which she pulled around as an invitation to a game. I was expected to chase after her, to get hold of the skin, and swing it onto a branch. If I succeeded, all three cubs climbed up after it and, cramped together at precarious angles, competed in pulling it down. If it fell to the ground, I had to grab it quickly while the cubs danced around and jumped at me as if I were a tree, and I could consider myself lucky if I managed to throw it up again before I was dripping with blood. Of course, they did not mean to hurt me and only scratched me accidentally in their excitement to get the skin. Pippa occasionally joined in the game and, to prove that she was still the boss, climbed much higher up the trees than her cubs could. She was very happy when I made a fuss over her, and rubbed my hand, but she purred only when we were well beyond earshot of her cubs.

They were now not quite eleven months old and were starting to become more independent of Pippa. Sniffing into holes or chasing after birds, they wandered off and sometimes stayed away for two to three hours. Though Mbili was the most adventurous on these occasions, she was also the most concerned to keep the family together. If one of her sisters roamed too far away she called persistently, prr-prr, until they were reunited; then she cuddled close to each in turn and all purred happily together. Mbili was obviously the pet of the family, and on the few occasions when she was nervous all would surround her protectively and lick her until she was reassured. She was still very thin in spite of the extra helpings I gave her. Of all the kills which George provided, the favorite with the cheetahs was zebra; waterbuck came last, and Grant's gazelles were acceptable only when freshly killed. This puzzled me, because only the Grant's gazelles were the size of beast a cheetah could kill on its own; they were also the most common of the local antelopes. When I asked Local for an explanation, he said that the meat of waterbuck clings to one's teeth and makes one extremely thirsty, and that Grant's meat, unless very fresh, develops a flavor disliked by predators. Since Grant's is a small buck and, under natural conditions, is eaten as soon as it is killed, Pippa's family objected to it only if we had kept the meat for a few days in the frigidaire. Supplying them with so much food became more and more of a problem, but as the cubs were still growing I continued feeding them whenever Pippa could not provide enough kills. She did her best to hunt and she and her cubs were often away for spells of up to six days, from which they usually returned well fed.

Our happy camp routine was upset when Local came back from a weekend's leave with a new wife. Though I was sympathetic, I could not agree that the pair should spend their honeymoon in the tent shared with Stanley and the cook. No one could understand my objection. I also disapproved of Local spending all his day with his new wife, whom I suspected from the start of only leading him toward another heartbreak. Grudgingly, he agreed to pass the nights with her at Kenmare Lodge and help me during the daytime with the cheetahs. After a week of passive resistance, during which he plodded behind me and daily invented new footsores to shorten our walks, he appeared one morning strangely serene and dignified and made no reference to his latest marriage. I did not embarrass him with questions, but when, a few days later, a truck passed in which I saw his wife and a younger Game Scout, I felt very sorry for poor old Local.

Luckily, he was so fond of Pippa and her cubs that our daily visits to the family soon cheered him up again. Pippa was now taking the cubs farther across the Mulika into plains which were bordered at the far end by the Murera River and ultimately reached Leopard Rock. If she remained within this area she would have an enormous hunting field during the rains without being cut off from our camp by floods. At the moment the plain was teeming with game, and one morning we found her stalking ten Grant's gazelles. At our approach they ran away, and Pippa, annoyed by our interference, climbed some fifteen feet up a tree to watch the Grant's. Completely ignoring us, she remained on her lookout while we fed the cubs below, and when she finally jumped off she must have ordered them to stay there while she continued her stalk. Anxious to know if she had made a kill, we returned early the next day, but judging by the appetite of the family she must have been unsuccessful.

Mbili, as usual, rushed along to get her titbits and, in her eagerness to drink the Farex milk, upset the bowl. I gave her a slight spank which made her growl. Next day she deliberately splashed the milk all over me and got a harder spank, with the result that, on the following morning, she drank her milk most carefully, and from then on she never misbehaved. Once I hung the camera bag high up on a branch well beyond her reach, but Mbili was not going to be defeated and, balancing along the branch, tried to get near it. Finally she managed to pull the strap up to her mouth with her right paw and, gripping it between her teeth, tore the bag off. She was the only one who enjoyed our chase after her, and even though she had to hold the cumbersome trophy between her teeth, she outran us. When finally we recovered the cameras we were tired out.

Next morning we found the ground patterned with lion pugmarks, and I was not surprised that our family had disappeared. I always marveled at how Pippa had managed to evade these natural enemies, even when her cubs could barely move. The fact that she had lived so close to lions on the *Born Free* film location might easily have impaired her natural reaction to these animals, but at the faintest sound of lion she always moved off with her cubs.

Driving along the road one morning, we were overtaken by two Land-Rovers identical with mine. Later, I saw, very far off, four dark spots which I could just identify as cheetah heads. Having kept in hiding from the other cars, the family now came trustfully to have their meal. I don't think that Pippa could have recognized us at this distance, and I wondered how she knew that we were inside the third of these similar vehicles.

Next morning we found the family waiting for us at the tree near the sandy patch where we had fed them during the last floods. They watched us cutting up the meat into four equal rations and mix-

Pippa with her third litter

ing the Farex milk into the bowl. While I was concentrating on dropping Abidec into small meat cutlets, a bull, a cow, and a baby elephant approached us swiftly and so noiselessly that we saw them only when they were within twenty yards; the bull was coming straight for us. Instantly we took to our heels. Local grabbed his rifle and shot into the air to stop the charge, but he had to do so four times, while running as fast as he could to keep ahead of the enraged bull. Finally the elephant turned and joined his family, who were being chased by one of our cheetahs. I thought it was Pippa gallantly defending her cubs, but when we returned to the tree we found her with Whity and Tatu greedily eating the meat. Then Mbili joined us and settled close to Pippa; she was so proud of having chased the elephants away. I gave her extra titbits while she allowed me to caress her.

During the following days we were unable to find the family.

I now had to go to Isiolo for a short visit. While I was away, Local went on looking for spoor. On my return, he greeted me with the good news that he had found fresh cheetah spoor along the airstrip at Leopard Rock. This was the first time that Pippa had taken her cubs so far, and she was obviously extending their hunting ground. Hoping to find the family, we started early and had not driven more than a mile when we met them on the road, coming straight from Leopard Rock. All looked fit but tired after their long walk. I wondered if Pippa had sensed that I was in the car when I passed the airstrip late on the previous evening and had walked the twelve miles during the night to get some food. Fortunately, we had some fresh meat with us, so we gave them a good meal. But evidently it was not mainly the hope of food which had caused the family to walk to camp, for after two days' rest they disappeared again. During their stay, Pippa's coat had been unusually silky and I suspected that she was in season. Because of her irregular visits to camp, I had never been able to ascertain the exact dates of her oestrus cycle. The only symptom occasionally indicating her condition was her resentment if I touched her when she had such unusually soft fur.

If Pippa kept me in uncertainty about her mating seasons, a pair of wire-tailed swallows left me in no doubt about their urge to breed. They perched on the laundry line, inspecting our camp commodities with a view to finding a suitable nesting site, and they decided on my sleeping tent, where, regardless of my presence, they

At loggerheads

flew in and out with beakfuls of mud. Unfortunately, I had just started preparations for replacing this tent, which the rains had rotted, by a more comfortable palm-log hut, so, as I did not want these friendly birds to waste their time and start a family inside a tent which I was about to pull down, I attached a small cardboard platform to the roof inside the studio palm-log hut which was close to the sleeping tent, hoping thus to induce them to use it as support for their nests. After investigating the construction, the pair decided against it and chose instead the distant spare tent. I did not know whether the birds disliked the cardboard platform or simply preferred a canvas tent to a palm-log hut. I watched them at work sticking tiny balls of mud on the canvas roof. Unfortunately, when they had almost completed a cup-shaped nest, a storm shook the tent and the nest collapsed. Trying to be helpful, I fixed another corrugated cardboard platform near the broken nest immediately underneath the roof angle. I hoped this would give them a base to stick the mud on, but they didn't like it and disappeared. I was very sorry to have prevented them from breeding in my camp, as I had become fond of these delightful birds.

The wire-tails are small compared to other swallows, but they make up for their lack of bulk by their exquisite coloring: a bluish sheen on their black wings and back, a deep red cap and a black cummerbund across their white underparts. Their elegance is further enhanced by two elongated, wire-thin tail feathers, from which they get their name.

As the spare tent was empty, I always kept it wide open to prevent snakes and scorpions, who like dark places, from occupying it. I did not enter it until nine weeks later when, to my surprise, the cook reported that there were birds inside feeding their young. I was surprised to find not only droppings underneath the platform but three naked chicks on the bare cardboard. There was no mud nest, no grass or feather lining to keep them warm. I could explain this extraordinary nursery only by assuming that the parent birds had taken so long to choose a nesting site that when they were overtaken by their breeding impulse, they had had no time left to build a proper nest and so used the cardboard as a substitute. Was this an "adaptation to circumstances" or even a "conditioned reflex"? Apparently, they simply had to breed at that time, whether a nest had been built or not.

Very extraordinary too was the behavior of the parents, who left the tiny chicks alone during the nights, reducing their parental duties merely to feeding the hungry trio. After ten days (by then I thought the chicks were at the most two weeks old), the parents tried to entice them to fly out. They perched close outside the tent and called. In response, the little chicks turned around and around along the edge of the cardboard, but it took another two days before they parachuted off it. It was a big event for them to fly straight to the laundry line and balance as best they could on the unfamiliar rope; there, looking around in bewilderment at the boundless space, the sky and the trees, they soon got tired and fell asleep on their precarious perch. This was the first chance I had of seeing them properly. I was amazed to observe how their plumage had already developed. Their fat little bodies were covered on top with pitch-black feathers; their grayish caps were already turning red, and their fluffy underparts were of the purest, silky white. Only their tails had not yet grown; they had just little stumps, which made flying rather difficult. During the next five days the parents took the chicks by turn every morning for flying lessons. Starting from the laundry line, they went in a big circle, landing on a small bush near the road where they had a short rest before the lesson was repeated. Invariably they all perched on the same bush, and I had to make a detour when driving out on my cheetah search so as not to interfere with their routine.

Daily their flights grew longer and the chicks' jerky movements soon developed into a smooth flight, even though their tails were still stumpy. Often they were out all day, but they always spent the night on their cardboard nursery. It was only after twelve days that they abandoned the tent. For a few more days I was still able to watch the trio, for they remained around the camp. I finally lost sight of this endearing family eighty-three days after the date at which the parents had started their first nest (June 18th to September 8th). The last I saw of the trio was on the laundry line, chirping away as though to say "Good-by."

Meanwhile we continued our search for Pippa and her cubs but only came across four lions; they were sleepy and merely raised their heads above the grass when we were within twenty yards of them, then moved off to the next bush. After four days we found Pippa's family half a mile from camp. They were all so hungry that they pounced on the meat we brought, scratching and biting one another. Mbili, however, soon climbed a tree to get clear of the growlings and spankings and remained there until I handed out her share, which she then ate in peace. During the next days a strong, high wind blew and we all, including the cheetah family, became rather cross; the cheetahs were very nervous and kept hiding even from Local when he went out to look for them and showed up only if I were close. In spite of this, Pippa twice walked into camp within the week. She went straight to the refrigerator and, hardly giving us time to put the meat into the basket, led us across the stream to the Kill Acacia where her cubs were hiding. As usual, Mbili was waiting on a branch for me to hand-feed her and joined her sisters on the ground only when their squabbles were over; by that time, of course, most of the meat had been eaten. This worried me, for how was she to survive if she could not fight for her share? Determined to build her up, I increased her supplementary vitamins: of these, the bonemeal was the most effective but the least popular, and I had to invent all sorts of tricks to make the cubs swallow it.

In mid-September 1967 the family again disappeared. Eventually we found their spoor at the broken Rojoweru bridge near the extreme end of their thirty-square-mile territory. Later I was told that two cheetahs had been seen on the far side of the river, and I feared that if the family had crossed the crocodile-infested river they might have got into trouble. I was still more disturbed when we saw a crocodile about eighteen feet long at one of the rapids where the cheetahs might well have jumped over. At another rapid we watched a club of seven turtles basking in the sun within six feet of a smaller crocodile. Continuing our searches into the plains beyond the Rojoweru took the best part of the day and in the present heat was most exhausting. Once we met a herd of twenty elands— the largest antelopes in Africa, weighing up to fifteen hundred pounds—among some fifty zebras. As soon as we approached, the elands split up, one group consisting of two females and a bull, surrounding five small calves, evidently protecting them, while the rest ran off with the zebras. When we returned to this place an hour later, the little group was still separated from the herd, which made us wonder whether elands went in for kindergartens as we knew impalas did. A welcome distraction during this worrying time was provided by the vervet monkeys who became more daring each day in their efforts to reach the ripe seed pods of the tamarinds which grew in camp. I loved these graceful monkeys, who often woke me up in the morning by munching the pods at the door of my sleeping hut, where they would consume their meal so long as I did not move. Less charming were the baboons, who also liked the pods and would besiege the camp all day long, waiting for an opportunity to invade the place. They jumped onto the huts looking like a miniature woolen army, stuffed the pods into their cheeks before we chased them, and then ran off yelling loudly to a nearby tree where they waited for another opportunity to invade us. Tamarind fruits are also much liked by people all over Africa and India: the juicy, sticky fiber, rich in vitamins, encasing the hard seeds, tastes like a bitter-sweet jam. It can be made into a delicious drink; the stony seeds are also used, when crushed to powder and then mixed with water, as a dressing to soothe the painful stings of scorpions.

Eleven days after we had lost the cheetahs, I went to look for them four miles from Leopard Rock in the neighborhood of Pippa's first camp. This was the only area we had not yet searched, because up to then Pippa had never taken her cubs so far away. I was therefore surprised to find recent spoor at the swamp which had been Pippa's first hunting ground two years ago. Obviously she had again widened her territory to include her old home. The spoor led us to within half a mile of Leopard Rock, to a bluff where tracking was difficult on account of the rocky ground; but, feeling that Pippa was close, I called and called and finally saw four cheetahs' heads peep above the grass, only to sink back instantly. This was the place where, two years earlier, we had surprised Pippa with a male cheetah. I approached cautiously, expecting the cubs to bolt, but they watched me come up to Pippa and sit beside her, then they began to purr. All were fit, and even Mbili had filled out. They followed me as I slowly made my way down the bluff until we reached a grove of tall acacias under whose shadow the family sat put. This had been one of Pippa's favorite lay-ups in her youth: from it she could overlook the airstrip and, in the early morning, see all kinds of animals playing games there. She could also watch what went on at distant Leopard Rock.

Leaving the family behind, I collected milk and Farex from the car, which I had left at the base of the bluff. I was very happy at having found them all in such good condition after eleven days and not even hungry. After I had given the cubs their Farex and milk, two of them played around an anthill while Mbili sat apart watching Leopard Rock. Knowing them all so content, I left to discuss with the Park Warden at Leopard Rock the urgent need to burn the grass before the rains began. Since our cheetahs were safe at Leopard Rock, I proposed that we should start burning the ground around my camp twelve miles from them. The Warden agreed and even offered to start by cutting proper firebreaks with a giant Michigan tractor which he had only recently acquired for the Park. This meant that this time we should run no risks. Next day the tractor bulldozed its way to camp, making wide firebreaks on both sides of the stream and even leveling its steep banks to ensure that in an emergency there would be a car crossing. When the Park Warden arrived he brought with him, not only a labor gang to help with the burning, but also a family of newly born ostrich chicks he had just picked up on the road to save them from the fire which he was about to light. Unfortunately, he had arrived too late to prevent a hawk from taking one of the chicks, but he had caught the rest except for two which had run off with their parents. I had watched this family for the last week strutting along the road, where the going was easier for the little ones than having to push their way through the grass.

We put the chicks in Whity's compound and started burning. The labor gang, placed at intervals upwind, beat the flames in the right direction as they raced past the camp, leaving it looking like a grassy island in a lake of ash. When it was all over the Warden went home and I found myself in charge of twelve baby ostriches. Looking at them carefully, I noticed that some of them were larger than the others; these were the males. Picking up grass and seeds, they huddled closely together and chirped away in a constant tremolo prrr-prrr. Obviously they were calling for their mother. They were cuddly at this age, but I knew how fast ostriches grow and visualized them in a few months' time tightly packing the compound in which I would have to keep them for at least a year. What was I to do? Luckily, at this moment George arrived; we discussed the problem and decided to try to find the parents and reunite the family. As it was only six hours since the chicks had been caught, they might still be accepted. We had not driven more than a mile when we spotted the white feathers of the cock on the burned plain; he was accompanied by the hen and the two chicks. Collecting the rest of the family and carrying them by armfuls to the back of my Land-Rover, their hard, brittle baby feathers pricked my skin. We then drove carefully across the smoldering ground until we were within thirty yards of the ostrich family, circled them, then separated the two chicks from their parents, who did their best to protect the youngsters, flapping their wings and fanning the ground with them. Next we maneuvered the back of the car close to the two chicks and, without showing ourselves, placed our cargo on the ground near them.

Instantly a tremendous prrrrrr-ing burst out and all rushed to their parents, who, with more wing-fannings, guided them all toward one of the distant grassy patches that the flames had left unscathed.

Meanwhile the fires blazed across the plains to Leopard Rock, illuminating the night sky and filling the air with smoke. On the cindery ash spooring was very easy, and though during the following days we found no trace of our cheetahs we often met our fire chicks. As I watched them grow stronger day by day I was very happy that we had been able to save them.

18

Mbili, Whity, and Tatu Go Off
on Their Own

I WAS enormously relieved to know that Pippa and her cubs were
able to look after themselves, yet I carried on the search for them
to find out when the cubs would start killing on their own. I also
wanted to know how far they might extend their territory and how
the final break with Pippa would happen.

On the fifth of October we found fresh spoor made by our cheetahs near the Murera River, halfway between the camp and Leopard
Rock. Never before had I seen the family here. I thought it must be
the nearness to the river which had made them extend their territory
over ground which was still smoldering. Their tracks led to a clutch
of twenty-one ostrich eggs, charred by the fires. Except for the ration of Farex milk we had given them two weeks ago, it was now
twenty-five days since the family had been fed by us. Had they been
hungry I would have thought they would have broken a few of these
eggs—Pippa was very fond of the yolk—but none of them had
been touched. I wondered if the cheetahs wouldn't touch the
eggs because they had been charred. I was curious also to find out
whether the fire had interfered with the incubation of the eggs and
decided to return within two weeks to see if any chicks had hatched.

At sunset I was taking a stroll near the camp when I suddenly saw Mbili, Whity, and Tatu rushing across the road and making for the stream. Assuming that they must be hungry after their
long walk, I drove to Kenmare and got a goat for them, but when I
returned they had gone. At first light Local went out to look

for them but though, as it later proved, he had been close to them, they did not appear till I followed, and even then only Mbili came, cocking her head and asking for her titbit. The rest were in no hurry to follow me to a shady tree to eat the goat we had brought.

I spent a happy morning with the family, who were all in excellent form; Pippa, as friendly as ever in spite of twenty-five days of separation, licked my face and nibbled at my hands. The cubs, however, had become much wilder, and Whity struck sharply at me whenever I dared to take a tick off her. I was therefore surprised when, during the next five days, Pippa brought the cubs twice into camp, demanding food. After she had gone to so much trouble to keep them away from camp, why should she have changed her tactics just now when the cubs seemed ready to live wild? But if she was prepared to break the rules, I stuck to them, and hoping to prevent more visits I carried three goat carcasses and a lot of zebra meat to the Kill Acacia during the next three weeks to satisfy their insatiable appetite.

On the eleventh of October I woke up to the thudding of an animal running behind my sleeping hut. At this moment the cook brought in my morning tea and told me it was Pippa chasing a buck. I went out and saw three cheetahs sitting near the road. I assumed they were her cubs. But I was wrong. It was Whity who had been running after the buck and Pippa and the other two cubs who were sitting still. Pippa now came to the refrigerator and made it plain that she was still hungry in spite of the enormous quantities of meat she and the cubs had eaten during the last few days. I had only a few scraps left to offer her; these she took upstream into a thicket and shared with Mbili and Tatu.

Meanwhile I followed Whity's tracks, which led to a thick bush by the stream. Suddenly, I almost stepped on her. She was on a duiker kill. She had suffocated it and opened it up between its hind legs. I felt proud of her, but Whity looked at me as though she had done nothing unusual and even left her kill to join the family, who now came into view on the far bank of the stream. When I picked up the duiker and waved it, Pippa quickly jumped across and I had to prevent her from getting at the buck's carcass until the cubs had joined us and could get their fair share. I was amazed to see how calmly Whity watched the others tucking into her kill, hardly giving her any chance to eat; she was the first to leave,

Whity with her duiker kill

The cheetahs trust Joy to hold "their" kill

while Pippa was the last to follow her children as they disappeared across the stream. I then measured the distance over which Whity had chased the duiker and found it to be 360 yards. Judging by the efficient way she had dispatched the buck, this could not be her first kill, though she was not yet fourteen months old.

This was a big day for me as I now knew that Pippa's cubs could if necessary provide for themselves, and I was glad that our feeding them had not impaired their natural development. Compared to Pippa they were precocious, for she, when she was twenty months old, could not yet tackle a chicken or a goat. It was interesting to have been able to verify the date on which cheetah cubs start killing, for it had been assumed that they were dependent on their mother for two entire years. Up to now I had taken many movie films of cheetahs as a visual record of their development. Recently I had been asked to add to these some scenes showing the animals with myself, as our relationship would be of interest for a possible TV film later on. It was suggested that a professional cameraman should do the filming. I had learned many new facts about cheetah behavior and development, but I was still no nearer to understanding their enigmatic character. This was brought home to me when, next day, I found Mbili suckling Pippa.

In spite of this infantile behavior I expected that the cubs would soon leave their mother and go off on their own, so if we wanted to get some films showing the family together we must hurry. The burned ground would also be a help since it enabled us to see the cheetahs at a greater distance; this was important in case they should resent the presence of a cameraman. In the end, however, George and I decided that he should do the filming. We hoped the family might accept him more willingly than a stranger. We spent many hours burdened with our heavy cameras, tracking the family, before we found them near the elephant forest. Pippa sniffed carefully at George and the cubs kept their distance until we dumped the meat we had brought. Then, forgetting George, the tripod, and the noises of the movie camera, they set to and he was able to film me holding food for the cubs, swinging a goatskin around while they jumped at it, and finally Pippa resting beside me. After this successful operation it was some days before the cheetahs turned up in camp early one morning.

While the men collected a sheep from Kenmare, Tatu chased a

Mbili still suckling Pippa

Mbili spots a skin

A tug-of-war

Retrieving skin

duiker but failed to get it. Perhaps this put her in a bad temper, for she reacted fiercely when we brought the carcass of the sheep to the Kill Acacia. Crouching low, trembling and growling savagely, she seemed ready to spring at me and watched every move of mine with hard eyes. Indeed, she kept me at bay for several minutes until Pippa came to my rescue and, walking between us, stopped her from charging. Did she blame me for having lost the duiker, or did she think the sheep carcass was her kill? I had never seen her in such a dangerous mood, and after this no one could make me believe that cheetahs are harmless animals: I had had my lesson.

From now on the family kept more and more away from camp. During our searches we investigated the clutch of ostrich eggs charred by the fire which I had found two weeks previously. All the eggs were broken into fragments, and since I could not find a trace of sticky yolk adhering to the inside of the shells, as would have happened had they been damaged before hatching, I assumed that the incubation had been a natural one and that the thick shell of an ostrich egg secured its contents against bush fire.

The November rains were due, and a sign of their approach was the sudden blooming of every acacia bush. Not only did they fill the oppressive atmosphere with a refreshing scent but their white flowers were in striking contrast to the burnt bush, and were very beautiful. This outburst of flowers preceding the rains was a reaction to the humidity of the atmosphere. It gave the insects time to pollinate the stamens before the heavy rains battered everything to pieces. Now, too, I understood why the giraffes kept their tails curled over their backs when moving fast, for watching a herd cantering through a belt of flowering acacias, which showed up clearly against their black surroundings, I noticed that their tails were level with the top of the shrubs; to press them, curled up, against their backs was an obvious way of saving the long-haired tassels from getting entangled in the thorns.

When, after ten days, the family appeared, all were in excellent condition except for Pippa, who was covered with ticks and sore bleeding patches where she had scratched. Why, I wondered, had the cubs not been infected but only Pippa, who should have the greatest immunity? She rolled herself into position for me to de-tick her and co-operated patiently. As soon as I had cleaned her of the ticks she went away, so I suspected she had returned only to get my help.

The first showers had fallen and we could watch the grass growing almost hourly; within a few days, the black plains had turned to expanses of waving grass interspersed with large patches of yellow, red, white, and blue flowers. The sky-blue pentanesia, in particular, made a superb background for the golden cheetahs, who remained for a short spell close to camp.

To get more films with the "human element" in this colorful setting, I had asked George to come and try his luck again. We had not walked more than a few hundred yards when we saw a cheetah running at top speed after a buck; both disappeared into a thicket from which we soon heard agonized bleats. They had ceased by the time we arrived at the scene and found Pippa breathing heavily as she grasped the throat of a duiker. Although it was already limp she held on for a few more minutes before straddling it and dragging it into the open. Then she called the cubs. They had been sitting still about 150 yards away, watching the hunt, and now came racing up. Pippa deliberately waited for their arrival before opening the carcass, at which all tore so voraciously that within an hour there was nothing left except the small horns. These were not worth burying, and Pippa moved off while Mbili had a little game with them before she joined the family. It was the first time I had seen Pippa killing, and we were very lucky to have been able to film this in still and motion pictures. We also shot scenes in which Pippa allowed me to hold her kill while they all ate.

By now the grass was too high for the cheetahs to stalk prey, so, being hungry, they wasted no time in coming to camp for meat but went straight to Kenmare to get a goat. I didn't want them to get into this habit and decided that the only way to prevent future visits to the Lodge was to keep a good supply of food in camp. This soon became known to two jackals who hung around and finally grew so cheeky that they sat within twenty yards of the cheetahs, even in bright daylight. They barked and teased them, and whenever a cub made a rush to put them in their place they played hide-and-seek. Jackals are most endearing and intelligent creatures and could be turned into delightful pets if nature had not protected them from such a fate by making them effective carriers of rabies.

Eating in "star" formation

Meanwhile, the grass grew taller and taller and finally Pippa moved to Leopard Rock, where the vegetation was less thick and she could watch the animals playing in the mornings along the airstrip. We found the family there one afternoon. Though they seemed happy to see us, they made no attempt to follow us to camp and remained in that area for nine days. Next time we spotted them was a mile upstream from camp on the far side of the water. By the time we had collected meat and crossed over, the cheetahs were gone but many vultures loaded the trees around the place. We searched for two hours for the kill, as well as for the family, but did not find a trace of either until it got dark. Just then I noticed four cheetahs' heads within a hundred yards watching us until we dropped the meat in front of them, and then, although their bellies were bulging, they gulped it down as fast as they could. Whity and Tatu had grown a good deal and were now bigger than Pippa, and even Mbili was now well padded. She was the only one who was still friendly; when she came up to me I saw a bleeding gash on one of her hind legs, but judging by her antics, it can't have hurt her much. Next morning, within half a mile of the place where the vultures had been sitting, we found the leg of a small buck surrounded by flattened grass and other signs of a struggle. Remembering Mbili's wound, I wondered if she had killed the antelope.

During the following months the cheetahs called occasionally, but once they were absent for fifteen days. We found several remains of kills along their tracks and one time came upon them just in time to watch them stalking six Grant's gazelles. Fanning out, they wriggled in a circle, bellies close to the ground, till they were near the grazing herd, then the Grant's got their wind and raced off.

As the cheetahs' kills were mostly dik-dik, duiker, and guinea fowl and these were not enough to fill four large, empty stomachs, I still helped them out with meat. While doing this I noticed that a new relationship had developed between Pippa and the cubs. Formerly, she had taken the initiative in all their doings; now she often watched me feeding them and joined in only after they had their fill, and she never showed any jealousy when I spoiled Mbili. Tatu, on the other hand, had become a bully and several times charged me for no reason.

On the sixth of December, when the cubs were sixteen and a half months old, we fed them within a few hundred yards of the camp. Hoping to take some photographs, we went back to see them again at teatime, but found only Pippa on a tree looking anxiously in every direction and calling for the cubs with her worried i-hn i-hn. It was plain that she had lost them. Sniffing the ground, she led us for about half a mile through thick grass where it was impossible for us to spoor until we reached an open patch on which we found pugmarks. Here Pippa sat down, purred, rolled into position, and invited me to de-tick her. We played together until the sun started to get low and I became anxious about the cubs. Pippa made no effort to join me when I walked away, calling the names of her children. I found them only three hundred yards away, peeping out from under a tree. Of course, it was Mbili who came and followed me to Pippa, who must have known all the time that they were close. Licking each other affectionately, she and Mbili waited for Whity and then moved off leisurely into the dark, followed at a safe distance by Tatu, who did not come near her mother while I was there.

From now on the cubs went off together for increasingly longer periods until, on the twentieth of December, Mbili disappeared by herself. This happened when I was in Nairobi for a couple of days seeing a doctor. While I was absent, Local met the family downstream on their way to Kenmare, where later in the afternoon Pippa was seen. Next morning he observed Mbili hiding under a terminalia within sight of the Lodge. We always called this tree "Dume Tree" because Pippa's mate unfailingly passed under it when he was in the area. Mbili was hungry and, expecting food, let Local come close to her. As he had nothing to give her he went back to camp to get meat, but on his return he saw no sign of Mbili or the other cheetahs. The following night several lions kept the Scouts at Kenmare awake by their roars. My return from Nairobi at teatime coincided with Pippa's arrival. She did not come into camp but stayed out on the road until I took her her meat. Stranger still, she did not touch it but trotted determinedly back along the road to Kenmare. Believing that she might lead us to the cubs, I asked Local to follow her while I rushed back to camp to collect more meat. When I caught up with Local at the Dume terminalia he was still out of breath from running after Pippa; he told me she had continued trotting along the road up to this tree and had then bounded off into the plains at such a pace that it was impossible for him to keep up with her. After he lost her he had come back to the road to meet me.

We followed her spoor until it became dark and started off again next morning. On our return at lunchtime we learned that Pippa had been to the camp and, after a good meal, had left and gone along the road to Leopard Rock. This was the opposite direction to that in which she had led us yesterday. It seemed to me that she was probably avoiding the lion we had heard on the previous night calling from across the stream. We did not find any trace of her but met Whity and Tatu the following day at the Mud Tree two miles from camp. Both were extremely shy but could not resist the meat we dropped. They dragged it into a thorny bush, after which we left them to try to locate the rest of the family. It took another two hours before we found Pippa, although she was only half a mile away. After I had de-ticked her and fed her, she followed us slowly to her two daughters and, without the usual lickings, settled within a short distance. But where, I wondered, was Mbili?

She had been missing for four days. Remembering the concern Pippa had shown when little Dume and Whity had been taken from her, I hoped to rouse her help in finding Mbili by calling for her, but Pippa showed no interest and soon dozed off. Although we spent the rest of the day looking for Mbili, we failed to find her and on the following day found only Pippa and the other two cubs at the Mud Tree. It was the twenty-fourth of December, and we were determined to give them a good Christmas meal.

For the last three years Christmas had been a sad time for us. This year it was not only my anxiety about Mbili which spoiled the holidays but the dreadful news that poor Arun Sharma had been drowned while spending his holiday at the coast. We had expected him to come to us for Christmas, and the shock of his death affected us deeply. On Christmas Day we found only Whity and Tatu at the Mud Tree. Pippa's spoor led first to the distant plain where she had given birth and then on for some three miles, which was the farthest we had ever known her to go up till now. The ground here was arid, open bush where on the reddish sand we could easily trace the spoor of duikers and dik-dik. During the following week we twice saw the spoor of a single cheetah and once the tracks of two, the smaller of which Local thought to be Pippa's, since

Mbili was now bigger than her mother, but we had no clue as to whether the large spoor was hers or that of Pippa's mate.

Meanwhile, Whity and Tatu remained close to the Mud Tree and behaved as though they had been ordered to stay there. Both grew wilder every day and made it plain that they only tolerated us because we brought them meat. If I dared to get close to them, they struck at me. I tried not to worry about Mbili, hoping that she was with her mother. Then, on New Year's Day, Pippa turned up in camp, alone. She walked in very early, sniffing the ground and calling in her worried voice, i-hn i-hn. I assumed that Mbili was hiding close. Hoping to make her show up I offered Pippa meat, but it didn't bring Mbili into view, nor did Pippa touch it. She walked off in the direction of the place in which last week we had seen Whity and Tatu. She covered the distance of two miles very quickly, as if she knew her cubs were at the Mud Tree. It was here they joined up, and I was surprised at their behavior. They just sat down to a good meal. Pippa's behavior was very strange. It seemed as though she had left the two cubs in my care for the eight days she had been away; if not, why had she come to my camp and then started calling for them, and why had she refused to eat until they were together? Her determined walk to the Mud Tree seemed to indicate that she knew that these cubs were safe. Was I to interpret her indifference to Mbili's absence as a good sign? Mbili had now been away for twelve days.

We went on with our searches till we were almost at breaking point, but except for a report by a Game Scout that late one afternoon he had seen two cheetahs near Kenmare, seemingly unafraid of people, we were without any clue. We hunted from dawn to dusk, including the hot, midday hours, while Pippa continued her customary routine calls at the camp, completely unconcerned about Mbili, who had now not been seen for seventeen days.

One morning I fed almost a complete goat to the three cheetahs at the Kill Acacia before setting out to look for Mbili. On my return, late in the afternoon, I found them not far away, very sleepy from the heavy meal. I rested my hand on Pippa's shoulder and relaxed as much as I could, but I was very worried. The fact that Mbili's disappearance had coincided with the invasion of the lion made me fear the worst. I called her name. Pippa listened and looked up. By now it had got so dark that Local came to fetch me. I was touched by his concern and followed him home. Halfway there, I suddenly saw a cheetah head peeping through the grass. It was Mbili, asking, with her impish expression, for titbits. I had nothing to give her except the head of a goat, which I asked Local to smash up so that she could get the best of this meager meal. Meanwhile, I offered her the milk her sisters had not drunk. She lapped the bowl clean. Her coat, in spite of being full of sticky burs, had a beautiful, glossy sheen and she looked very fit.

I coaxed Mbili to follow me in the direction of her family. Before we arrived, Local returned with the meat which she gobbled up to the last scrap, just in time to save it from Whity, whom we spotted craning her neck above the grass. The next moment she pounced on Mbili and licked her. They were soon joined by Tatu, and all three rolled around affectionately and then tumbled happily over to Pippa. Without moving, she welcomed Mbili, purring loudly. The cub clasped her tenderly and rubbed against her; she was more affectionate than I had ever seen her before. I could hardly believe that skinny little Mbili had been the first to show her stronger sisters that she could live successfully on her own for such a long time. But, judging by Pippa's behavior—who had gone off at sixteen and a half months for even longer escapades in the company of males—it was perhaps only natural for one of her cubs to be already showing an interest in the other sex. They were not ready to mate, yet nevertheless I assumed it had been Mbili with a boy friend whom the Scout had seen at Kenmare.

The fact that Mbili was around again made me very happy, and she seemed to share my feelings: she was full of fun and accidentally splashed the milk in her bowl into my face. While I was wiping my eyes she got hold of a piece of goatskin and clowned around most disarmingly as if to make up for the milk splash. Finally, she flung herself close to me and purred her best.

After a few days Pippa came to camp limping badly on her right leg. I manipulated it from the shoulder to the toes but found no injury, nor did she react as though it pained her. Nevertheless, during the next week the limp got worse till she could move only with difficulty. I was therefore surprised that she took her cubs each day over a long distance toward the base of the Mulika ridge, where she stopped at a group of trees. Here they remained for some days, Pippa resting in the shade of a large terminalia, while the cubs had endless fun climbing up and down a fallen tree. It was an ideal place for Pippa to recover in, provided she need not use her injured leg for hunting. I helped with meat.

It was interesting to observe how Whity and especially Tatu now accepted Mbili as their leader. I felt sorry for Tatu when I saw her watching us from a safe distance, playing with a goatskin but, in spite of some daring attempts to join in, never allowing herself to trust me as Mbili did. Pippa's attitude had changed, too. She was exceptionally gentle now, and when she nibbled at my hands, she seemed to be thanking me for helping her. I could not imagine what injury she was suffering from; she usually took great care when placing her right foot on the ground and walked slowly, but sometimes she raced around, playing with her cubs, without a sign of pain.

We lost trace of the family for three days. Then a party of visitors who called at my camp mentioned seeing four cheetahs in the morning near the road, of which one was so friendly that it even posed for photographs. When they heard that I had lost Pippa and her cubs, they offered to lend me their cook to guide me to the place where they had seen the cheetah family. Taking meat and Farex milk, we drove for sixteen miles, passing Leopard Rock and on to Pippa's first camp, where, sure enough, we found the four of them near the Haraka Lion Villa. Pippa was still limping and didn't like my touching her belly; I saw that her nipples were in milk. It then dawned on me that the two spoor we had found six weeks ago on the arid plains must have belonged to Pippa and a mate, whose cubs she now carried. It was an interesting fact that as soon as Mbili, Tatu, and Whity could kill and lead independent lives, she had become pregnant again.

What would she do if her new family arrived while the earlier litter was still with her? I knew of a cheetah mother in Nairobi National Park who had found herself in a similar predicament. She solved the problem by sneaking through the fence outside the boundary of the Park, and there, out of reach of her already independent cubs, gave birth. When, after a few weeks, the Warden coaxed her and the little ones back into the Park, she chased her old cubs off fiercely. But how could Pippa scare away her daughters when she was so handicapped by her limp and also needed my help with food, which would tempt the cubs to remain with her? Since she had started to limp twenty days ago she had moved eighteen miles, which was not going to help her lameness. Next morning we found the family half a mile farther away, resting on one of the large earthen mounds which had been piled up at short intervals along the new main road then under construction. This road was three lanes wide and went straight as an arrow through the Park, connecting all the smaller tracks. Since there was still little traffic on it, it was used as a dust bath and playground by many animals, as well as providing a good lookout for predators. Pippa took full advantage of it. She could not have chosen a better training ground for the cubs: the adjoining plain was never swampy even during the rains, and it was always teeming with herds of Grant's gazelles, waterbucks, zebras, kongonis, and oryxes. From atop the mounds of earth the cheetahs could survey the road over long distances, and the scrub along it gave them splendid cover for ambushing their prey. The cubs made the most of their opportunity, and today we found them stalking two warthogs. They sneaked cunningly up to them, but then they must have looked at their formidable tusks and decided against giving chase, for suddenly they gave up the hunt. During the next few days we observed the family moving steadily along the road toward the entrance gate—the last place I wanted them to frequent.

One day two Vets who were visiting the Park called at my camp and, after hearing about Pippa's injury, offered their help. One of them was Dr. Sayer, a friend of the Harthoorns; he worked at the Veterinary Laboratory in Nairobi. Describing Pippa's symptoms was not enough to allow him to make a diagnosis, so we decided to drive out to her. By watching me manipulating her leg through the binoculars, the Vets might be able to determine the cause of her limp.

By the time we located the cheetahs it was midday and all were resting sleepily under a bush. Leaving the Vets inside the Land-Rover, I walked over to Pippa and, pretending to play with her, moved her right leg into various positions. This assured them that she had not dislocated her shoulder or torn a ligament, but they said that to diagnose her injury one of them would himself have to manipulate the leg. Not knowing if she would allow a stranger to do this, Dr. Sayer and I approached very carefully. The cubs bolted instantly, but Pippa co-operated as if she knew we had come to help her. She allowed the Vet to handle her until he discovered that the small bones of her wrist were strained. If she rested they would return to normal but, if not, the inflammation of the joints might develop into a painful permanent rheumatism. At the present stage, this could be prevented by giving her butazolidin. Promising to send a supply from Nairobi, the Vets left. I was most grateful for their help and only hoped that when the drug arrived I would be able to administer two tablets for seven days, as prescribed.

Meanwhile the family moved still farther up the road, far beyond the area in which I had ever known them to venture. Pippa had again widened their territory, but I hoped she would not extend it beyond the Park boundary. There was nothing I could do about it, but I pinned my hopes on the six white rhinos which, since they were imported from South Africa two years ago, had been living within restricted ground near the gate. This part of the Park was the least infected with tsetse fly and for this reason had been chosen to acclimatize them against trypanosomiasis. Weekly blood tests had proved that these rhinos were now immune to trypanosomiasis, and it had recently been decided to move them to the center of the Park. To prepare them for the long walk they were now kept outside the compound during daytime, and it was a hilarious sight to see the huge, bulky beasts being herded like cattle by their keepers. I trusted the bustle involved in this exodus might prove too much for our cheetahs and would make them return to the plain.

So far as Pippa was concerned this proved true, but one morning we found the cubs almost opposite the rhino camp. We had tracked their spoor for three hours from the Mulika stream, which here ran close to the left side of the road, while the Murera River flowed parallel to the right side. The cubs were very hungry but often interrupted their meal to look in the direction of the Murera River and sometimes even walked short distances toward it. Assuming that Pippa was there, we searched the area in vain for the best part of the day while the cubs, to my surprise, remained immobile on the spot at which we had found them. Returning next morning, we found Pippa and her family about a mile short of the gate, being photographed by a tourist party. Pippa was obviously so suspicious of what was going on that I had to beg the visitors to leave the cheetahs alone, and only then did she settle down. While feeding her I put her first dose of butazolidin in the meat. I was only just in time, for immedi-

Joy with a white rhino

ately afterward she walked off toward the gate, never stopping to look back for her cubs. They watched her disappear without attempting to follow her and amused themselves with a bit of goatskin until they retreated to a bush and dozed off, apparently content to be alone.

They were seventeen and a half months old now. Little did I realize at that moment that I had witnessed Pippa's final parting from her cubs.

Since we had seen the family ten days ago near Pippa's old camp, they had explored new hunting fields. Here they would always find plenty of prey and water, because both the Mulika and the Murera were not far off, and it was an ideal stretch of cheetah country some seven miles long and two miles wide. Pippa had gradually introduced her cubs to a territory of sixty-three square miles by way of four ever-widening circuits. Now they were familiar with everything they needed to know to be able to live on their own. I was amazed to observe how unconcerned the cubs seemed to be at the absence of their mother, although they had not moved from where they had parted yesterday. They never looked for her, nor did they seem to miss her when they had their meal. Afterward they had a grand game around an earthwork mound.

We found Pippa's spoor half a mile away near the remains of a fresh duiker kill. Nevertheless, when we came up with her on the following day she was very hungry and greedily gulped down the second dose of butazolidin. I had concealed it in a small piece of meat which I gave her before her large meal. She was very irritable and growled at me whenever I tried to touch her, and as soon as she had had her fill she went off into the plains toward Leopard Rock. The cubs, whenever we saw them, seemed quite happy to be alone; they played most of the time and hardly touched the food we had brought them. Eventually they became intrigued by the appearance of a zebra herd which also interested me, for in the middle of twenty-five normal zebras was an albino with stripes so faint that it looked almost white. As if conscious of its oddity, it never left its well-protected position. On the few later occasions when we again saw this herd, the albino always remained at its center.

19

Pippa's Third Litter

DURING THE following ten days we spent most of our time looking either for Pippa or for her cubs. Though they were never more than one and a half miles apart, they remained strictly separate. When driving for long distances up and down the road in our search, I always called for the cheetahs by using the same succession of honks on the horn. They came to recognize them and at once approached the car.

Often we did not find Pippa, but the cubs were always waiting close to the road to welcome us, or rather the meat which we brought. Whity and Tatu had become extremely wild, and only Mbili kept up a friendly link with me. She always asked for a game, and I had to watch our belongings attentively, for if I didn't she would career off with them. In spite of my care, she did, once, get hold of my topee and leapt from bush to bush, shaking the helmet teasingly at me while I ran after her. It was midday and very hot for chasing a cheetah who was determined not to give up her toy. I really was quite exhausted by the time I managed to pull a dead branch off a tree which startled the cub and caused her to drop the topee. It was in poor shape by then with many punctures left by Mbili's teeth. Two days later she disappeared.

When, on the following day, all the cheetahs had vanished I began to think that they might have joined up again. But I realized how little I understood the working of the mind of cheetahs when I discovered that Pippa had cleared out of the area. The last time we had seen her had been within two miles of Leopard Rock, heading in that direction. I had taken the occasion to give her the fifth dose of her medicine. Her limp had improved but was still noticeable.

On the seventeenth of February we spotted the three cubs some five miles beyond Leopard Rock, far out on the plains. We just could see the white tips of their tails above the grass. Responding to my honking signal, they came bounding along and hardly gave us time to cut the meat up into equal portions before they pounced on it. As usual, I held Mbili's share for her to gnaw at leisurely. When they retired, each to a different tree, their bellies looked like balloons. George was with me, and he photographed us all together. These pictures proved to be a record of the last hours I shared together with all of Pippa's children.

On our way home, seven miles from my camp we found fresh spoor, undoubtedly Pippa's, superimposed on our morning tracks. It was six days since we had seen her. Obviously she had abandoned her cubs. I marveled how painlessly the ties between them had been broken. Since we had watched Whity at fourteen months so efficiently killing a duiker, Pippa had never been perturbed when the cubs were absent for increasingly long periods; she must have realized that they could now fend for themselves. It was while Mbili had been on her long safari when she was sixteen months old that Pippa had looked for a mate and had started a new family. Then she had taken her cubs to the farthest part of her territory where she knew they would always find plenty of food and water. She had remained with them for ten days more, but as soon as they were well acquainted with the area she had gradually withdrawn and was now looking for a suitable nursery for her next litter. After she had left the cubs we gave them food for another thirteen days. During this time they never once made an attempt to find their mother but behaved as if they were obeying her wish in starting to live on their own. They were now eighteen months old.

George had come over to discuss the last details of a trip we had planned in order to move our belongings from Isiolo to a new home at Lake Naivasha. We were to start the next day. As this entailed hiring transport and labor and making three 240-mile journeys, we decided that we could not cancel all these arrangements at such short notice, even though I would have liked to watch Pippa's behavior during the next few days. The best I could do in the cir-

Joy feeding cubs after Pippa had abandoned them

cumstances was to leave a generous supply of meat in camp and ask the Warden to help Local by providing a car for long-distance searches for the cheetahs. Next day George and I left to supervise the move.

We were lucky to get all our business done before the rains broke, especially as this happened three weeks sooner than we expected. But break they did when we were nearing home. The last eighty miles of our return to camp were a nightmare, driving in a howling storm, splashing through knee-deep lakes and muddy ruts, slithering helplessly into ditches. We arrived exhausted and only just before another downpour started. Local was glad to see me, for only once during our ten days' absence had he met the cubs. Then he had found them close to where I had last seen them. They had been very hungry and had devoured the meat he gave them. He said they were all in splendid form. With Pippa he had been luckier, as after two days she appeared in camp and since then had called in regularly for her meals. This morning when she left she had crossed the stream, which since then had become a raging torrent. After a night of heavy rain the flood increased to such an extent that it was teatime before Pippa could cross the swollen stream. Then I heard a splash and soon a wet Pippa rubbed herself against me, purring loudly. Her pregnancy was now well advanced, and after eating as much meat as she could hold, she went off along the road to Kenmare and we drove off to look for her cubs. We did not find them, nor did we see them next day; after that, unusually heavy rain put a stop to any further searches.

Listening to a downpour drumming noisily on the palm-log roofs all night, I watched the water rising rapidly in the stream. Luckily, the flood only reached the camp after dawn, so at least we could see what we were doing. Wading up to our waists, we rescued our belongings from the huts, which were under two feet of water. The only creatures in the camp who were still comfortable were two baby wire-tail swallows who had hatched in my absence. Like Pippa, the parent birds of our "cardboard chicks" had lost no time in starting a new family. They had made the best use of the fresh supply of mud and had built their nest inside a palm-log hut which I had erected to replace the spare tent. Standing knee-deep in the water inside it, I watched the chicks snuggling cozily inside their nest, which was attached to the roof; they were quite unaware of how enviable their position was. It was three weeks before the ground inside the huts had dried out and we were able to use them again; meanwhile, I slept and worked inside the Land-Rover, which was the only dry place in the surrounding swamp. Poor Pippa, she had no such refuge and, during the rains, found moving very difficult and finally cleared out. To make things worse, Local was again due for a month's leave, and this just at the time when Pippa was likely to be very sensitive to any change. Her cubs should be born within a month, and I hoped that Local would be back in time for the event as Pippa preferred him to Guitu, who was replacing him.

Together, we waded in deep mud searching for Pippa. I often wondered whether she could hunt across this boggy ground and get all the food she needed during her pregnancy. So I was greatly relieved when, after five days, she appeared in camp. She was very hungry, and I was glad that I had enough fresh meat to give her a good meal. Later she moved off toward the road. Guitu and I followed her. Wandering undecidedly about and making many small detours, she made it plain that she was not going to let Guitu "spy" on her, so I sent him back. Only then did she guide me to the plain where we had released little Impia, and lay down in the shade of a thornbush. There were plenty of similar bushes within a short distance, any of which I thought might provide an ideal nursery. Pippa seemed to agree with me, for she did not move far off during the next days. However, when we visited her she never let us see where she came from and always suddenly appeared in the open. In all other ways she was very friendly; she let me pluck out her mud-clotted hair and even allowed me to touch her milk-swollen teats.

Meanwhile it rained and rained, which made long drives to search for Pippa's cubs impossible. Limited to walking, I sent Guitu spooring daily as far as he could go on foot while I looked after Pippa. One morning he returned with the good news that he had found a running cheetah's spoor together with those of a running buck along the Mulika track close to Pippa's favorite sand patch. Hoping to find one of her cubs, we went to investigate, but though we searched every likely place on the adjoining plains, we found no further traces of the spoor or of a cheetah. During the following days, whenever the weather permitted it, we drove to the plains where we had last

The flooded camp

Joy feeding Mbili after she had been on her own for one month

seen our cubs, cruising along all those tracks which we could risk taking without getting bogged. The place was teeming with all kinds of animals—except cheetahs.

Pippa came off and on to camp, and she never moved far away. Of all the areas she frequented she seemed to prefer the Impia plain, although the grass there had grown into a thick, wooded jungle, and besides, to reach it she had to cross the swollen Mulika. Luckily, its waters never rose to the height of our stream, and she probably felt less cut off from camp there than on the Gambo plain, where the grass was comparatively low.

On the seventeenth of March, exactly one month after I had seen the cubs for the last time, Guitu met Mbili eight miles from camp along the road to Leopard Rock. By the time he had walked back to tell me this very exciting news and we had driven to the place, more than two hours had elapsed so I was not surprised that she had gone. I called her name and observed her racing through the grass to us from a great distance just at the moment when two cars arrived bringing a party of visitors to the Park. Instantly Mbili vanished, but she reappeared after the cars had left. She followed me to a tree and while she tucked into the meat I prepared her Farex milk. She was a little thinner than a month ago, but her beautiful, glossy coat and general condition proved that she was very fit. She seemed happy to see me again and allowed me to touch and even to de-tick her. Otherwise she behaved like a wild animal, looking around suspiciously and jerking nervously at the slightest snapping of a twig. I was so happy at being again with Mbili that, not knowing when I might see my favorite little clown again, I dragged out the time we spent with her as long as I could. But, thinking of her future, I finally left a small piece of meat to keep her occupied while we went off, for if she had followed us to camp it might have upset all she had so far achieved in terms of going wild. We moved quietly to the car and tried to start the engine, but nothing happened. Using the crank had no effect either, and our last resort, pushing it along the bumpy road, was equally unsuccessful. There was nothing left to do but to send Stanley to Leopard Rock and ask for a mechanic to come and repair the Land-Rover. I hoped that this might at least give me more time with Mbili, but when I looked for her she was gone. Assuming that the noise we had made in coping with the car had driven her away, I sat in silence for two hours, only now realizing that Mbili had no wish to share her life with us any longer and had vanished back into her wild world. It proved that the rehabilitation was a great success. If Mbili could now live on her own, her stronger sisters could certainly do so too, especially as they had always stuck together and could help each other.

It was another twelve days before I was told of a cheetah having been seen halfway between the gate and Leopard Rock. Investigating, we found vultures guarding the remains of an antelope, but the prints of their claws had spoiled the spoor on the surrounding ground so that we were unable to identify what animal had killed the buck. We thought it must have been a cheetah, since a lion or hyena would not have left the smaller bones.

It was still early, so I asked Guitu to search across the plains where he had last seen Mbili while I drove on to look for Pippa. He found a single cheetah spoor leading toward the Mulika, where he lost it, but following the rivulet until he came to within five miles of the camp he was almost run over by a buck fleeing from some predator. A few seconds later Mbili appeared. Realizing that Guitu had spoiled her hunt, she went up an anthill and watched him calling her but made no attempt to follow him when he eventually walked home. Hearing Guitu's report, I was divided between my wish to see Mbili and the consequences this might have. If she followed me to camp, this could upset Pippa's plans, for she had kept the cubs away from her during the last weeks. If Pippa was big enough to let them live their own lives I should do the same—the more so as by now I suspected that she might have given birth to a litter.

She had come to camp on the twenty-fifth of March at 5 P.M., just before a heavy cloudburst. While I fed her she had continued looking nervously across the stream, and she had left as soon as she had eaten. She had gone toward the road, sinking instantly into the grass whenever she saw me watching her. Half an hour later I had followed her tracks, which had been joined by those of another cheetah, both leading to the Mulika ford. By then it was becoming too dark to carry on and next day, after a night's rain, all spoor had been washed away. In the afternoon Pippa appeared from the same direction. I had prepared a goat for her. I thought it would be the last meal she would have before her labor, since I expected her to give birth within forty-eight hours. Her behavior indicated that I was right: she was as irritable as she had been before her previous litters. She growled with flattened ears, struck at me and scratched me whenever I came close, and even tore my shirt. However, she ate an unbelievable amount and then left for the Gambo plains. Sitting still, she had made it clear that I was not to follow her. I had done so only because I was sure that she had crossed the stream so as to lead me in the opposite direction from the one she intended to take. I did not expect to see her again for a few days, but when there was still no sign of her after a week, I became worried.

It had rained heavily most nights, which made my searches very difficult. I always went alone, fearing that Pippa might resent Guitu's coming near her cubs, which I assumed had been born on the twenty-eighth of March. One night we had 4.9 inches of rain and I was alarmed for Pippa since the vegetation on the Impia plain was already far too high for her to be able to see above it.

Owing to a recent reshuffle of Wardens in the Park, there had been no burning before these rains; consequently the old grass retained the floods and the plains were waterlogged. As a result, the vegetation grew in such profusion that it had become a trap rather than a grazing ground. Concentrating my searches on the Impia plain, I looked into every promising thicket, calling through a megaphone to save my voice, but I found no trace of Pippa. I had, however, a strong feeling that she was close by.

When I returned from another futile search at midday, Pippa suddenly appeared. She had lost a lot of weight since she had given birth and was very hungry but also in a hurry, so after gulping down the meat she trotted off toward the road. Guitu and I followed her. It was unfortunate that I had to take him with me, but this very morning I had almost run into a buffalo and could not risk walking without protection. Pippa looked disapproving and fooled us by various devices. She rambled aimlessly upstream on our side of the Mulika and even crept inside two thornbushes, pretending to look for her cubs. When at last she realized that she was going to have to put up with us she sniffed the air, leapt across the Mulika, and then walked toward a double bush some sixty yards away. Splashing through the water and leaving Guitu behind, I followed her and found her lying under the right-hand bush, while from under the left-hand bush I heard tiny noises. Pippa looked at me with hard eyes and did not budge. I took the hint, returned to Guitu, and sent him home. She watched his departure attentively and did not move over to her cubs until he was out of sight.

It was some time before in the dim light under the dense foliage I saw that there were four of them. Turning their blind faces toward me, they spat and spat until Pippa placed herself between them and me and made ready to be suckled. The little cubs could barely crawl and had a tough job reaching her teats before settling down for a drink. Judging by their size and movements, they were probably eight days old. In spite of the ghastly weather we had had since their birth, they were in wonderful condition. Pippa lay with her back to me and never once looked around so I withdrew quietly and went home. Her nursery was only half a mile from camp and looked as if it had been occupied for some time. I had passed within some fifty yards of this double bush twice in the last twenty-four hours. Why, I wondered, had Pippa not responded to my calls? After all, she had taken me to see her last litter when they were three days younger than the present ones.

CHAPTER

20

The Cubs Disappear

THAT NIGHT IT RAINED without stopping, and next morning I was not surprised to find the little ones lying in wet mud and soaked by dripping leaves. Pippa soon emerged, looked carefully around, then walked stiffly to a distant tree where Guitu was waiting with the meat. She only ate a little and hurried back, obviously trying to keep her babies warm. Two of the cubs had three leathery, lentil-sized patches (where, later on, their sex organs would be) which puzzled me. They could not be ticks, since they were in the same tri-angular position on both cubs and never moved though Pippa often licked the place. I expected these cubs to be males because they had larger heads than the other two. Pippa was touchingly concerned about her children and spent all the time nursing or cleaning them by licking the mud and excrement off. Soon it started to rain again and we went home. It drizzled all day and when we re-turned at teatime the nursery was extremely wet. So we cut grass and then waited until Pippa left the cubs to have her meat some twenty yards away. While she ate I covered the muddy ground around the cubs with grass without touching them. Of course, they spat at me. I knew that Pippa might resent my help, but I believed this would bring less harm to her young than leaving them lying in a quagmire. To my relief, she settled as a matter of course on the grass bed, and by the way she played with the cubs I knew she was not worried by my interference. One of the little ones tried to catch her tail and to hang on to it whenever Pippa snatched it away. Today all the cubs could crawl quite well, but they soon got tired and then dozed off, their heavy heads falling back at most uncomfortable angles.

Thank God, that night it did not rain. By morning Pippa had pushed the heavy foliage away from the entrance to her nursery and the sun could reach the suckling cubs. They looked very happy and I could now take some photographs of them suckling. It was interesting to see how at this early age the spots on their flanks and hindquarters followed distinct parallel lines, though later they looked rather haphazardly patterned. The marking leading from the eyes across the temples to the neck was still an almost solid line which only later separated into spots; this was also true of the spots at the root of their tails. This made me wonder if, at this early stage, the cheetah showed some slight resemblance to the markings of the now exterminated king cheetah, who was marked almost like a serval cat. The skin on their bellies was still deep purple; by licking Pippa kept them spotlessly clean in spite of the muddy ground. I took the opportunity, while Pippa was having her meal some distance away, to cover the sludge with grass, which made the nursery cozy again. I then sat for a while with Pippa, holding her meat. (I removed all trace of it from the ground before we both returned to the cubs.) Strangely enough, today Pippa seemed to disapprove of the grass bedding and carried the cubs by the scruff of their necks to the farthest corner of the lair, where the ground was wet; there she settled till she eventually moved them out from the bush and hid them under the foliage of a large-leafed plant where they remained until I left.

In the afternoon we found that the family had moved some seventy yards into a bush much woodier and less muddy than the earlier one; its branches were so thick that I could only get glimpses of the cubs clambering up Pippa's back and sliding off again. Of Pippa herself I saw nothing but her eyes, and even these she turned away as soon as I dangled meat outside the bush. I waited for half an hour, but as she never moved and continued to look in the opposite direction, I then went home. She had eaten very little for two days, but when I looked up my notes on her behavior when she had borne her last litter, I saw that then too she had eaten very little after giving birth. No doubt this was to allow her body to recover and also to keep her digestion functioning while she took hardly any exercise.

On that occasion too she had carried the cubs for the first time to another lair when they were ten days old and still blind, although the weather had then been fine and there was no mud.

By next morning the little cheetahs had opened their eyes. Discovering a visual world seemed to tire them and they were very sleepy, except for one cub who caressed Pippa's face for a long time; this she seemed to enjoy with her eyes half closed. Although it had not rained much, the ground inside the bush was very wet because the foliage was too thick to allow the sun to get through and dry the mud. It was also too thick to permit me to creep inside and cover the lair with grass. When Pippa emerged for a short walk I noticed clotted blood around her vagina which seemed to make defecating difficult. She again ate very little and soon was back on duty. Seeing the cubs so tired, I decided not to disturb the family in the afternoon. This was just as well, since on my return to camp I found George there and a baby buffalo. He had heard it calling for its mother, of whom he found no trace. As he had searched all morning for her, he now assumed that she had been killed by lions.

The little calf had its umbilical cord still attached and the sprouting horns were hardly visible, so we guessed it to be about two weeks old. We put it into Whity's compound and tried to give it milk, but it seemed too upset to drink and only wanted to rest. However much I should have liked to help the little orphan, I could not possibly confine it in my camp because of Pippa and other predators who might be attracted by its scent and bellowings. Also, if there were a sudden flood it might be drowned. So we took it to the Warden at Leopard Rock. It was a very skiddy drive, and by the time we arrived there the calf was exhausted and fell asleep. We gave it two hours in which to recover; by then the Warden had arranged for an enclosure to be prepared for it close to his home.

While all this went on, the old bull buffalo who had lived for many months at Leopard Rock appeared, ready to retire to his favorite bush within three yards of the Warden's kitchen for a sleep. It seemed incredible that such a formidable wild beast should behave like a pet. He spent his nights and many hours every day close to the armory, which was guarded by Rangers, or near the Warden's house, as though he knew that here he would be safe from lions which because of his age he might no longer be able to repel. In spite of the constant movements of the Warden's family and staff close to the old buffalo, he never showed the slightest wish to harm anyone. He felt safe from lions and knew he was accepted as part of the family. Watching him lumbering around the kitchen corner, we wondered if he would adopt the little calf or whether he might regard it as a rival and attack it.

Meanwhile I had tried to comfort the calf by stroking it gently and succeeded in making it drink by dropping diluted Nestle's Ideal Milk into its mouth. Later, when George and I were ready to go home, he started up the engine and immediately the baby buffalo staggered to its feet and tried to follow the car, which it seemed to regard as its mother. It ambled after us for a few hundred yards and finally had to be carried off and put into its enclosure. It was astonishing that during the few hours which had elapsed since George had found the orphan it seemed to have accepted the Land-Rover as the substitute for its mother. Was it because the calf felt safe near this large shape, similar perhaps in its bulk to that of its mother? Perhaps the illusion could be explained by the fact that the milk it had received had been given it near or in the car? When, during the night, I was kept awake by the chuckling and howling of at least three hyenas, mingled with the agonizing barks of a baboon which they killed close to the camp, I was particularly glad that the calf had now found a safe home. I followed the hyenas' spoor with apprehension next morning; it crossed over the Mulika ford and continued along the road about five hundred yards from Pippa's lair.

When I got there I found the family close to the entrance of their nursery. Pippa must have found the mud inside the bush too wet, so now all were enjoying the morning sun right in the open. I watched the cubs having their breakfast while Pippa licked them affectionately. After they had finished suckling she allowed them for the first time to play between herself and me. The cubs too seemed more at ease and didn't spit when I took photographs but only blinked at me with their large eyes. Later I was able to hand-feed Pippa the first good meal she had had for four days. Suddenly it began to drizzle. Pippa quickly pushed the cubs beneath some large leaves and protected them still further by covering them with her body as best she could. She remained in this uncomfortable position until the drizzle stopped, and I then realized that the excellent condition the cubs were in was due to their mother's dedication in keeping them warm and dry, however foul the weather. She had

Pippa with her third litter, 9 days old

hardly left the cubs since they were born, and I wondered what she would do when they started to move about, for the vegetation between the bushes had by now grown so thick that walking through it had become difficult even for us. After luncheon we visited the family again and found them still at the same spot. Pippa seemed badly in need of exercise and, making the best of our presence, walked farther than she had dared to so far. I followed her with meat and was amazed that she could eat so much after her large morning meal. Afterward she rolled around and around, stretching her legs and purring contentedly while I de-ticked her and played with her.

Recently I had read in a report from the Krefeld Zoo that the cheetah cubs reared there could retract their claws up to the age of ten weeks. I had never seen Pippa's cubs sheathing or retracting their claws and doubted the statement. As all our cheetahs seemed so relaxed today, I thought it a good opportunity to find out if they could retract their claws. So, leaving Pippa to rest, I went to the cubs. Without stepping on the flattened grass around them, I tried to tuck the claws of one of the cubs back: it did not move. Satisfied, for the rest of the afternoon I watched Pippa and her family playing together, the cubs toppling over each other and prodding Pippa with their soft paws. She bore patiently with their antics, fondling and nuzzling them. Finally she clasped one between her front legs, where it snuggled down comfortably against her chest, while the others fell asleep in a heap. When it was time to go home I turned around and saw the head of a hyena only fifty yards away, peeping at us. It vanished instantly. Yelling and throwing stones, Guitu and I rushed after it, but in the fading light we could not see where it went, though we believed that it crossed the road and ran toward the stream. I felt very worried and could only pray that nothing would happen to Pippa and her cubs.

After dark some lions started a squabble across the stream close to camp. It must have been an exceptionally large pride: their roaring and growling were so terrifying that I was frightened. Unless they were fighting over a kill I could not imagine what could have upset them so much, but their brawling continued far too long for such a dispute, and the longer it lasted the more anxiety I felt about our cheetahs. Finally one of the lions crossed over the stream, and his grunts, coming from behind my sleeping hut, kept me awake until dawn. Then suddenly all went silent. This lion must have gone back to his pride, for we later found no spoor along the road and, much relieved, I went on to Pippa's lair. It was empty. There was no indication of lions or hyenas having come near it except for a tiny spot of blood which I could not explain, as there was no evidence of a fight, no broken leaves, no churned-up earth. Pippa must have heard the lions during the night as well as we did, and we decided that she must have taken the cubs to a safer place. We now searched every bush within the area to which she could carry the cubs in four trips. Eventually, some hundred yards away, at an extremely dense thicket, we found a few broken leaves where an animal had evidently crept in and then left by the opposite side. Cutting through the thorny stronghold, we saw a small patch of mud at its center which looked as if the cubs had lain there. Fifty yards beyond this thicket we came on a single pugmark but too spoiled by rain to enable us to identify it as made by a hyena or a cheetah.

We searched for another hour, calling all the time. Suddenly Pippa appeared as if from nowhere, at least five hundred yards from the thicket. By the way she seized the meat and wolfed it down, I believed she was in a hurry to return to her cubs, so I was astonished when she became playful and did not move off for half an hour. Feeling anxious about her family, I walked away, hoping thus to induce her to guide us to them. She followed reluctantly and finally sat still at a bush next to the thicket as if she were guarding the entrance to her lair. I sent Guitu home, with the result that she immediately moved to a sheltered place between this bush and the thicket and lay down, purring. While I played with her I noticed two small bleeding scratches on her front legs about half an inch long. Could these be responsible for the spot of blood we had seen in her lair? Fearing that the lion had scared her so much that today she would not trust even me with the cubs, I went home to give her a chance to nurse her hungry children. On my way I again examined the lair where last we had seen them together. While concentrating on finding an explanation for the blood spot I almost bumped my head against Pippa, who had followed me and now sniffed the ground intently. Later she climbed up a tree and, after surveying the surroundings, jumped off and walked in a large circle until she finally settled under a tree about six hundred yards away. By now it was 1 P.M., so I went home for lunch, hoping that she would go to her cubs, who by now must be starving. I was very glad to find old Local back in camp. Relying on his talent for spooring, I took him with me after lunch to try to retrace Pippa's movements. Starting with the twin bush, we had a narrow escape when we found it occupied by a buffalo who was resting on the grass matting. Dodging around the sleepy beast, we next inspected Pippa's second lair. Since it was undisturbed, Local attributed the blood spot to Pippa's scratches, for if even a python or eagle had taken the cubs there would have been signs of a fight. We continued to look for Pippa and found her sound asleep exactly where I had left her. Yawning and stretching, she gave Local a friendly welcome and flung herself between us, ready for a game. Local examined her scratches and was convinced that they were caused by sharp sticks rather than bites. Later Pippa led us in a casual manner back around the circle we had made this morning. On the way she climbed a few trees or rested in their shade. When we approached the thicket she suddenly rushed off, crept inside, and sniffed around its center for a long time. Afterward she rambled about in such an indifferent manner that I became alarmed. By now it was 5 P.M. and still she showed no intention of leaving us, so we went home, hoping that she would return to her cubs before it got dark.

Pippa had been an exceptionally good mother and I could not believe she would starve the cubs for a whole day, just for the sake of hiding them from me. To add to my worries, it rained again all night and the downpour continued throughout the next morning. Wet through, we searched every bush within a two-mile radius of Pippa's lair. We scrutinized broken leaves and called her name, but, except for the sound of dripping rain, there was a deadly silence. Believing that Pippa could not carry the cubs in four trips over a great distance, next day we searched the area beyond the Mulika— not that it was likely that she could have jumped across its swollen current four times, carrying the cubs with her mouth. We looked into every place where she might have hidden her family. Plodding through deep mud, mentally and physically worn out, we returned home only at dusk. That night the rain was even heavier. Watching the rising stream, I tried to put myself in Pippa's place. Since the poor cubs had been born two weeks ago, she must have spent most of her time drenched to the skin as she watched her surroundings turn into a soggy bog. How could she keep fit in these circumstances if she had to remain immobile with her cubs in order to protect them?

Reflecting that Pippa's first litter had disappeared in similar weather conditions, I considered the possibility that, obeying the instinct for survival, she could have killed her young; but, having seen the extent of Pippa's devotion to her family even in the most trying circumstances, I rejected this solution and inclined to the belief that the cubs had fallen victims to a hyena. I felt sure that Pippa knew what had happened to them, for she did not search for them or show the anxiety she had exhibited when Dume and Whity were taken from her. It was distressing to think that of the eleven cubs which she had borne in two years, only three were alive, and even of these Whity might well have died if we had not helped to cure her leg. Frequent leg injuries among cubs, their being killed by predators, and climatic calamities on top of all this make it understandable that natural mortality is high among cheetahs. Man also contributes to their extermination by his ruthless killing, and does this only to please the vanity of women, or turns these strikingly handsome creatures into pets. No wonder, then, that the cheetah population is on the decline.

21

The Spotted Sphinx

IN THE MORNING the stream was still very high, so I was suprised when Pippa suddenly appeared outside my sleeping hut dripping wet after crossing the torrent. She was very hungry but gave herself barely time to eat and soon walked off to the road. Seeing Local and me following her, she hesitated, then suddenly hurried off, splashing belly-deep through the flooded Mulika ford, after which she continued determinedly. A little later she stopped and, staring intently at the stream, started to walk toward it but then, glancing back at Local, changed her mind and turned in the opposite direction toward the Impia plain. When she came near her former lairs she looked at Local with such a murderous expression that I asked him to keep as far as he could behind without losing sight of us while I followed closely behind Pippa. But however cunningly he tried to hide himself during the next hour, Pippa knew he was behind me and fooled us by making many small detours. Three times she tried to cross the Mulika, then gave up, frightened by the raging torrent. She seemed particularly interested in the plains beyond and, since she could not reach them, climbed high into an acacia from which she watched the bush across the water. We waited for a long time for her next move, but when she finally flopped onto a comfortable branch, dangling her legs along its side and dozing off, we left. I could not understand her behavior. Preserving a spark of hope that the cubs were still alive, I determined not to be in Pippa's way and so did not return that afternoon. During the night it again rained heavily and next day Pippa did not show up.

It was Easter Sunday. In spite of the bad weather, a film party was spending the holiday in the Park and had camped for a few days between the gate and Leopard Rock. Churning bravely along the slippery road, they brought me news of two cheetahs who had appeared early that morning within a hundred yards of their camp and apparently quite unperturbed had watched the people moving close to them. One had seemed to be shier than the other and had moved away as soon as their photographer drove his car near to take pictures. The other had remained on the spot even when the cheetah found itself separated by the Land-Rover from its pal and had finally followed the car for a short distance before disappearing. These were most likely Whity and Tatu, for they always kept close together, whereas on two occasions we had found Mbili far away on her own. Comparing the photographer's Land-Rover with mine, they proved to be identical in shape and color, and by a strange coincidence the photographer's wife resembled me sufficiently to be mistaken for me at a distance. Obviously the cubs had expected food from her and had moved away only when there was no response. Although we found no further trace of them when we looked for them, the news that both had been seen in excellent condition, after living independently for almost two months, made Easter a very happy day for me.

Another unexpected Easter present was a fragment of the shell of a swallow's egg. It fell as a result of the hatching of two chicks of the third generation of wire-tails to be born within our camp. The parents had again used the nest inside the palm-log hut, which they seemed to believe had been built for their special benefit. Calling the little ones "Shanti" (Peace) and "Sunday," I hoped to ensure them a happy life.

After another night's rain, Pippa turned up in camp. She came along the road from Leopard Rock and only called for a quick meal. While I fed her I noticed that her teats were dry and almost back to their normal size. She was in a most irritable mood and hurried off along the road to Kenmare as soon as she had eaten. She ran so fast for about a mile that I had difficulty in keeping up with her. Repeatedly she looked back to reassure herself that only I was following. When we reached the Dume Tree she slowed down and sniffed all around this terminalia, then bounced off into the plains. As I splashed across the marshy ground after her, she growled at me and made it plain that she wanted me to leave her alone. A week later we tracked her spoor across the distant arid plain where, barely three and a half months earlier, she had found the father of her latest cubs. Was she again planning for a new family?*

During the following weeks Pippa came in for meat only when she was unable to kill for herself; otherwise, she kept clear of the camp. Surely she must often have felt lonely after having lived for eighteen months with Whity, Mbili, and Tatu, but even though she knew where she could find her cubs she never moved into their territory, and neither did they trespass into hers, which she had recently restricted to within two miles of the camp. The heavy rains had made the roads impassable and I could not drive alone to Leopard Rock to try to see the cubs until, on the sixteenth of May, I had an opportunity to join George, who had to shoot a buffalo a few miles beyond the gate outside the Park. Driving with him in convoy, I suddenly saw Whity and Tatu close to the place where we had seen them three months earlier. Both were in excellent condition, Whity still very light, contrasting with Tatu's beautiful dark color. As they moved near the road they were indeed a handsome pair, their muscles rippling under their glossy coats. George drove on to deal with the buffalo, and, hoping that he would return with meat, I waited. It was 5 P.M. and the cubs had obviously been on the prowl to look for their dinner. They sat close to the car for two and a half hours and disappeared only when it became dark. This was just as well, for when George appeared he had no meat. He had shot the buffalo too late to be able to move the car near to it and intended to collect the carcass early next day. We arranged that he would start at first light while I would follow two hours later and wait on the road for his return.

Next morning I located the cubs and offered them Ideal milk. Cautiously they approached the bowl, which I held as usual in my hand. Whity was the first to test whether I was still trustworthy: she lapped the milk eagerly. Only then did Tatu pluck up enough cour-

---

* Later I learned that a female cheetah or lioness, prematurely losing her cubs, immediately comes in season, which enables her to mate again and have another pregnancy.

Joy feeding Whity and Tatu, who had been on their own for three months

age to join in, after which she pushed Whity's head away in no un-
certain manner. Both seemed to hope that there might be some meat
to follow and, resting under a bush close by, waited for two hours
until George arrived. He had already prepared three large chunks
of buffalo meat for them, of which I gave them two, which they
dragged hurriedly into a thick bush. There we left them to enjoy
their meal. It was exactly three months since I had been together
with all three cubs, and finding two at least so fit made me extremely
happy. I asked George why he had prepared three chunks, and he
told me that he had seen Mbili early in the morning about half a
mile from Leopard Rock, but as he would be driving home in a
hurry he had got the meat ready for me to give her in case I should
find her.

We set off, calling for Mbili, and soon saw her sneaking through
the grass and finally hiding in a bush. This was unusual, and when I
came close I found that she was blind in one eye. The right eye was
the size of a ping-pong ball and covered with a fleshy, bloodshot
tissue. She also had a partly healed scar on her forehead which I
reckoned to be two to three days old. I fed her the meat, which she
took from my hand, and left her with a very full belly under a shady
bush. Afraid that the injured eye might be lost and even affect the
healthy one if it were not treated immediately, I radio-called the
Harthoorns. Unfortunately, we could not get through and had to
wait until the next morning to send a message. I spent the afternoon
collecting more meat from George and repaired the enclosure at my
camp in case we needed to confine Mbili.

Next morning we found her at the same place where we had left
her. The eye was worse and the lower lid red from broken blood
vessels. I gave her a large meal and dressed the scar with sulfathiazole. Then, leaving Local in charge, I went to Leopard Rock, where
I heard that the Harthoorns would fly in at 4 P.M. On my return I
found that Mbili had moved a few hundred yards into the plain;
Local was close behind her. As soon as she spotted me she disappeared. Local and I looked for her and had a narrow escape from a
rhino which emerged from a thick bush just as I was trying to peep
inside to look for Mbili. Searching desperately to find her by the
time the Harthoorns arrived, we went on looking until 4 P.M.,
when, at last, I saw two ears above the grass which vanished instantly. Mbili had moved about a mile and was inside a thicket from

which she overlooked the swampy plain from the lower end of the airstrip right up to the ridge of the Mulika circuit. Leaving Local to watch her, I now drove quickly to the Warden's house, where I met the Harthoorns. They were prepared to operate on Mbili during the night if necessary as they had to fly back next day at 2 P.M.

There was no time to be lost. They injected a hundred milligrams of sernilan into a piece of meat. The dose was calculated for a body weight of a hundred pounds. It was the same as what we had used when immobilizing Whity. We then drove off to find Mbili. As soon as she saw us she bolted, and although Local and I searched the surrounding area until dark, we didn't see her again that day. I was in a panic in case the Harthoorns should have to fly back before we could find her. By now she had obviously sensed that we were after her.

As soon as it was light we went to look for her and were lucky: we found her at 8 A.M. right on the airstrip, watching eight crested cranes. She seemed suspicious when I offered her the meat containing the sernilan, but by sheer luck I managed to push it into her mouth before she walked away. This was at 8:30 A.M. I sent Local to fetch the Harthoorns, who had spent the night with the Warden. For three hours we watched Mbili getting sleepy; yawning frequently, she rested on the airstrip in the open sun until it got too hot, then she moved slowly to a tree close by. Toni Harthoorn and I followed, waiting for a chance to inject more sernilan into her muscles; obviously, the initial dose had not been big enough. While I managed to divert her attention by giving her milk, Toni drove the syringe home, and Mbili leapt into the air as soon as she felt the prick of the needle. We then waited for another hour only to realize that she needed still more sernilan before she could be handled. Toni eventually gave her a further injection, bringing the total dosage up to that for 150 pounds of body weight. (Of course, by now the effect of the initial dose had partly worn off.) To make sure that she would keep absolutely still while he treated the eye he gave her an intravenous quick-acting anesthetic (intraval sodium thiopentone). Meanwhile, we sent for a badminton net, which the Warden kindly brought along. While he and I held Mbili safely in position under it, the Harthoorns tried to examine the eye. But the lids were so swollen that they could not be pulled apart under these improvised conditions. We therefore drove Mbili to the Warden's house, where he had prepared an operating table.

Here the Harthoorns gave her an injection of conbiotic cortisone, then they applied adrenalin and ice (from the refrigerator) to the eye to reduce the swelling, as well as cocaine to ease the pain. As soon as these had had an effect, the Harthoorns pushed the lids apart and pulled the very swollen nictitating membrane off the eye. With the aid of a special flashlight they could then see deep inside the mess of swollen tissue, and were able to tell that the sight was not damaged. The injury was luckily only an external one, most likely caused by a heavy kick from a hooved animal. The Harthoorns believed that within a day or two the bruises would go down, and they left me some terra cortril ointment, telling me to use it as often as possible on the swollen lids. They expected Mbili to come around early next morning and strongly advised me not to confine her in the compound at my camp at that time as she might not only revolt against finding herself behind wire and harm herself by trying to get out, but also Pippa might no longer tolerate her presence in her territory and might even attack her. So we decided to let Mbili wake up in the place where we had found her in order that she might continue her life where it had stopped for her in the morning.

By now the plane had arrived to take the Harthoorns back but, wanting to observe Mbili's progress, they postponed their return for a while and helped to settle her close to the swampy plain near the airfield. Placing her on a bed of grass under a shady tree, we watched her for two hours, by which time she had opened her eyes and raised her head. Satisfied at seeing her recovering from the anesthetic, the Harthoorns left. I was most grateful for all they had done, especially as they had sacrificed their weekend for this purpose. By now Mbili had relapsed into a deep sleep. Hoping to comfort her, I stroked her gently, but she lay limp and never stirred. When it got dark I covered her with grass to protect her from the cold early morning air and went to bed inside my car, which I had parked next to her to protect her against predators. Shortly afterward I heard a lion roar alarmingly close. Mbili was still immobilized, so I lifted her as quickly as I could into the car and drove to the Warden. He advised me again not to take her to my camp but to let her recover in her own territory. To guard her against lions, he very kindly provided two Rangers and a tent for the men to sleep in, then he helped me to find a suitable place right on the airstrip within half a mile of his office, and placing Mbili once more on a grass bed between the Rangers' tent and my car, he left us. Mbili's body was colder than was normal so I covered her not only with grass but also with a blanket, and watched her all through the night from my car, which was only a yard away from her. At 3 A.M. the Rangers and I heard the agonized bellows of a buffalo mingled with lion whuffs. When at dawn I noticed many vultures circling in the direction of the kill I was thankful that Mbili was safe.

Even now she could barely lift her head and looked around drowsily. The swelling of the injured eye had already decreased sufficiently for me to see her widely dilated pupil through a narrow slit. I managed to get her to swallow some Ideal milk, and by ten o'clock she was able to keep her head up long enough to nibble at some meat which I held for her. I could not have done anything worse, but unfortunately I only learned this too late. Filling up her stomach before her system was completely cleared of the drug retarded her recovery, and Mbili and I had to pay dearly for my ignorance. By now the sun was getting warm and I rigged up a shelter by attaching the Rangers' tent to my car. Under this Mbili and I spent the morning. At 1 P.M. she staggered to her feet, moved a few yards away, and produced some pitch-black, watery evacuations. Since the midday sun had become unbearably hot even under the canvas shelter, she now dragged herself toward a tree some hundred yards off; she swayed like a drunkard and collapsed several times before she was able to settle, exhausted, in its shade. I placed the meat and water close to her, then moved the car within a few yards and watched her all the afternoon getting gradually stronger. When the Warden called at teatime he agreed that Local and I should spend another night guarding her. But unfortunately Local made such a clatter with his cooking pots that Mbili became suspicious, and after we had both retired, he to his tent and I inside my car, she suddenly got up and walked off. We watched her moving in a very unbalanced way, but also determinedly, out of the headlights' glare and into the darkness. Driving after her might only have provoked her to walk farther, and fearing to lose her in the dark if I followed on foot, I was left with no alternative but to pray that she would not get into trouble before morning. Listening for a long time to the whuffings of two lions did not lessen my anxiety, though I thought they could not be hungry after their last night's kill.

As soon as the first bird twitter announced dawn, Local and I looked for Mbili and found her in a ditch some two hundred yards away. I sent Local for a goat I had stored at Leopard Rock and meanwhile gave her Ideal milk. Although she lapped it eagerly from the bowl I held out for her, she was very fierce and growled and snarled at me. This was not surprising considering all she had undergone in the last days, for in fact the sernilan had had an immobilizing effect only and she had been fully conscious except for the time when she had been anesthetized. Now able to move again, she naturally resented my coming close to her and walked away. Except that her hindquarters were still a little stiff from the many drugs which had been injected into this part of her body, her movements were normal. After watching a few zebras and baboons she moved with increasing speed toward the airstrip, hopped onto a stone roller, and, while surveying the surroundings, produced another black evacuation.

As soon as she spotted Local at the far end of the airstrip with the goat, she trotted off toward the swampy plain, too fast for me to follow her, and disappeared. By the time I had collected Local and the goat by car there was no sign of her. Fearing that she might bolt far off if we chased her, I decided to return at teatime with the goat; meanwhile she could have a rest and regain strength. But in the afternoon we found no trace of her and only met a lion on the road at exactly the spot where I had found Mbili ill four days ago. Feeling anxious, Local and I spent the night again at the landing ground. At 10 P.M. we heard a short but frightening lion roar very close. Later, I was alarmed by a jackal yelling right in front of the car. Switching on the lights, I saw a lion within fifteen yards of me. He was much bigger than the one we had met that afternoon and his belly was full. Switching the headlights off and on made him walk away, though we heard him whuffing for the rest of the night. I shuddered to think of the consequences if this lion had come here on the previous night when Mbili was lying within two hundred yards of the car, unable to run away.

For the next three days Local and I screened every bush and thicket, looking at countless mud puddles for spoor, we drove along all the tracks which Mbili might have crossed and walked over plains we thought she might have gone to, all the time calling her name without finding any trace of her. When passing a labor gang five miles from camp where Guitu had last seen Mbili two months ago, a tractor driver told us of a cheetah who, earlier in the morning, had watched the road men and seemed quite unconcerned about the people milling around. We searched the area but without result. Since this place was on the borderline of Pippa's and Mbili's territories, the cheetah might have been either of the two. Not to waste time in case it was Pippa, we drove home and found her in camp, where she had been all morning. After feeding her we took some meat and quickly returned to look for Mbili.

Leaving Stanley with the meat inside the car, Local and I searched the plain between the ridge and the Mulika, calling and calling, but only some vervet monkeys reponded to our cries. Soon, however, I detected Mbili hiding in the grass. I sent Local to get the meat, hoping meanwhile to keep Mbili on the spot by feeding her a tin of Ideal milk. This she lapped from the bowl which I held for her. Now I could see that her eye was normal again except for a hardly noticeable swelling on the lower lid. Her scar too was healed but for a tiny moist spot which I dressed with sulfathiazole to keep the flies away. We sat close together, waiting for the men. I did not dare touch Mbili or to talk to her, fearing she might bolt, but she seemed to have regained her old trust in me and waited placidly until the men arrived. Then, dragging it off a short distance, she ate it to the last scrap, all the time looking around nervously as all wild animals do when feeding. By then it was dark and we had to hurry home. Mbili could easily have followed us to camp, which was no more than one and a half hours' walk, and familiar ground to her, but when there was no sign of her next morning I realized that however ill or hungry she might be, she now rigidly adhered to the law of territorial rights. Returning to the place where we had left her the evening before, we had to look for fully two hours before finding her within two hundred yards. She must have heard me calling; why then had she not shown up? She was hiding under a small tree from which she could overlook the swampy patch with the fallen doum-palm logs along which, many months ago, she and her sisters had had such glorious games. Today she had only an elephant for company who rubbed himself against the logs, then splashed through a muddy puddle trying to cover himself with the cooling substance. The wind was against us and he did not notice us, so while giving Mbili a large meal we had to put up with his presence. She did not mind my holding the meat for her but snarled and growled at me whenever she

*The Harthoorns
treating Mbili's
eye*

*Eight days later,
Mbili's eye healed*

stopped eating and looked into my eyes. I felt I understood her dilemma in taking food from my hand. She was automatically reverting to her old habits but simultaneously found herself face to face with a creature whom her wild instincts now resented. The only way to help her to overcome this confusion was to leave her alone. Whatever the wrench might be for me, I must let her live the life of a wild cheetah in which I had no longer any part. As if she understood my thoughts she made the parting easier by moving away to a small tree from which she watched me going my way, while she remained in her own world.

How glad I was when on returning to camp I found Pippa there. She was unusually affectionate. While I played with her I noticed that her nipples were again in milk. Gently stroking her soft belly and the forming lives inside it, I felt closer to Pippa than I had ever been before.

A week later George arrived to tell me that he had just seen two cheetahs near his camp, one very light in color and friendly, the other dark and rather shy. These he felt sure were Whity and Tatu. I could hardly believe that they had ventured right to Mugwongo Hill, where they had never been with Pippa and which was some twelve miles in a straight line from where we had last seen them. I went back with George, taking meat and milk, and after I had called for a short while Whity appeared. Was it chance that she came from almost exactly the same spot where a few days ago I had seen a wild male cheetah? Soon Tatu also showed up, but as usual she kept at a safe distance and only joined Whity quickly when I dropped the meat. Both were very fit but wild and nervous, and whenever I went near them to take photographs they growled, though, strangely enough, they had no objection to my squatting next to them while holding the bowl with milk, which they lapped eagerly, almost banging their heads against mine.

It was the second of June and the cubs had been living on their own since the seventeenth of February. To reach this place they had had to explore new ground as well as cross the Rojoweru River. I wondered if they had done so to find the company of a male or if they wanted to extend their territory without infringing on those of Mbili and Pippa. Five days later both were seen not far away, and on the twenty-first of June George found the larger bones of a kongoni calf with fresh cheetah spoor around and shortly afterward the remains of a young ostrich—both in the same area. Meanwhile, on the tenth of June, Mbili was seen by the Park Warden within two miles of Leopard Rock, and on the fifth of July I found my clown on the airstrip. Crouching low, she let me approach to within five yards —then she bolted as fast as she could with such a heavy belly that I believed her to be pregnant. I was very intrigued to know if she could already be in cub, and in order to find out I collected meat from camp which I assumed she would refuse if her stomach were full from a large meal. But we did not find her again that day and had to wait until next morning, when we discovered her half a mile away. Her belly had returned to its normal size and by the way she gulped the meat down it was difficult to believe that she had eaten such an enormous meal only yesterday. While she tore at the meat and lapped the milk I held out for her, she allowed me to sit within three feet of her; but once I got up she growled savagely and charged whenever I dared to move. She had now lived on her own for four months and twenty days. Although she still fell into old habits when I held the familiar milk bowl and kept low, she was now wild enough to resent me as soon as I stood up and moved about close to her. Whity and Tatu had reacted in the same way. A month later George again saw one cub some four miles farther off on the Mugwongo plains, also in perfect condition. She came up to his car while he searched for his lions; for these he had brought some meat and water which he now gave the cub. She ate it within ten yards of the car. Next day we searched but did not see the cub; however, from the photographs George had taken I identified her later as Whity. Obviously the cubs were extending their territory, and though I often scanned the plains through my binoculars, hoping to see the white tips of their tails, it would now be a matter of luck if I were to see them again. The remarkable fact that none of the four cheetahs intruded in each other's hunting ground seemed to indicate that female cheetahs limit their territory more strictly than the males, who appear to roam around at random. How Pippa succeeded in confining her daughters to areas where they would not interfere with her new family is one of the secrets she is keeping to herself.

Recently she had made me believe that she would choose for her new nursery the place where her last cubs were born. She did this by cunningly spending most of her time there. Right up to the last

The fourth litter, 14 days old

The Spotted Sphinx

she fooled me by retreating to this spot deep inside a bush and showing all the symptoms of her hour being near.

When, after nine days' absence, she reappeared in camp she was extremely hungry but hardly gave herself time to eat before she went back on her tracks along the road toward Leopard Rock. She allowed Local and me to follow her, and after two miles she turned into the plain where I had found her together with Whity, Mbili, and Tatu a year previously on an ostrich kill. Anxiously looking around, she led us to a thorny bush (again *Acacia mellifera*) under which four cubs were hidden. Two already had their eyes open, and, since they were much larger than the others, I believed them to be males. Later I saw that there were indeed three males in that litter, but one was smaller than the female. All her other cubs had opened their eyes when they were between ten and eleven days old, so I assumed the new cubs had been born on the fifteenth of July. Allowing for a gestation of ninety to ninety-three days, this meant that Pippa must have mated within a week of the disappearance of her last litter.

These tiny cubs crawled over on very shaky legs to their mother and, while she licked them tenderly, settled down to suckle. Watching this peaceful scene, I wondered what the future had in store for us. Would Pippa again allow me to share her happiness and sorrows until the time came when these cubs could live free and independent, like Whity, Mbili, and Tatu, who soon might start having families of their own? Would Pippa recognize her children and grandchildren if she went on breeding so successfully, or once the young could fend for themselves, was the break final? To this—and to so many still mysterious habits of cheetahs—I hoped to learn the answers if Pippa would agree to share a further part of her life with me. But I knew that, whatever happened, I would never be able to fully comprehend the character of my lovable but aloof friend who, for me, would always remain a spotted sphinx.